MW00476528

Playing the Lying Game

Playing the Lying Game

Detecting and Dealing with Lies
and Liars, from Occasional Fibbers
to Frequent Fabricators

GINI GRAHAM SCOTT, PhD

 PRAEGER

AN IMPRINT OF ABC-CLIO, LLC
Santa Barbara, California • Denver, Colorado • Oxford, England

Library of Congress Cataloging-in-Publication Data
Scott, Gini Graham.
  Playing the lying game : detecting and dealing with lies and liars,
from occasional fibbers to frequent fabricators / Gini Graham Scott.
     p. cm.
  Includes bibliographical references and index.
  ISBN 978-0-313-38351-9 (hard copy : alk. paper) — ISBN 978-0-313-38352-6 (ebook)
1. Truthfulness and falsehood.   I. Title.
  BJ1421.S358   2010
  177'.3—dc22   2009046112

ISBN: 978-0-313-38351-9
EISBN: 978-0-313-38352-6

14   13   12   11   10   1   2   3   4   5

This book is also available on the World Wide Web as an eBook.
Visit www.abc-clio.com for details.

Praeger
An Imprint of ABC-CLIO, LLC

ABC-CLIO, LLC
130 Cremona Drive, P.O. Box 1911
Santa Barbara, California 93116-1911

This book is printed on acid-free paper ∞

Manufactured in the United States of America

Contents

PART IV
Lying in Personal and Private Life

Introduction

In recent years, lying has become of increased concern, as has ethics. Numerous reality/game shows have involved deception, most notably *Survivor*. The hit TV show *Lie to Me* is about an investigator who detects lies. Numerous films highlight lying and deceit, such as the box-office smash *Hangover* and the Julia Roberts–Clive Owen star vehicle *Duplicity*, Recently, lying has been very much in the news because of deceptions by a string of finance tycoons charged with cheating clients of millions and billions of dollars, such as Bernie Madoff, whose 50-billion-dollar Ponzi scheme netted a 150-year sentence. And many authors have been found guilty of creating their memoirs out of imagined incidents, such as Herman Rosenblat's fabrication about his experiences in meeting his wife as a child in a concentration camp. The list goes on and on.

Because of such controversies, a renewed debate has swirled around the question of when lying is acceptable and when it should be excused. Ironically, when I first published *The Truth about Lying* in 1994, no one seemed to think lying was much of an issue; publishers seemed to think people either didn't lie or wouldn't want to admit it by reading a book about it. But then the 1997 film *Liar, Liar,* with Jim Carrey, about a lying lawyer who commits to telling the truth, triggered interest in the subject, leading to discussions of the topic on popular programs such as *Oprah* and *Montel Williams*. And the following year, President Clinton created an explosion of interest in lying with his 1998 deceptions about his affair with Monica Lewinsky and his stern pronouncement that he had never had a relationship with "that girl," leading to lying becoming front page news as the specter of the Starr Report and impeachment proceedings fueled the news and late night talk show jokes. In fact, during this period, I was a featured expert guest on *Oprah, Montel Williams,* the *O'Reilly Factor,* and other shows talking about how and why people lie and describing the different types of liars, from those who virtually never or occasionally lie to the out and out Pinocchios and compulsive liars, who could flip out a lie like turning on a car ignition switch.

So, given this growing interest, *Playing the Lying Game* is designed to look at how, why, and when people lie, and how to understand the different styles people use to lie. These styles refer to the frequency with which people are apt to lie in different situations, and they range from the person who is almost always honest to the usually deceptive person—and, at the extreme, the compulsive or conscienceless liar: the sociopath. This range forms a continuum of lying, from the primarily honest person to the person who lies all the time—a distinction that especially fascinated interviewers when I was on *Oprah*, *Montel Williams*, and dozens of other TV and radio shows—though these distinctions and the quiz identifying them were only a short section at the back of the book.

But now these distinctions are front and center, because they provide a key to understanding and relating to different liars. Now you can better determine when someone is lying to you and whether to do anything about it—from ignoring the lie to avoiding or confronting the liar or even filing suit. As described in Part II, this continuum of lying can be divided into five major types of liars:

- The model of absolute integrity, who only lies in the rarest of circumstances;
- The real straight shooter, who is honest most of the time but is open to an occasional pragmatic lie;
- The pragmatic fibber, who lies as necessary when practical to do so but tells the truth where possible and convenient (where many of us fall today);
- The real Pinocchio, who often lies but does so in a very convincing and compelling way;
- The frequent liar, who freely exaggerates and presents a false but desirable self-image, or in some cases may even be a pathological liar who will lie about anything and may not always know the truth because he or she tells so many lies. While these may be two separate categories of lying, I have combined them here because the pathological liar is relatively rare. It can be hard to tell the difference, and in some cases, a frequent liar can turn into a pathological liar as the number of lies increase.

Playing the Lying Game focuses on recognizing and applying these five styles of lying in personal and work relationships, and on better understanding everyday events in the news. It also provides a new lens for looking at styles of relating in different cultures and throughout history. As the book points out, all of us lie at times, and some of our ordinary social lies (such telling someone you like a hate tie or not saying something to be sociable or hide negative feelings) facilitate everyday social interactions. But when lying goes too far it can break relationships and tear society apart, though sometimes it can be hard to know what's acceptable and what's not.

As *Playing the Lying Game* describes, in looking at lying from a popular sociological and psychological perspective, people vary greatly in how and why they lie—and what they consider lying. It asks the questions: "Why do we do it?" "How do we do it?" and "What can we do about it?"

For example, some of the reasons that people lie are to protect themselves, escape blame, avoid hurting others, gain financially, cover up social gaffes, step out on a mate, conceal secret activities, and for countless other reasons. However, people vary on the continuum on how frequently they will lie, with whom, and the types of lies they tell—from the harmless white lies that many people feel are fine to the serious, harmful lies that hurt many people.

By understanding these distinctions, you can better understand where you fit on this continuum yourself and better deal with others. These strategies include better recognizing when others are lying, deciding how to respond to a lie, and assessing when it may be necessary to be deceptive in a difficult situation, though the truth is the ideal.

Why should understanding lying be so important, both for individuals and society as a whole? The simple answer is that trust, born out of honesty and truth, is the glue that holds personal relationships, communities, and societies together, and polls for the last 20 years have found that over 90 percent of the people questioned stated that honesty was an extremely important attribute or quality in a friend. And when I did my own research, interviewing dozens of people about their perceptions of lying in everyday life, I found broad agreement on the importance of honesty and integrity, combined with an awareness of the commonness of lying and its dangers. Though people might lie for various reasons at times, for the most part they considered themselves to be honest, respectable, and responsible.

Indeed, the more I thought about lying, the more I realized its complexities. On the one hand, if lying becomes more common and if people thereby lose their confidence in each other or in national institutions, this threatens to undermine the social contract in society that binds us together with others in relationships and groups. On the other hand, there are many reasons to lie, not only for personal advantage and gain, but to help or protect others, or even to facilitate the operations of ordinary social discourses (such as the white lie to give an acceptable excuse or comment, rather than tell a truth that might be hurtful or disruptive). Yet while those who lie might feel that the particular lie is justified or appropriate, those experiencing the lie may not; they might rather know the truth, whatever the hurt.

But would they really? The subject of lying comes in many shades of grey, though we all might admit that there is some kind of ethical crisis that has led a growing number of businesses to introduce ethics-training programs, universities to start classes and programs on ethics, law schools to introduce classes on professional responsibility, and individuals to start going to workshops on being authentic to be true to both themselves and others.

To this end, the book probes such questions as:

- When do people lie? To whom?
- What kinds of lies do they tell?
- How do people differ in how they lie? What are the different types of liars?
- How do people feel about lying in different situations?
- What strategies do different people use to be convincing?
- How do they conceal their lies? When do they reveal them?
- How do they feel when others lie to them? What do they do?
- What makes them suspect a lie?
- When do they feel it is acceptable to lie? When do they feel it isn't right?
- Where do you and people you know fit in the types of lies you tell?
- How can you tell if someone lies to you, and what should you do about it?
- How should you respond to different types of liars?
- And more.

More specifically, the book features the following sections and chapters.

PART I: WHY DO WE ALL LIE?

We all lie under certain circumstances, though some people are more prone to lie than others. The chapters in this section provide a brief look at the pervasiveness of lying and the reasons and justifications for it, drawing on examples from history, other cultures, and psychology. This section categorizes the many motivations for lying, such as survival, escaping blame, and looking good, and describes the range of philosophical and ethical views about the role of lying in society and when it is justified.

Chapter 1: The Pervasiveness of Lying
Chapter 2: Why the Lie? The Reasons and Justifications for Lying

PART II: IDENTIFYING THE DIFFERENT TYPES OF LIARS

This section focuses on the range of approaches to lying, from the individual who tries to be a model of integrity to the individual with little conscience who feels free to lie when it suits his purpose or enjoys lying to get away with as much as possible. The chapters in this section discuss how and why different types of people make these different choices, using examples from interviews with several dozen interviewees. It includes the Lie-Q Test, designed to help readers examine their own style of lying and better understand the approach of others, and includes examples of individuals representing different categories or lying styles. It suggests ways in which readers can apply these results in everyday life to examine their relationships and make desired changes.

PART III: LYING IN PUBLIC AND PROFESSIONAL LIFE

The chapters in this section look at a variety of situations in which different types of people make different choices and employ varying styles of lying in their public and professional lives. It illustrates how people may be guided by the different lying styles of their work and professional peers in different types of organizations and occupations. This overview is designed to help readers better identify and respond to these different choices, using examples from the interviewees. Suggestions are provided on how to deal with the lying styles of different types of people more effectively.

PART IV: LYING IN PERSONAL AND PRIVATE LIFE

Generally, people are expected to be more honest and forthright in personal relationships, compared to their work or professional lives, where practical considerations are more apt to influence whether they lie or not. But in some cases, particularly in male–female relationships, lying can become common—and often may be a source of conflict in the relationship. However, lying styles still vary widely based on personal qualities and social circumstances, from the individual who highly values integrity to the person who is more likely to lie when it serves his purpose. The chapters in this section focus on how people with different lying styles approach a variety of situations. Here, too, readers are not only helped to recognize different styles but are provided with guidelines for improving their relationships with others.

PART I

Why Do We All Lie?

CHAPTER 1

The Pervasiveness of Lying

Every so often there is a backlash of concern about lying, such as when Governor Mark Sanford was caught lying to his wife, his staff, and the nation about his affair with his Argentine mistress or when Bernie Madoff's lies cost his trusting clients billions. But despite such recurring condemnations of unethical behavior and lying in everyday life, and despite the power of lying to threaten the bonds that link human relationships and society as a whole, lying is ubiquitous. It goes back to the dawn of human history, is found in all human societies, and occurs throughout the animal kingdom—even in some plants. Moralists, religious leaders, and philosophers decry it as ethically and morally wrong, as something that destroys trust, love, friendship, the social contract, and so forth.

But as long as there have been societies—from the simplest to the most complex—there have been lies. Most basically, lies protect the individual. Sometimes they can be used to protect the individual's relationships, community, and national groups, too. Biologists even suggest that this capacity or propensity for lying has been wired into our genes as an adaptive mechanism that has helped us and other forms of life survive.

Just how pervasive is this thing called lying?

WHEN IS SOMETHING A LIE?

What is lying? People have different definitions, and "lying" can depend on how narrowly people define it. In this book, I will be using the broadest, most inclusive definition. Also, I distinguish between more-serious and less-serious lies, sometimes called "white lies," that are often an accepted part of everyday social discourse; sometimes lying becomes a type of social convention not even considered a lie by some.

For example, in her classic book on the moral implications of lying, Sissela Bok focuses on "clear-cut lies"—lies where the liar has an obvious intention to mislead, knows that what he is communicating is not what he believes, and where he has not deluded himself into believing the lie.[1] Others have suggested the lie must involve some kind of misstatement disbelieved by a speaker who has the intent to deceive, though there may be exceptions, such as when a misstatement is said under duress or as a joke or a bluff.[2] There have also been scholarly efforts to attempt to distinguish among lying; bluffing, which involves faking something rather than falsifying; and bull-shitting, which involves weaving a web of fakery that goes beyond bluffing in a particular situation to fake on a greater scale.[3]

Lying need not be confined to deceptive statements. It also can occur through behaviors—such as actions or gestures used to support a lie—or concealments of relevant information. Making a promise or agreement without the intent to keep it can be a lie, too, though if one's intent is initially pure but circumstances undermine the promise or agreement, then that's not a lie—but it can often be hard to determine what is one's real intent.

Thus, out-and-out fabrications are only a small part of lying when the word is defined broadly. Rather, from this perspective, lying is ubiquitous—in animals and plants as well as in humans from the beginning of time.

HOW ANIMALS AND PLANTS DECEIVE

Do animals have the ability to plan their acts of deception? While many animals do engage in deceptive behavior—such as using a hiding place to elude predators or entrap prey, some seem to actually plan ahead, such as when a mountain lion picks a path on which to lie in wait, anticipating the subsequent arrival of a tasty deer. Or as one *U.S. News and World Report* article put it over two decades ago: "At its most elementary level, deception is a protective strategy, woven into evolutionary design."[4]

A good illustration of this design is the use of camouflage in nature as a way to protect the organism through disguise so it will be less likely to be eaten by some eager predator. Examples from the insect kingdom include bugs that look like sticks or stones; moths with spots on their wings that look like owls' eyes; and viceroy butterflies with the wing patterns of the poisonous monarch butterfly. Supposedly, this deceit will make a bird think the insect is inedible and pass it by.[5]

Plants use their own ploys. They may be bright and beautiful to entice insects to come to help them disperse their pollen. In other cases, insect eaters such as the Venus flytrap lure with their beauty. Then when the insect enters, expecting a treat, the trap snaps shut.

Moving up in the animal kingdom, there are numerous examples of birds, such as the plover, that try to lure predators from their nests by pretending to have a broken wing or otherwise leading the predator on a wild-goose chase.[6]

Among primates, trickery becomes even more complex and more obviously planned and intentional, showing clearer parallels with the kinds of lies humans tell. Baboons, for instance, have been found to use deception not only to get food but to attain other goals, such as dominance or protection from attack, as R. W. Byrne and A. Whitten discovered. In one example, a young juvenile began screaming to suggest that an adult female who was digging for food was attacking him, with the result that his mother came and chased the other female away. With the adult female gone, the juvenile was able to eat her food.[7]

Likewise, Jane Goodall's studies of chimpanzees in the Gombe Reserve in Africa have provided numerous examples of their deceitful behavior and tricks. Some less powerful adult males found that they could make others submit if they made loud noises by banging on the pots or garbage can lids they found in Goodall's camp, and for a while this strategy made them the dominant males. But after the other chimps realized that these chimps had no special powers from these devices, they fought back, and the less powerful males soon were back to their former status.[8]

Biologists such as R. H. Wiley suggest that this deception has evolved because camouflage, mimicry, and intimidation contribute to the organism's survival.[9] As a result, because lying and deceit have proved to be adaptive, they have been programmed into our ancestry. We have learned to lie, because for survival, lying works. Or as the social psychologists Charles Bond, Karen Kahler, and Lucia Paolicelli have put it:

Genetic capacities for deception have evolved through natural selection . . . In conflicts between predator and prey, in struggles over scarce resources, deception confers a selective advantage. For hundreds of generations, the less cunning have left behind fewer offspring, and deceptive capabilities have come to dominate the gene pool. Some of the resulting adaptations are anatomical (like coloration that offers concealment), while others are behavioral (like bird songs that mimic an opponent's rivals) . . . Although we (may) marvel . . . at the wonders of animal dissimulation, Homo sapiens is the master of deceit, for the brain our ancestors evolved to afford the most flexible deceptive repertoire—a repertoire which is influenced by genetically transmitted differences in aptitude.[10]

Given this adaptive quality of lying, traced back to our animal ancestry, is there any wonder there is so much lying today and throughout human history?

Yet, paradoxically, the ability of the person who is lied to to detect lying has evolved in tandem with the ability to lie, much like the power of viruses to cause disease has evolved as people have gained the immunity to defeat other viruses. It is like a continually changing game of cat and mouse in which as the mouse gets better at eluding the cat, a cat comes along who is better at catching mice, so the mouse has to be even more elusive to survive, and so on.

In turn, there is an underlying evolutionary science behind this, according to researchers Bond, Kahler, and Paolicelli. The reason for this constantly evolving dance of liar and lie detector is because "the liar gains evolutionary advantage at the dupe's expense, so dupes have left behind fewer offspring, and an aptitude for lie detection has evolved."[11] But that has led to a kind of evolutionary arms race in which the dupes get better, but the liars adopt still newer and better deceptive tactics for survival through natural selection.

THE TRICKSTER FIGURE IN HUMAN MYTH

Liars have also been honored as heroes, as well as being reviled through human history. Consider the example of David, who outwitted a much stronger Goliath, on the one hand; on the other hand, the devil is often depicted as the ultimate deceiver. This notion of the trickster figure as hero has long been celebrated in story and myth.

Possibly the roots of this trickster hero idea go back to our ancient hunter-gatherer past, where a person had to use his cleverness, trickery, and deceit to lure game. It's an idea suggested by ancient cave paintings, such as the figure of a man with outstretched arms and an erect penis near a bison-like creature with a spear through it that was found in the famous cave of Lascaux in the Dordogne Valley of France. The image may represent a man engaged in hunting magic designed to help bring game to the family or clan.

Commonly, the trickster gains what he or she wants through trickery and deceit or uses this trickery to help the culture as a whole. But sometimes the trickster is fouled up by such tricks.

A classic example of this archetype is the Coyote figure among native North Americans. In a typical story, he is presented as a selfish buffoon using tricks and deceits to gratify his big appetite for food or sex. But his elaborate deceits often backfire, so he ends up looking foolish.[12] In other myths, the trickster figure is seen as representing the spirit of creativity or chaos that exists in all of us or as being a "fun-loving, irreverent, crude, directly sexual, irresponsible, and unpredictable" character, representing a way of breaking free of the traditional order. And in still other stories, the trickster is presented as the creator of the earth, the slayer of monsters, the teacher of cultural skills and customs, and a cultural transformer.[13]

According to scholar William Manson, these opposing themes in the trickster's character represent the tensions that exist within all individuals and society. One is the instinctual desire for gratification and the expression of powerful yet socially proscribed desires and fantasies. The second is the development of civilization and culture, based on controlling these desires.[14] The trickster stories represent a playing out and reconciliation of these two impulses, showing our appreciation and admiration of the liar on the one hand, and our distrust of and anger at the liar on the other.

These devious heroes can take different forms. The image of Bre'r Rabbit, from the Southern black American folk tales, is another example of the pervasiveness of this wily trickster, as are the fox and wolf in the folk tales of Western Europe and the spider and jackal in tales from Africa.[15] The ancient Greeks had their own trickster in the person of Hermes, the Olympian messenger, who often tricked his way out of difficult situations. In Europe, the medieval jester and the irrepressible Tyl Eulenspiegel figure took this role.[16]

The Bible also offers a large cast of characters seeking an advantage by using deceit because they had less power. Many of these deceivers are women who are low on the power totem pole, such as Tamar and Judith, who combined sexual wiles with crafty speech, and Rebecca, who schemed to win the first-born's blessing for Jacob from her husband.[17] Still others are males, such as David, who used trickery as a boy to defeat Goliath. But their rationale is the same—they use trickery as a person in a position of social disadvantage to influence the course of events.[18]

Another reason for using deception by the trickster figure and others is to get outside the strictures of society and escape taboos, such as used by the Plains Indian tricksters and clowns. As described by Joseph Epps Brown, an authority on Plains Indian culture, these figures, in engaging in the "wisdom of the contrary," would do things to break with traditional norms or to fool people. If they go too far, they can be punished by their own tricks, such as happened to one medicine man, Black Elk, playing a trickster in a ceremony. He claimed he was going to make the earth rise in front of everybody within the tepee, then put gunpowder just under the surface of the earth, and when he called on the earth to rise, he touched it off. The earth did rise. But the gunpowder flared up and singed his eyes, and from that time on, he was nearly blind. So Black Elk had been punished for going too far in fooling people.[19]

Yet, by unknowingly overstepping boundaries, the trickster can help to define what is acceptable, since he is reined in whenever he goes too far, much like a modern liar might be able to get away with small social lies, such as exaggerating stories to be more dramatic or feigning interest so as not to embarrass a host. But once the lies become too bold, the liar falls into social disfavor, just like when a trickster who fails to recognize the proper borderlines between order and a lack of order in society acts against the social structure.[20]

Taken to extremes, this trickster figure becomes a devil figure, such as the devil character in Christianity who sets himself in opposition to God and the spiritual world and reflects the more material, biological, and animal qualities of the human being.[21]

So while the trickster can be a hero who uses his wiles and can advance his culture as a source of innovation, in another aspect the trickster is a demonic figure that challenges the everyday order.

It is this central paradox and ambiguity of the trickster, so universal in human culture, that affects how we view lying in everyday life. We disparage the liar and the idea of deception. But at times the lie is necessary to help and protect, as in the whole category of social or white lies. And many justify lying to advance a social good, such as to protect someone's life or to preserve a cherished value or the nation.

Another paradox is that lying appears to be part of our biological nature—we are programmed to lie; it's in our genes—while all societies denounce lying as being harmful to human relationships and the social order.

THE MORALITY AND SOCIAL DYNAMICS OF LYING

How should we deal with lying? What lies are acceptable?

The ideal has been to speak the truth, particularly in the Judeo-Christian tradition, where lying is viewed as morally wrong, evil, even a sin. Familiar quotes from the Bible speak of the virtues of truth:

- "Great is Truth, and mighty above all things" (Apocrypha, Esdras 4:41)
- "Rejoiceth not in iniquity, but rejoiceth in the truth" (Corinthians 13:1)
- "And ye shall know the truth, and the truth shall make you free" (John 8:32)

On the other hand, the lie and the liar are much disparaged. The Bible explicitly warns against lying:

- "You shall not bear false witness" (Exodus 20:13)
- "Keep far from a false matter" (Exodus 23:7)
- "Neither shall you deal falsely nor lie to one another" (Leviticus 19:11)

Still other examples come from the Jewish Talmud, among them: "Such is the punishment of the liar—even if he tells the truth he is not believed" (Sanhedrin 89b).

Likewise, the Greek philosophers found virtue in truth. As Plato observed: "The philosopher is in love with truth, that is, not with the changing world of sensation, which is the object of opinion, but with the unchanging reality which is the object of knowledge."[22] (Symposium, 201).

Theologians, philosophers, and jurists, too, have emphasized the need for the truth to protect the very foundations of the social order. For instance, in the fifth century, Augustine, the church father, stated that truthfulness was necessary because "When regard for truth has broken down or even slightly weakened, all things remain doubtful."[23] While some lies might be pardonable, such as those that harmed no one or saved someone from a serious injury, Augustine thought that some lies were much worse, especially those stated in the name of religion.[24]

Later, in the Middle Ages, the 13th-century theologian Thomas Aquinas inveighed against mischievous or malicious lies as mortal sins, though he excepted two types of lies—those that were helpful and those told in jest.[25] But some were much stricter in their approach, such as the 18th-century German philosopher Immanuel Kant, who took an absolutist position against all lies, claiming that all should be prohibited, regardless of their nature. In his view, truth is an "unconditional duty which holds in all circumstances" and should be limited by "no expediency," no matter how great the disadvantage to oneself or another. Why should truth be so important? Because, according to Kant, lies always harm humanity in general, even if they do not wrong any particular person. Why? Because the lie "vitiates the source of law" and destroys the human dignity of the liar—a view far different from the more casual attitude many have towards lying today, where lying is often the most practical approach in many situations—and if you can get away with it, why not lie if it's to your advantage?[26]

Between these extremes, the circumstances under which lying might be acceptable has been a subject of wide debate. Some thinkers, for example, have tried to delineate the conditions under which lying is acceptable, such as Hugo Grotius, a 17th-century Dutch scholar. He suggested that a falsehood becomes a lie and should be forbidden only if it prevents someone who deserves it from hearing the truth.[27]

Another school of thought advanced by the casuist thinkers permits a person to use a mental reservation to make a misleading statement true. The idea here is that a speaker can't be held responsible if someone else misinterprets his statement. For instance, if you say, "I didn't do it," even though you did, but think to yourself "I didn't do it when you said I did," that would no longer be a lie.

Still other thinkers question the premise that every untruth is morally wrong, suggesting that if a deception is designed to benefit the person deceived, it may as a matter of sense sometimes be right, an approach taken by the 19th-century English philosopher Henry Sidgwick.[28]

Because of all this quibbling throughout the centuries about the value of truth and the morality of lying, religious leaders, philosophers, and others have tried to come up with guidelines about what is appropriate. A list of admonitions is suggested by religious leader Mark Dratch, who proposes some of the following:

Absolute veracity is essential in judicial proceedings . . .
Lying is forbidden when it results in harm to another . . .
One may deviate from the truth for the sake of peace as well as for other ethical imperatives such as humility, modesty, and sensitivity . . . Even in those cases in which mendacity is permitted, habitual falsehood is forbidden . . .
In those cases where lying is permitted, ambiguity is to be preferred over an outright falsehood. It is preferable to make an equivocal statement that is truthful in its intended version but that may be misinterpreted by the listener.[29]

While such moral and ethical guidelines have been designed to keep people in line, for many people the inbred belief or fear that truth will out may be even more powerful.[30] Even if one no longer cares to tell the truth because of a weakening of conscience, the concern is about getting caught, though some recent exposés of a continual pattern of lies by financiers, politicians, and others suggests that many people think they won't. Just by repeatedly getting away with a series of lies, they have come to think they are invincible. But many others do refrain from lying in many cases out of a fear of being exposed.

Perhaps the more modern version of this concern is the oft-quoted phrase "What goes around comes around."

While the original strictures against lying may derive from a moral force urging good behavior (and presumably honesty) in order to get good behavior (and presumably honesty) in return, the modern attitude seems to reflect the pragmatism of the modern world. "Don't do it if it's wrong, because if you do, someone may do the same thing to you." The change is subtle, but it reflects the decline in the hold of traditional moral and ethical thinking about controlling behavior and marks the rise of a more secular, pragmatic, results-oriented thinking reflected in daily life and in the news every day.

Yet despite the potential danger of the lie being found out or coming back to harm us, we lie, and the texture of lying is woven into everyday life, because we make unconscious—maybe even conscious—cost-benefit analyses of lying in a situation. We weigh the risks of being found out and the losses of not lying against the potential gains.

It's as if people lie and expect lies to the point that common falsehoods are so common they are no longer considered lies. Should this be? In doing my interviews, I found that some people were quite bothered by this, though they experienced or sometimes did it themselves. "Just why do we have to lie?" some of them were asking, even as they saw lying as a common reality. And when I spent two years living half-time in LA, I found that lying was an even more pervasive part of the culture, much of this due to the influence of the film business. After all, as they say in LA, throw a rock and you'll hit an actor, and it's true that at almost every social gathering you'll run into some people with visions of silver screen or video discovery. Well, the essence of acting is being someone else, of being a trained poseur. And since status, money, and celebrity are the currency of the realm, people want to give off that aura of success, even if they have not achieved that yet. Even if they have to lie, that is a survival strategy for gaining acceptance and prestige in what some describe as the "brutal" competitive culture of LA.

In short, throughout history and even more today, we live in a culture of lies, despite all the moral and religious strictures against lying. So how much do we lie? According to one classic study by Daniel Goleman, the average adult lies—or admits to doing so—13 times a week.[31] So if you take the morality out of the equation, lying becomes as common and normal as eating ice cream. Or as Arthur Goldberg, a professor of psychiatry at Rush Medical College in Chicago, has stated: "Lying is as much a part of normal growth and development as telling the truth."[32]

But lies vary depending on what different people feel are important or what they fear happening if they don't lie. According to psychologists, the key areas that motivate people to lie include the following:

- To gain a sense of independence from the control or intrusiveness of others;

- To gain power and control; to repress or deny a source of conflict or unpleasantness; and
- To express a wish or increase self-esteem, say, by embroidering the truth or embellishing achievements to appear more "sought after, accomplished, or admirable."[33]

Some authors even suggest we live in a culture where lies have been institutionalized and are used routinely by our leaders. For instance, in a thoughtful article two decades ago on "The Culture of Lying" in *The New Republic*, Mark Hosenball used examples from the Iran–Contra affair to illustrate four types of lies:

- The outrageous lie, repeated frequently and vehemently until others believe it;
- The crafty lie, which creates a fog of confusing statements and evasions;
- The patriotic lie, which uses a sincere conviction as justification for the lie; and
- The muddled lie, in which perpetrators maintain their stories are confused rather than false.[34]

Well, exactly the same distinctions could be used to describe the lies told by different groups of people within the former Bush administration to support the Iraq War, using terrorist tactics in interrogations, and suspending of usual constitutional protections to permit surveillance in the name of national security. The debate over these different types of lies has become front page news today.

In short, lying is everywhere, and takes multiple forms. The following section lists some of the most common lies, many of which you may have heard or told yourself.

COMMON LIES PEOPLE ENCOUNTER

Social Lies

"Five pounds is nothing on a person with your height."
"It's delicious, but I can't eat another bite."
"Your hair looks just fine."
"You made it yourself? I never would have guessed."
"So glad you dropped by. I wasn't doing a thing."
"You don't look a day over 40."
"The baby is just beautiful."

"You can tell me. I won't breathe a word to a soul."
"Having a great time. Wish you were here."

Sales Lies

"It's a good thing you came in today. We have only two more in stock."
"The river never gets high enough to flood this property."
"You don't need it in writing. You have my personal guarantee."
"This is a very safe building. No way will you ever be burglarized."
"This car is like brand new."

Man–Woman Lies

"Sorry, dear, not tonight. I have a headache."
"Of course I will respect you in the morning."
"You have nothing to worry about, honey. I've had a vasectomy."
"Put the map away. I know exactly how to get there."

Parent–Child Lies

"Go ahead and tell me. I promise I won't get mad."
"The puppy won't be any trouble, Mom. I promise to take care of it
    myself."
"Our children never caused us a minute's trouble."
"I've finished my homework."
"Dad, I need to move out of the dorm into an apartment of my own so
    I can have some peace and quiet when I study."

Work Lies

"Sorry, the work isn't ready. The computer broke down."
"The new ownership won't affect you. The company will remain the
    same."
"I gave at the office."

Doctor–Patient Lies

"It's nothing to worry about—just a cold sore."
"The doctor will call you right back."

Lies to Officials

"But, officer, I only had two beers."

Self-Lies

"I'm a social drinker, and I can quit any time I want to."

All-Purpose Lies

"I did it. I didn't do it. I can't remember."
"I'll do it in a minute."[35]

The reason lies are so common is that the motivation to lie can be extremely powerful, whether we use a lie as a sword to go after something or as a shield to protect ourselves. As psychologist Beverly Palmer of California State University put it in a *USA Today* interview: We commonly use lying to protect ourselves "from the other person's angry or hurt feelings. We lie when we feel insecure, scared, or we're trying to escape consequences of our actions."[36] But then we run into the consequences of lying—the moral taboos, the threats to relationships and community, and the possible damages to ourselves if caught.

It was this central paradox that guided me as I explored this subject and asked questions in my interviews. When did people lie, and why? When and why did others lie to them? How did they feel about lying? What did they do to deal with it? When did they feel the lie was justified? What did they do if they thought someone was lying to them? Bring it out in the open? Let it lie? Pursue other strategies? How could they tell if someone was lying? And how did people differ in the extent to which they lied about different things—which led to the continuum of liars—from the models of absolute integrity (at least almost always) to the people who readily or even compulsively told lies.

In these interviews, I spoke to a representative sampling of dozens of men and women who could be considered successful business and professional people, in both informal and formal interviews. I also spoke with experts—psychologists and therapists who have encountered and dealt with lying in their own practice; specialists on male–female relationships, often a prime area for lying; and business consultants working with corporations and small businesses.

The following chapters describe the results of these explorations, as well as my own reflections and reactions to the central paradox of how and why we lie in everyday life.

CHAPTER 2

Why the Lie? The Reasons and Justifications for Lying

Just about any situation where people interact holds the potential for lying. Even when alone, people can lie to themselves. It's no wonder that most people I spoke with about lying agreed that it is at least somewhat common and comes in many forms—everything from the outright fabrication to the evasive half-truth, concealment, or unintended promise.

What is common? The people I spoke to reported that others lied to them about once or twice a week, and they averaged about one or two lies each week themselves—though most were so-called white lies committed to save people's feelings and smooth over social relations.

There are so many types of lies that turn up in so many different situations and that are told for so many reasons that it can be hard to determine whether a statement really is a lie. Was it intended as a lie? Was it perceived as a lie? Did it feel like a lie?

TYPES OF LIES

Lies are like soup—they come in a variety of packages with different contents, sizes, and costs—and as will be described in the next chapter, liars do, too— ranging from those who almost never lie to those who readily lie about everything.

Some lies are much bigger and more costly than others (think Bernie Madoff), while some are smaller and less expensive (think saying you like the hostess's terrible soup when you don't), and just like more costly items are rarer, so are the bigger lies, whereas the little lies spring up like weeds in a garden.

In turn, people have different ways of defining what they consider a lie. For example, many people will dismiss an exaggeration as just that—a good story rather than a lie, while others may prefer to see any embellishments as lying. And some exclude lies of omission, thinking that if you don't say it, it's not a lie. But omissions to conceal truths are definitely lies—in fact, they may even become torts like misrepresentation or crimes like fraud, such as when a realtor or financial agent doesn't disclose certain risks to lure you into buying or investing.

The type of lying most clearly perceived as lying—and which is usually thought of as worse than any other type—is the outright fabrication of something presented as true or fact. You know it's three o'clock, but he says two. It's the overt lie or lie of commission.

Such a lie differs from the mistake, for the person knows what he is presenting as true is not; he is directly seeking to deceive—the essence of the lie.

But then, the out-and-out falsification is the least common type of lying. What seem to be more common are the *half-truths*, which contain some but not all of the true information or present what's true in a misleading way; the *omissions or concealments*, which leave out something important and relevant; and the *commitments and promises* made that one doesn't intend to keep.

Though lies are commonly spoken, they need not be verbal; they can be made with gestures and nods—even silences can be taken to be an assent or a disagreement with something said.

I've tried to define lying broadly to encompass these different views, but these varying viewpoints still can lead to different ideas about why people lie and when lying is appropriate—and how to categorize the different types of liars based on the frequency and the seriousness of their lies.

For example, take concealing. It could be considered a lie when the information covered up or not stated is something one would be expected to reveal, such as a husband concealing an affair with a mistress. He doesn't tell his wife he has a mistress, because she doesn't ask, so he is not misstating the truth—he is just not telling it. In such a case, not telling would become a lie, because the understanding with his wife is that he will not have an outside intimate relationship. So concealing his failure to honor this fundamental agreement in the marriage becomes the lie.

Similarly, only stating a partial truth when the whole truth would give the full picture could be a lie, too. An example is when a person says "I'll have to cancel our appointment because my car is in the shop," but the real truth is that he decided to do something else and took the car to the shop, because he no longer needed it to make his appointment. If he didn't take the car to the shop at all, that would be an out and out lie.

Sometimes the purpose of the person lying can confuse things, as when some people think that concealment for a good purpose isn't really a lie, such as withholding an unfavorable bit of news from someone with a bad heart. As one woman told me: "I don't think that's lying, if you're assessing what you can safely say and are looking out for someone's welfare." But it still is a lie to conceal something for a good purpose, though it is one of those white and beneficial lies—and commonly people tell them. Even so, some people—most notably those who rarely lie—don't like such concealments, claiming it is better to tell or know the truth.

As one man I interviewed put it:

For me, withholding information would be lying if you knew that not withholding it would make a difference in your relationship or transaction or you used it to influence the outcome. Or if you knew this was important information you should reveal. Then I would consider it a form of lying.

Similarly, views about the relationship between keeping commitments and lying vary greatly. While some people might not consider breaking a promise or commitment a type of lie—"It's just a lack of integrity," as one man said—while others might see it as a lie if the promise or commitment is made without the intention of keeping it. As one man put it, "If someone consciously intends to not be there, and they say they're going to be there, that's a lie to me." Another woman made this fine distinction: "If you don't intend to do it at the time you make the agreement, that feels like lying. But if you have the intention to do it but then you don't do it, then I think it's just not keeping agreements and having a lack of integrity." If the reason for not doing it is error or forgetfulness, that's just a "mistake," as one man said.

In other words, what defines a lie in making agreements is your intention at the time. If you make an agreement in good faith, but then circumstances changes, so you really can't keep the agreement—not just that you'd rather do something else, then that's not a lie. But if you enter into an agreement knowing that you don't expect to fulfill it or that you probably won't, then you are lying. As Roger (not his real name. Names have been changed throughout to protect privacy.), a college philosophy teacher, pointed out:

Breaking an agreement or lying are two separate things. An agreement is something that's going to happen in the future, and you may or may not be able to keep your agreements, based on what occurs. So there might be contingencies that prevent you from keeping an agreement, such as one time when I made an agreement to substitute-teach for a friend, and it was raining, and I couldn't get there because it was so slow on the freeways. So I got there late. But it was beyond my control to get there on time to keep the agreement, so there was no lie. And if I had forgotten, that wouldn't be a lie either. It would show a lack of integrity, but it wouldn't be a lie.

However, a lie might be involved if one makes an agreement in bad faith. For instance, there was a man who was living upstairs from me who borrowed $100 to fix his car. He promised to pay me back. But he lied, because there was nothing wrong with his car; he was just out of gas. And then he didn't keep his promise to pay me, either. He promised that he was going to take the money to get his car going and then he was going to get his paycheck. As I found out later, he didn't have a job then. So that was a lie, too, because he was making an agreement that he knew he couldn't keep. He was making the agreement to get some kind of benefit for himself, but he had no intention of ever keeping the agreement. And that's a lie.

The whole area of self-presentation and image-making also is ripe for exaggeration and lies, though when does presenting an improved or anticipated self-image become a lie? I found this question especially relevant after living half-time in LA for two years, where presenting a false but embellished self is embedded deep in the culture. So what might be accepted there as a common part of getting ahead, as long as one is good at this choice of self-presentation, might be frowned upon elsewhere for being phony. Again, the key factor seems to be the individual's intent in making the presentation and whether he or she is leaving out information that would be considered important or relevant or adding information that might mislead. The notion of affirming or presenting oneself in a positive light seems fine, though when this shades over into exaggeration and bragging about something that is untrue or unrealized, this gives birth to a lie.

As Roger, the philosophy teacher, expressed this paradox in defining this sort of lie:

I don't consider presenting the truth in a favorable perspective to be lying. Say you're applying for a position, and there's a two-year gap between your graduate school and your first teaching job, because you had a difficult time finding yourself. I don't consider it lying not to put down the details, because that's personal information and it could directly interfere with your getting a job which you can do. So as long as you can do the job, I think it's appropriate to present the information on your résumé to your best advantage.

Roger gave an example of a man he knew who did this.

He was a professor who was applying for a job at a school where I was teaching. He did not have his Ph.D. so on his vita he simply did not list his degrees. He was interviewed, and the committee liked him, so he got the position. After he was in the position for a few years, a committee came around to verify his credentials, and they found out he didn't have his Ph.D., though he had been doing a good job. Eventually he was fired for misrepresenting himself. That's the case where I'd consider it dishonest to misrepresent oneself in that way, because letting people assume that you have a Ph.D. when you do not, to gain an advantage, is a case of deliberately withholding certain critical information you should disclose. So that's a case of telling a lie through falsely presenting the self.

In other cases, this emphasis on the positive and withholding of the negative seemed fine. It was part of the philosophy of affirming the self or making others feel good by accentuating the positive. So it wasn't a lie. If it was, it was one of those benevolent white lies, and therefore fine, as Roger explained:

When you go for an interview, certainly you don't declare all of your frailties. You try to put yourself forward in the best possible light. Or when you go out on a date, you don't go into the details of your sexual behavior until you really know the person. In my case, I do want to share every aspect of my life with another person that I'm intimate with. But not all at one time or in the beginning. So I don't consider that I'm misrepresenting myself when I don't tell all in the beginning.

It's the same way when you're trying to impress someone, say at a mixer. In a certain way, you're presenting an aspect of you that's not the total you, but I don't consider that lying. For that's the crucial difference—the difference between presenting your-self in a positive light and deliberately withholding some information that one would normally expect to be there.

For some people the idea of couching a critical evaluation in a positive light is not a lie, either. For example, while purists on the absolute integrity side of the continuum might consider anything less than the complete truth to be lying, albeit for the best of intentions, the philosophy teacher quoted already, more of a pragmatist, described this more positive approach as a way of framing or shaping reality to get a better response. As he observed:

I don't consider presenting the facts in a favorable perspective to be lying. For in-stance, if someone asked me: "How do you like my dress?" or something like that, I think I can express the fact that I don't think it is the best or that it doesn't bring out the best in a person and still make the person feel affirmed. In other words, I'm pre-senting a perspective on the situation. It may be a favored perspective on the situation, but it's still an interpretation of events. . . . I'm finding something positive to say; I'm not trying to put the negative in some positive context. But that's not lying, because I don't see lying and the truth as direct opposites, so that whenever you don't tell the full truth, that doesn't mean you're automatically lying, as if these are direct contrar-ies. Rather, lying involves deliberately trying to mislead or deceive someone. But just putting things in a positive light doesn't do that.

In short, lies can run the gamut from the outright, overt misstatement of the truth to those other half-truths, concealments, and broken promises that some people think of as lies only in some circumstances. In any case, if someone con-siders something to be a lie, whether he does it or someone else does it to him, then so be it—that's a "lie" for the purposes of this book. The essence of the lie is the conscious intent to deceive, no matter what forms that deceit takes.

THE REASONS FOR LYING

When I interviewed people, some of the same reasons kept coming up for both the women and men as to when they lied or someone lied to them. The most popular reason—especially for the women—was to spare someone's feelings or make someone feel better, the altruistic side of lying, while the men were apt to lie to enhance their achievement, status, or power, reflecting the com-mon female/male differences in what is most important to them—nurturing and relationships are high priorities for the women; presenting oneself as a success is especially valued by the men—and we tend to lie about what is most important to us.

Most other reasons revolved around gaining an advantage or improving one's appearance, such as by

- Getting out of some activity or event,
- Appearing more skilled or knowledgeable,
- Improving one's reputation,

- Hiding a mistake,
- Covering up something,
- Keeping a secret, or
- Gaining a financial advantage or position in business.

In addition, another reason for lying was revenge or jealousy.

Beyond these situational reasons are deeper motives for lying, for at its roots—and why the tool of lying and deceit has been programmed into us—lying is a defense mechanism to protect the individual or others he chooses to protect. As Mark, a business consultant, firmly noted, we lie for survival. As he said:

What human beings do is primarily for survival, and survival includes looking good, being right, justifying ourselves, dominating the situation. That is, if we are right, we survive. So we do everything to survive. So we will lie, cheat, steal, all in the name of our own survival. And so we always have some way to justify the lie. It may not work—I don't think it does in the long run. But lying is absolutely congruent with survival. And to survive, we can justify anything—including cheating on our wives and our husbands, cheating on our taxes, whatever. We're seeking the short-term gain and justifying it to ourselves. Because the lie is about survival—lying for our own advantage to survive.

In turn, this use of lying as a defense mechanism may lead to lying to the self and to others to avoid facing an unpleasant reality. A psychotherapist I spoke to, Robert Young, a practitioner working with mentally ill patients, explained:

Sometimes as a defense, people may deny what is true or even conjure up images of multiple personalities, because they so need to defend against the truth as to provide a reality they can live with. So they have to lie to themselves and other people.

For example, a classic case is the woman who has experienced sexual molestation or abuse. Some women who have been abused cannot really consider that it is true. So they might say, no, it never happened, or it was a dream, or people are lying about it.

Then there are other sorts of lies that in their more extreme form reflect personality or character disorders, such as the narcissistic personality disorder, where a person has such grandiose thoughts of himself as important, valuable, or good that his ideas become pathological.

What are the major factors that trigger such uses of the lie? Common triggers are stress, attack, or risk. As Stephen, a writer, commented:

Generally, I would say I've lied to others when I have felt under stress or maybe under attack for some reason. Either there's some sort of stress occurring in my life or in my relationship with someone. So the lie is a way to protect myself or gain an advantage somehow. . . . And then I found I have lied when I felt at risk in some way, either emotionally or physically, though emotionally mostly. For example, suppose the woman I'm with asks me a question about herself or asks for my opinion on something, and I think she's expecting or wants a certain answer, but my answer isn't that. I might lie to smooth things over, such as saying "I love you," or "I agree with you," when I'm not feeling that emotion or that opinion at the time.

Such feelings of stress or attack can help the person justify the lie, as Robert Young pointed out. As he explained:

Stress tends to make lying less of a sin. Stress tends to make it more allowable to lie. Say if you have to get something done by a deadline, and the boss asks, are you going to have it done? You may know you are not going to have it done. So you may say, yes, you'll finish it, just to get him off your back, and hope that maybe it will get done after all. So stress in general can tend to make people be less truthful.

Under stress, people may look to all sorts of excuses to justify the lie. As Young commented:

I think drugs and alcohol are a bit of a fad excuse now for excusing yourself for your own personal behavior. "It wasn't me, it was my substance abuse." So these substances can be used to excuse lies as well as other kinds of behavior, particularly since the general population is now coming to see alcoholism as a disease, and hence beyond one's ability to control. This disease theory may not be true. But whether it is or not, people use the excuse of drugs or alcohol to say "I couldn't stop myself," Or "I couldn't control myself," Or "I didn't mean to do it," "It's not my fault, I was drunk," or "I was on drugs."

In turn, this stress theory of lying suggests that people subjected to economic stress—people earning less money—might be more likely to lie, which I have found myself in the recent recession. For instance, people who have encountered a sudden downturn—from failing in a business to losing a job— may want to look like they are still successful to others. So they may describe themselves as consultants or experts in a particular area to maintain the aura of success, rather than acknowledge their growing desperation. That way, they feel, they may be more likely to find acceptance and other opportunities.

By contrast, those who are successful and feel economically secure are better able to maintain high ethical standards, unless they are among the strivers who define success by obtaining more and more. Then, like the financiers on Wall Street who engaged in all sorts of schemes to build capital and left their ethical principles behind, until the financial dominoes began falling in the fall of 2008, they may leave these standards behind.

I found this distinction again and again among the people I interviewed. While the successful professional and business people I interviewed emphasized their own generally high ethical standards, a woman transcriber, earning much less money and living in a small apartment, felt she didn't have that luxury and, if necessary, would lie to keep her head above water. As she commented:

It's nice that somebody in such a secure financial position can afford to be so honest. But when you have to keep it together financially, you have to think of your own survival. Sometimes you have to lie to survive.

In short, one factor influencing the propensity to lie can be income. Or as the popular phrase goes: "Fake it till you make it." Well, once you make it, you no longer need to fake it. You just have to lie to claw your way up. And then, like a king or queen on a throne, you can afford to be generous and don't need to lie as much, since you already have it made.

While economic insecurity can create the fear that leads to lying, people can be insecure for all sorts of other reasons that lead to lying, such not having enough confidence or feeling a lack of prestige. That's a theme Judith Briles noticed when she studied the ethics of the women and men in the corporate world, reported in her two books, *Women to Women: From Sabotage to Support* and *The Confidence Factor*. As she observed in an interview:

Often people feel drawn to lying and justified in doing it because they feel they aren't getting their worth recognized. They aren't getting their due. They have not been honored. They haven't been credited for something. . . . Something has happened to make them feel diminished, insecure. For the act of lying is birthed out of fear. It's birthed out of insecurity. It's birthed out of low confidence. Sometimes you can have jealousy and other things thrown in as well, but that's the bottom line—insecurity and fear.

Still another common reason, born out of insecurity, is a desire for increased self-esteem, noted by numerous people I interviewed, including Frances, a computer-systems supervisor in a large manufacturing company, who noted that

I've run into lying a lot with people seeking a job or a better position. They don't feel good enough about themselves to tell the truth. So they're compensating for a lack of security and self-esteem. They have to puff themselves up to make themselves look better. . . . And we've all seen this with people in the public eye as well. For instance, some candidates have lied about their undergraduate work. And there was one woman here in San Francisco, running for supervisor, who said she had done certain things on her résumé when she had not. So that's a big one, I think, self-esteem.

Robert Young, the psychotherapist, backed up this influence of low self-esteem on lying from his own practice. He saw many people with eroded confidence engaging in lies to deny their sense of failure to themselves, create a protective fantasy that things would really be fine, or try to maintain a good face for others. As Young observed:

Society has become so dynamic and changing today that it tends to disrupt people's confidence, such as when a person loses a job and can't find another. A concrete example might be the guy who's trained as a tool-and-die maker. He gets out of tool-and-die–making school, but then he's out of a job in five years, and a lot of his sense of self-worth is shattered because now he's no longer able to provide for his family. He's out of a job, or maybe he's working at a low-income job, such as the 7-Eleven at a minimum wage. . . . The person has been trained with certain skills for a skilled job and suddenly has nowhere to use them. So his self-confidence is eroded, which can happen to anyone who suddenly encounters closed doors and feels his sense of self undermined.

And then, as a result of this lack of self-confidence, the person mostly wants to deny. So lying becomes a way of covering up, of trying to maintain a facade, or of saying to himself, it's not so bad, it will get better, I'll get another job doing this, when in fact, there are no jobs. The lie becomes a way to protect against the lack of self-worth and confidence the person feels.

But such lies to protect one's self-worth need not only be to other people. This desire not to admit or to hide something can additionally lead to lies to oneself—to avoid facing something unpleasant, as well as lies to others—to avoid feeling shame.

For example, Raphael, a counselor and healer, encountered many people lying to him, both clients and associates, because they were afraid to be direct and revealing:

I think people often are not direct and open about what's happening, because they may not want to admit to something to someone else. Or they may not want to look at something in themselves.

For example, that happened with some of the people I worked for who decided our working arrangement wasn't working out. They were in authority, and they could use their power to make it seem like I wasn't doing things the way they wanted. But the approaches I was using were working, and I wanted them to look at their own issues and reasons. But they said no, trying to make me seem in the wrong, because they didn't want to see what was going on in themselves.

Raphael also encountered the concealing and hiding.

It happens when you don't want people to know something about you which may affect how these people treat you or think about you. So you say things that aren't true or leave things out—lies of commission or lies of omission. But they can be used for the same reason—to try to hide something. For example, you are asked something directly: you say no or you don't know. It can be an easy way of getting off the hook or keeping someone out, instead of maybe being more direct and saying "mind your own business." I know I've used that sometimes; and others have used it on me. I think we all sometimes have things we want to hide, and lying, or maybe more accurately, concealing, can be a way to do this.

Likewise, Stan, a usually honest high school teacher, used lies to hide a smoking habit from his wife. He suspected that she knew, because there was the smell of smoke everywhere—though she never said anything—because it would be too stressful to deal with the subject.

Another type of lie, born of insecurity, is the passive-aggressive style of lying, described as a common dynamic in lying by one of the therapists I spoke with, Sylvia Mills, a psychotherapist in private practice, who deals with primarily professional and business clients. In this case, the passive-aggressive person feels insecure and so hangs back from being assertive and saying what he or she really wants. Instead, he or she says something, agrees to something, or goes along with something he or she really doesn't want, and so, in effect, lives a lie. That failure to be authentic can lead to anger and resentment, which can be expressed through open hostility, distancing in relationships, or covert behavior, such as back-stabbing or sabotage. As Mills explained the process, illustrating it with an experience with two friends:

Basically, what happens with the passive-aggressive person, is he or she seems very agreeable. It's like he or she is Mr. Nice Guy, so nice and ready to do things your way. But all the time they're agreeing, they are burning up with resentment, because they are "giving in" and not doing what they want to do.

For example, if I'm a passive-aggressive person, which I'm not, I might agree to go to a movie with you, saying: "Okay, I'll go to the movie you want to see," but I'll sit through that movie thinking: "I don't want to sit through this movie. I want to go to the other movie." And meanwhile, I'll be angry or hating you, because I've gone to your choice of a movie instead of speaking up for myself.

Finally, after numerous occasions of giving in, the resentment is voiced. These angry feelings are typically directed at the other person for being "inconsiderate." It's hard for Mr. or Mrs. Nice Guy to take responsibility for their own passivity—and so much easier to project out all the responsibility and blame.

The irony of all this is that the other person is usually feeling quite warm toward their "considerate" partner. Thus it's a rude shock to discover the partner has been lying about his or her real feelings.

How does this happen? I wondered, and Mills explained:

In one case, the woman—I'll call her Judy—was friends with another woman, Sally, whom she thought was a real friend. And then one day, when the two of them were in a group of about half a dozen people, Sally suddenly announced that she really didn't like something that Judy did. She thought Judy was bossy and controlling, that Judy always wanted to do things her way, and so she had gone along with Judy in the past. But now, she griped about how she resented that.

And Judy was shocked because she had known Sally for three years, and Sally never complained about anything. Now Sally was saying she had felt this way for three years. To make matters worse, she was making this accusation in a very public group with Judy's friends.

Judy was really furious and disgusted. She felt her relationship with Sally for over three years had been based on trust. They had both shared so much of their lives with each other. Now in this very public way, Judy suddenly felt that Sally had come out and negated that trust. So that ended the relationship, since Judy now realized the lie Sally had been hiding for all these years; her feelings of trust were shattered.

Another big reason for lying, which can also be traced to fears of insecurity, is the desire to avoid embarrassment or save face to make oneself look better.

Don, a 50-something engineer, for example, felt embarrassed telling the store owner his real reason for getting a dog whistle. When the owner asked whether he had a dog, he quietly fibbed and said he did. But the real reason, Don told me, is that

I wanted to get this whistle to annoy this dog next door to get him to stop barking. I wanted to train him so that every time he barked, he would hear this unpleasant whistle, and that might get him to stop. But then, I thought it might not be proper to use the whistle in this way. You're supposed to use it to get the dog's attention so you can train it. But this isn't what I was doing, and maybe if I started explaining my real reasons, the owner might think I might want to blow the whistle to have the dog bark more so it would bother other people, and then we could all get together to get rid of the dog.

A few days later Don encountered a case of someone lying to make himself look good. It was one of those name-dropping situations, where Don and a girlfriend had gone to a party and had sat with a man who was telling stories about his successful exploits in building companies and making high-yield investments. He also described exciting international adventures where he had eluded some potential robbers or killers, presumably after some of his expensive belongings or his money. People had listened in rapt fascination.

But when Don and his girlfriend drove the man home and Don asked him more detailed and pointed questions, it soon became apparent that some of his stories could not have happened. As Don explained:

Things just didn't jibe right or hang together. So we concluded he must be a pathological liar. He was just trying to make himself look good or more important. And he could do that—he could say anything he wanted to impress—because no people bothered to check out or question his story, or maybe didn't know enough to do so. So that's what he was doing—building himself up to impress everyone with what a guy he was.

Another reason for lying is to gain power—a reason often used for lies in business or politics to gain an advantage, or in conflicts of lovers and spouses, usually by the woman, because she has less power.

For instance, as Dee, a real-estate investor, observed:

If people lie to me, I would lie back to them if I feel that it's necessary to be on a more equal footing with them. As I see it, the lie is a way of gaining power in a situation. So in that case I would use it if someone isn't going to be straight or fair with me. It's like my way of evening out the deck if someone else is trying to play with the cards.

Conveniently, there are lies of convenience, too. In this case, it is just easier to lie than raise issues that might be discussed, give explanations, deal with feelings, or risk hurting someone's feelings by telling the truth.

Lies can also be used to get someone to do something or to get out of doing something. Roger, the philosophy teacher, described how one of his colleagues, ironically a professor of ethics, did this by using promises he didn't expect to keep to gain an advantage. As Roger told me:

This teacher, Jack, got a one-year sabbatical from his university for a year of study at a big eastern university in some ethics program, and so he had to move there. Well, he knew a graduate student who had a truck. So Jack promised this student that "You move me to Harvard with your truck, and I'll set up interviews with all of these teachers I know there to help you get into Harvard."

The student brought his truck around, loaded up Jack's furniture, and drove him from this school in the South all the way to Massachusetts—a distance of almost 1,000 miles. But a few months later, when the student returned to Massachusetts, wanting to set up the interviews, Jack had totally forgotten about his promises. "What promise?" he said. "I didn't promise you anything."

So the graduate student didn't get his interviews, didn't get in, and was furious, because Jack reneged on what he said he was going to do. Maybe the student wouldn't have gotten in anyway. But the point is that Jack used the student to get what he wanted. Then, after he was moved to Harvard and didn't need the student anymore, he reneged.

Still another category of lies are those that hurt or wound others. Often they are born of jealousy or revenge. If true hurtful evidence isn't available, sometimes someone will make up something, as happened to Don, the engineer, when he and a former lover were having a fight. As Don described it:

She said some very insulting things to me—making up insults to hurl against me. She claimed I couldn't do this, couldn't do that, said I didn't have the feelings I said I had, that sort of thing. And then she said I didn't do things that I did.

I knew the things she was saying weren't true, and I don't know whether she had spaced out and literally forgot things that had happened or was making things up, just to have things to throw at me. I suspect the latter, and when I tried to confront her, to point out how these things weren't true, she replied she was just joking. But I don't think she was. She clearly wasn't saying things in a joking way. I felt she was saying them to put me down and was trying to make me think she thought these things about me, whether true or not. So she was just trying to get me, I think, by making up lies.

Revenge, too, can be an underlying motivation, which is what happened to Reba, an inspirational speaker. By mistake, she disclosed information about a former coach and trainer, and he was very angry about it, so angry that that ended their teacher—student relationship, and he barely spoke to her for years. But he did even more, as Reba later found out.

I learned about it from my boyfriend. The man was spreading stories about me, claiming I was unreliable, that I wasn't as good and competent as I presented myself, things like that. And then, when I confronted him about it, he told me: "Well now you know how I felt, because you disclosed something I had told you in confidence about me."

Well, until then I never realized I had let anything slip before—he had never told me, just acted odd and distant. And then he further retaliated by telling false stories about me. I feel like he should have told me what was bothering him in the first place, because I realized when I spoke to a couple of friends about this that I could have inappropriately disclosed things. But then, I don't think that justifies what he did against me—I had just made a mistake, but he was out to actually hurt me, to get back at me for revenge.

While most reasons for lying reflect the dark side of lying, there are some good reasons for some lies. Some are designed to help and protect someone else and are commonly called "white lies," although the term also refers to the trivial lies about things of small importance and consequence. As Stan, the teacher, explained:

There were a couple of times that I lied to my wife, but this was to help her. What happened was that she was very ill with cancer, and she was on chemical treatment for a year. I had to continually reassure her that she was doing fine, that she was getting better, although for a while it didn't look that way. But I felt I was helping her, at least to brighten her spirits, even if she couldn't be cured. But then, eventually, she did beat it, and it could be that maybe the lie helped. So I think sometimes it is possible to help someone by lying, and then I think it's okay to lie.

Stan similarly used lies from time to time to encourage and motivate his students. Again he felt lying was justified, because it was done to help. As he told me:

It's okay to lie when it's making people feel okay about themselves or encouraging them to do something. I've done this with my students. For instance, a kid comes up and asks me: "Am I really flunking?" and the kid probably is flunking now. However, the kid by law is going to be in my class until June, with several months to go. So if I was to tell him he is flunking, I'd probably never see him again. So instead, I would tell him, well, maybe if you really buckle down and start coming and make up this work, maybe you'll pass.

In a way it's a lie, because the student is probably not going to do what he needs to do to pass, and I suspect the student feels he can't pass anyway. But I think it's a worthwhile lie because it helps and encourages him a little.

Then, of course, there are the self-lies to protect and build up oneself to oneself. Such lies can start off as deceptions to others, but as the person tells them again and again, they can turn into self-deceptions. So the liar comes to believe his or her own lies. Or as psychotherapist Robert Young explained:

When someone creates a fantasy to impress people, that could be an example of narcissism. And sometimes they believe in what they are saying themselves, sometimes not; or the fantasy could be a blending of both.

Often the story they tell can grow into them, so they come to believe it more and more as time goes on. Just the process of telling and retelling can help them believe, so after a while, truth and fantasy become so artfully blended or they have repeated the imagined claim so often that they think it is true.

Moreover, as Young suggests, if the fantasies and deceptions become great enough, this turns into a syndrome that psychiatrists call "grandiosity," which often appears in manic-depressives in the manic phase. And often it is accompanied or eased by alcohol or drugs that support the fantasy.

Why would lies and deceptions go so far as to turn into such a syndrome of mental illness? Because they protect the person from even greater internal struggle. Or, as Young noted, the syndrome occurs because:

The narcissistic or grandiose lie has become a defense against a more serious inner turmoil, such as a defense against either depression, which is most probable, or some other sort of trauma. The lie becomes that much greater, because it is a defense against more serious problems.

So even if such self-lies don't go so far as to become forms of illnesses, they can still be used as a psychological defense against reality.

This is what happened when Blanche's husband Mack lost his job. He was an engineer who lost his job in the defense industry and couldn't readily find another. So Blanche, as an act of love, not because she needed him, hired him to work in her start-up business. Soon Mack began to think he was important to the company, though he wasn't; instead he was inefficient and ineffective in his managerial duties, though he didn't want to admit this when Blanche tried to point it out.

"That's a good example of denial to escape facing reality," Young told me. "These kind of false build-ups of self are always a kind of defense against reality. After all, if her husband was to really see himself as he is, he would have to face the fact that he is a failure, and then, who knows what could happen?"

Then, too, some lies may be used like a Trojan horse to help the social good, to gain a strategic advantage in a conflict, or cover up something in the name of national security. Plus, a lie might be used to save a life other than one's own, as in the classic "he went-that away" ploy used to protect someone from being hurt by another. As Young observed:

Classically, the philosophers and moralists have said, "Don't lie." Kant said that one should never lie.

But then there's the classic counterargument showing there are times when the lie can be appropriate. For instance, what if a man comes running through your room and says, "There's a murderer chasing me and he has a gun in his hand?" And then, after the man runs off, the murderer comes in, saying: "Where did that guy go?" If you tell the truth, you might be responsible for the man's death, whereas a lie might save him. So there can be times when lies are appropriate. This may be an exaggerated example, but there are times.

Then there is the lie, which may be benign, that allows us to step into another reality for a while by creating not just a better image but another self-persona. It is a way, as the philosopher Elizabeth Kamarck Minnich describes it, of giving us "an almost magical sense of our own power and freedom," and as such it is "like imagination, like creativity, like play." It is a way of lying "for fun," to show that one is "not bound by the facts of the matter."[1]

Raphael, the healer and counselor, gave a good example of this when he described how he created a new character for himself when he went to a local restaurant—an exaggerated, eccentric, free-spirited, looser, freewheeling, and entertaining image of his usual self. This way he could be more fun and free. As he put it:

I can be whoever I want to be. It's kind of fun. I can step into this other role and be light-spirited. If I'm really in a magical mood, I can say some nice things. Or I can wear something unique and different. Sometimes I wear black. Sometimes a unique hat. Sometimes some earrings, or other touches. It's just interesting to create this public versus my private person. I think there's something exhibitionistic about what I'm doing. And it's fun.

JUSTIFYING THE LIE

Ironically, people generally say they don't like to lie and sometimes feel guilty or bad about lying, though they do it, while feeling angry and betrayed when others lie to them. Yet they commonly feel their own lies are justified or appropriate. In fact, people sometimes feel proud of certain lies. This sense of justification is due to what psychologists call "homeostasis"—achieving a sense of psychological balance so that one can feel good or comfortable about however one has acted.

When I spoke with psychotherapist Robert Young, he explained justifying the lie this way:

Lying is fundamentally wrong. Everyone would generally acknowledge that. Though many people have a relativistic ethic, making it okay to lie to certain groups of people or under certain circumstances. For example, it's okay to lie to an enemy like the Iranians. It's okay to lie to someone who has lied to you before. It's okay to lie to ruin someone's reputation, because that person has already done something to do me in and therefore deserves it. And then we define some lies as okay, because they are done to help people.

In other words, lies are normally justified. There's always some hidden agenda in the lie, some good reason or bad reason that justifies the lie. And the underlying dynamic behind this is the psychological process known as homeostasis, which is a way of keeping balance. We use justification to not be out of balance. So if you have a good reason to lie, you'll feel much healthier and calmer about yourself.

In some cases, an outside observer wouldn't agree with that reason. He may think it's a bad reason. But the person engaging in the lie will think it's a good reason; he'll feel it is justified; it's his way of staying in balance, in homeostasis with himself.

Otherwise, without doing this, the individual might feel some internal or intrapsychic dissonance, resulting in feelings of anxiety or paranoia. So people will come up with reasons so they feel comfortable about what they do.

As Young pointed out, some of the reasons might not seem to be valid justifications to someone else. For instance, a sleazy salesperson might not tell a customer that the brakes on the car he was buying were bad because the salesman might tell himself: "If the customer didn't bother to check, he's stupid and deserves what he gets." Or on the national scale, a government official might justify a lie in the interests of national security, such as "I lied to the Koreans to get the hostages back." Psychologically, the reason, whatever it is, has enabled the person to achieve a state of balance or homeostasis.

That seemed to be the main distinction among the people I spoke to in what justified a lie or not—if it helped or didn't hurt anyone, it could be justified, even if it might not be morally condoned or right. But if it hurt or harmed, it became a bad, unjustifiable lie.

In turn, such justifications can be used to shore up everyday business and social practices, because they make the reasons given for lying in particular situations appropriate. Dick, the sales manager in a large company, gave an example.

I don't ascribe to lying. I don't condone it. But I think a good example of when it's okay would be a situation which occurred for a client of mine from the Northwest. He had a will agreement for all of the relatives to sign, and when he asked some of the relatives, he told them that another relative some asked about had already signed the agreement, and later that relative did.

Should he have said that? His view was that everybody was going to sign the document anyway; nobody got hurt by signing; everybody was going to gain from the document; and he was just trying to keep things moving and get it signed in time. And since everyone was going to sign—and did—why not do it as efficiently and effectively as possible? The results were exactly the same whether he directly told the truth, evaded the question, or massaged the truth as he did. So he felt his lie was justified. There was no cost to anybody; the lie didn't hurt anybody. So why not do it? At least that's how he justified what he did as being all right, and I suppose if I was in that situation I might, too, though I think lying in general is wrong, because it involves being evasive or not stating the truth as it is.

Then, too, a major justification for lying might be to serve some higher principle or good, such as the code of ethics of one group, country, or god. For instance, one might argue that Dick Cheney and others justified their deceptions to support interrogating suspected terrorists in Guantanamo and using CIA surveillance of Americans without warrants on the grounds they were serving a higher law to preserve the values of this country. It is an approach used by many others in the political arena to support their particular causes.

Sometimes religious leaders or other group leaders may use this, too, such as in justifying their lies in the name of their Christian mission or God to raise funds for certain ministries and then use these funds for other purposes.

And even hardened criminals use justifications to support their lies and crimes, such as blaming the pressure of a parent, spouse, or lost job for their decision to rob or steal.

Thus, whatever the nature of the lie, the individual explains it in terms of his own value system, so it becomes appropriate to use the lie. This helps to support the individual's own values by helping him to stay in balance—in homeostasis—with himself.

In some cases, this process of justification can even help the individual to feel proud of the lie, because he has been successful in using it to conceal something or to achieve a goal.

For example, Storm, a journalist, once used lying to get a woman he thought was particularly vicious in denigrating others to talk to him. As a result, she said things that discredited herself—a completely justifiable result from his point of view. As he explained:

I felt this woman was going around spewing out vicious stuff about gays, and even though I didn't think that she thought of herself as a vicious person, I felt the attitude of homophobia she was fostering was wrong. So I led her on to believe that if she talked to me for an interview, I would make sure that the world would get a chance to hear what she had to say and the interview would be unbiased. Which was true.

But what I didn't say is that I would ask tough questions, and I led her to think I would give her a supportive hearing. For instance, I told her she would feel better for doing the interview, and that the world would know where she really stood. However, after the interview came out, showing what she said she believed, she had tons of ridicule heaped on her; she lost three contracts and proceeded to divorce her husband.

I feel that was directly related to the article I did, and I was proud of it. She said all sorts of things in the article that turned people against her, and I was proud of what I did. Let's say I let out the red carpet and she walked upon it. She exposed herself for what she was, and I was very proud of what I did in setting the stage for her to do this.

REACTIONS TO THE LIES OF OTHERS

As much as we may justify and explain our own lies, we feel bothered or disturbed when others do it, except perhaps for the lies that have become everyday social conventions. When I asked people how they felt about lies aimed at them, the typical responses I got were: "I don't like it." "It bothers me when people lie, just as I don't like to lie to other people." "I don't think most lies are necessary—people could easily tell the truth."

Some people interpreted lying as a sign of lack of respect. Stan, the teacher, commented:

Well, I would always feel that someone really didn't respect me very much if they were lying to me, at least in the case of major kinds of lies.

I don't feel this way about the run-of-the-mill sorts of excuses you sometimes get, such as when the kids in school fake a reason for an absence or someone doesn't feel comfortable saying their real opinion. But if someone close to me, such as a friend or colleague, was really lying about something serious, then that's what I think it would be—a lack of respect for me.

Others felt even more adamant about not wanting to hear lies. Susannah, a financial planner, felt "disgusted" by lies. She spoke with an intense fervor, the result of experiencing many serious lies in both her personal and business lives.

I feel a great deal of contempt for the lie. My style is to want to get everything out in the open, and to confront things I feel aren't true. I know confrontation upsets a lot of people. They don't like to look at the truth. But I much prefer getting everything out in the open than dealing with someone who uses a devious, manipulative style, maybe because that was typical of some of the people in my family. So really, I hate it when people lie.

Nancy, a personal-growth counselor, summed up some of these feelings:

How do I feel about others lying to me? Generally, very badly. I immediately think they're on a very low level of development. And I don't want them in my life on a personal level. And in business situations, I have real high standards. If somebody doesn't come through that I'm doing business with, say I'm paying them money for something, I just don't give them any more business. If I don't feel a high level of trust for them or they don't keep their agreements, or if they're not into integrity, I don't want to deal with that.

It's different if clients come to me and lying is one of their problems, because they need to change that, and I help them with that. But I won't deal with it in my own business or personal life. I feel such people can pull me down, because their own level of development is low. So I would rather shut them out of my life.

PART II

Identifying the Different Types of Liars

CHAPTER 3

How and Why Different Types of People Lie

In the early 1990s, when I wrote a book *The Truth about Lying*, I didn't classify the different types of liars based on their propensity to lie. Those distinctions only emerged after I had written the earlier book and hundreds of people began taking the Lie-Q (Lying Quotient) Test. Then, these differences emerged, which I have classified based on a continuum of lying from those who only rarely lie and consider this the moral, right thing to do to those who lie often, and often well, on the grounds that it is more pragmatic, or practical. Their motto is "Do it if you don't get caught."

THE MAJOR TYPES OF LIARS

As I'll describe in more detail, the continuum of liars breaks down into these five major groups:

- The model of absolute integrity, who is determined to be upright and honest and avoid lying at all cost.
- The real straight shooter, who is straightforward and honest most of the time, but occasionally will tell a lie, usually of the white lie variety.
- The pragmatic fibber, who alternates between being straightforward and honest, especially to those he or she is close to, and telling lies where practical, especially in a work situation to get ahead.
- The real Pinocchio, who commonly exaggerates, lies to get something he or she wants or to make a good impression, and often lies to people he or she is close to, such as to cover up an affair. Plus, he or she readily tells lies in the work arena if that contributes to his or her success. The bottom line is what matters, not the lie, so he or she feels no guilt about lying;

lies are like tools to facilitate personal and business relationships and to achieve goals.

- The frequent liar. This is the person who not only lies for practical reasons, but out of a deep compulsive need or pattern of lying dating back to childhood. In fact, such liars may be apt to lie to themselves and confuse what's reality and what's based on a lie, because they may come to believe some of their lies. Such people exaggerate, shade the truth, misrepresent, present hopes as reality, and conceal information under virtually any situation. Thus, while they may be charming, they can't be believed because it can be hard for anyone to know what is true or false—and they may not even be clear themselves.

There are, of course, shadings between different groups, and at different times and with different people, individuals may vary in how much and about what they lie. But these groupings provide a convenient set of guidelines for distinguishing these different types along the continuum of lying, which looks something like this:

Model of abso-lute integrity	Real straight shooter	Pragmatic fibber	Real Pinocchio	Frequent Liar

THE PARALLELS BETWEEN LYING AND MAKING ETHICAL CHOICES

As I thought about these distinctions, I also thought about the parallels between this propensity to lie and the different ethical approaches that people use, since the decision to lie is tied closely to one's ethical values. Those who lie almost never or rarely tend to be more committed to traditional moral principles, whereas those who lie more often do so for practical reasons and tend to be more pragmatic in their ethical approach to life.

By the same token, those who lie less tend to follow the rules, whereas those who lie more are more apt to be rule breakers or create new rules as they think would be appropriate for that situation.

Also, those who lie less are more apt to be other-oriented, taking into consideration the concerns of others or society as a whole, whereas those who lie more tend to be more self-centered, thinking about what's in it for them when they lie, rather than how a lie might hurt others. If they can get away with it, fine; they are glad to tell others or let others think what they'd like them to know.

Finally, those who lie less may be more likely to make this choice because they feel or know this is the right thing to do, so they are more intuitive in their decision to tell the truth, based on what they have been taught is right. By contrast, those who lie more may be apt to be more rational in their approach as they decide whether it makes sense to lie or not in a particular situation—is the gain of lying more worthwhile than the loss they might experience for telling the truth?

Thus, to recognize and better deal with the different types of liars, it helps to understand this ethical context that shapes their behavior. Accordingly, I want to briefly review these different approaches before providing some examples of different types of liars, how to deal with them, and how to assess yourself. I developed this system after examining the ethical systems of dozens of philosophers and ethical thinkers, and first described them in my book *Making Ethical Choices, Resolving Ethical Dilemmas.*[1]

THE MAJOR ETHICAL APPROACHES
WE USE IN EVERYDAY LIFE
The Major Ethical Approaches

While dozens of ethical systems have been proposed by writers on ethics, we all use a few basic approaches, sometimes in combination with one another. The six major approaches most commonly distinguished by ethical theorists are the following:

1. Looking to moral principles—deciding what's right and wrong by drawing on traditional morality, which provides a code of general principles and rules for action.
2. Applying moral strategies—deciding what's good and bad or when the ends justifies the means using a pragmatic or utilitarian approach.
3. Evaluating the situation—deciding what's fitting or not fitting by following the appropriate rules, or using situational ethics to fit the particular circumstances.
4. Following one's intuition—looking to one's inner voice, inner eye, inner knowing, or gut-level instincts by using an intuitive approach.
5. Following the pleasure or power principle—choosing what has the most personal benefit by responding to one's own self-interest.
6. Seeking the greater good—choosing what will help the most people as a result of being concerned about others.

In addition, after interviewing dozens of people about how they made ethical choices, I found two other approaches, not often included in categorizing how we make choices, leading me to develop the Ethical Choices Map. These two other approaches are:

7. Being an innovator in creating new rules.
8. Using a rational analysis to decide the best thing to do under the circumstances.

However, while these are different approaches, they often overlap. For example, someone might look to his intuition to help decide what's right or wrong, or a person may follow the pleasure principle to choose what has the most personal benefit, because that seems to be the most appropriate—and appealing—thing to do in that situation. Or a person may seek the greater good as well as what's best for himself in deciding that the end justifies what he wants to do.

However, despite such possible overlap, these categories were chosen as a starting point in exploring ethical decision making to learn the major reasons ordinary people give for why they do what they do and how they choose what to do when faced with an ethical dilemma. By the same token, these factors can influence how and under what circumstances a person will lie, because choosing to lie is an ethical choice. While these guidelines may come from different sources—traditional religious teachings, family values, accepted standards among peers, principles inculcated by educators, codes of ethics from work— they are what influence the way people make decisions in the here and now. Think about what approaches you are likely to use as you read about these different approaches that people use.

The following section describes each of these six approaches with an example to illustrate.

Looking to Moral Principles — Deciding What's Right and Wrong (Drawing on Traditional Morality)

This moral principles approach is the one that is most wedded to the traditional ideals taught by our religious leaders, teachers, and parents about how we should act. These principles are the laws and rules we start learning as children about what's right and wrong—"Do this" . . . "Don't do that." When rules conflict, we learn other principles for choosing the higher value, such as when we learn that "It's wrong to tell a lie," but later discover that telling a "little white lie" may be all right, if it's done to protect someone's feelings or to keep someone from being hurt.

A good example of this "looking to moral principles" approach is the teacher who decides to enforce the school rules or the judge who decides to go by the letter of the law, no matter what.

Applying Moral Strategies — Deciding What's Good or Bad or When the End Justifies the Means (Using a Pragmatic or Utilitarian Approach)

The moral strategies approach represents the more pragmatic, practical approach many people use to make decisions and resolve ethical conflicts. It's the approach we as a culture tend to use, especially in work and business situations, since the emphasis is on what seems to be the best, most effective, or most useful approach in light of the potential outcome or consequences of a situation. It might sometimes be referred to as the utilitarian approach.

Someone using this approach might engage in a cost-benefits analysis, weighing what he would like to do for gain against the costs of doing it. Also, someone might consider the value or worth of the end goal in relationship to the methods he or she might use. If that goal is important enough, its attainment might be used to justify a less than ideal or acceptable means. Or if the risks of a negative outcome are low enough, this might justify using such a means, too. The focus here is on what is good for the individual or for the group making the decision, rather than the more altruistic social motivation underlying the "greatest good" approach.

Many examples of this approach can be found in everyday business and work situations, where an individual plays the odds to gain a hoped-for outcome. Sometimes it works; sometimes it does not. For instance, someone using this approach might lie about his income on an application for a home loan or mortgage in order to get the house, figuring that he desperately needs the house and will be able to support it through his earnings, even though his past income tax records might paint a different picture.

Some other typical examples might be: an employee up against a work deadline who decides not to run a computer test to check there are no bugs in the system, though the usual procedures at work require this; the man who files an inflated insurance claim, thinking he won't be found out; or the woman who decides to hide a past abortion from a prospective suitor, thinking he will be better able to accept this after they are married.

Very often, such calculated risks work—the moral gamble succeeds. But when it fails the results can be very costly—a computer system may collapse because the bug wasn't discovered, resulting in a huge data loss; financial penalties and even criminal charges may result when an investigation uncovers the truth; a husband may file for divorce after he finds out a truth he can't accept.

Evaluating the Situation — Deciding What's Fitting or Not Fitting (Following the Appropriate Rules)

This is the approach where the person looks at what is happening at the moment and decides what the best thing is to do given the circumstances. He might be guided by fairness, feelings of loyalty or friendship to another person, priorities of the moment, the attitudes of his peers and associates, or the policies of his employers. The emphasis is on what is the most appropriate, suitable, practical, or optimum thing to do right now, based on present considerations. For instance, a person might decide to lie to conceal his or her real negative feelings about someone else if it's advantageous to do so in order to get a job or promotion or to smooth over relationships when it's necessary to visit a disliked relative.

Often, this kind of ethical response occurs in situations involving one's family or personal relationships, since clear guidelines or rules may not work that well in complex situations that are often full of feelings and countervailing pressures. Also, the more strategic cost-benefit analysis that seems so fitting in the work and business environment may appear less appropriate here. However, while family and relationship situations may provide a particularly fertile ground for such an approach, it can occur anywhere.

Following One's Intuition — Looking to One's Inner Voice, Inner Eye, Inner Knowing, or Gut-Level Feelings or Instincts (Using an Intuitive Approach)

Though one may use one's intuition to make any of the choices already described—say by feeling a strong intuitive pull to follow a certain rule, select a certain strategy, or decide that a certain action is the most fitting in the circumstances—people think of an intuitive response as a distinct approach. They feel a strong inner, intuitive, or emotional call to do something, rather than trying to reason out what to do by weighing this factor or that. For instance, a person may feel a sudden impulse to tell a lie to someone else, such as exaggerating one's personal income, because that person will think less of him as a person by knowing the truth.

In using the intuitive approach, people find that the knowledge or feeling of what choice to make can come on very suddenly, like a flash of insight, illumination, or compelling impulse to do a certain thing. Often such feelings come in very personal or emotional situations, such as when a man decides to follow his heart and run off to marry the woman he loves, while lying to his family so they can't try to talk him out of taking that action.

The underlying ethical foundation for the validity of this approach is the view that we can intuitively know what is right, good, or fitting, and act accordingly. Indeed, this often appears to be true—people follow their intuition and the outcome leads them to feel they have made the right choice. They feel good; other people affected by their decision feel good; the outcome is generally successful. Thus, the result validates and reaffirms their intuitive leap.

On the other hand, the potential danger of the intuitive, visceral response is that the person responding may think what he is doing is good, but the results in reality may be very destructive to him or others, such as when a lie about past achievement to get a job results in a person who can't perform well and may endanger others through his lack of experience. Still, when the call of inspiration or revelation is for a beneficial purpose, the results can be very good, such as when a quick learner conceals negative information to get a job and then does it very well.

Following the Pleasure or Power Principle — Choosing What Has the Most Personal Benefit (Responding to Self-Interest)

The pleasure or power principle comes into play when people choose to do whatever gives them the most immediate satisfaction or gain at the time. For example, someone opts to have an affair because he is so powerfully attracted to a woman at work and hopes his wife and his coworkers won't find out about it—and he tells lies about where he is to keep the affair a secret.

This approach is different from the self-interested moral strategies approach in that the focus is on one's immediate desires rather than on long-term gains.

In some cases, the two may go together very well, when there are both immediate and subsequent benefits. But in other cases, the long-term consequences may not be so favorable, as reflected by the phrase: "Pay now or pay later." In fact, sometimes the later consequences can be very severe, such as when the lie is revealed, leading to a scandal later or someone contracting an illness because the other person didn't take precautions and lied that he had.

Seeking the Greater Good — Choosing What Will Help the Most People (Being Concerned about Others)

This final principle is the opposite of the pleasure/power principle in that its focus is on what will bring the most benefit for others. It's the most altruistic of the ethical approaches, since it emphasizes helping and serving others, and frequently these "others" are defined in a general, abstract way: such as helping the poor, the homeless, the indigenous peoples of the Americas and Africa, or the world as a whole. And, commonly, those committed to this principle will seek to avoid lying, too, because they are committed to acting out of integrity and are willing to engage in personal sacrifice to put the group first, though in other cases, they may choose to lie in the service of this higher good.

For example, several people I met involved in humanitarian work to help animals reflected this connection between altruism to others and being completely forthright in what they did, even if it meant not getting a grant for their work, because they didn't want to violate their principles. On the other hand, there are animal activists who lie about who they are and what they are doing in order to interfere with the work of animal researchers or injure them to make a statement about their political cause.

Applying the Major Ethical Approaches in Everyday Life

In summary, these six major ethical approaches have been recognized as guiding our life by philosophers and ethical thinkers. They all underlie different approaches to lying: drawing on traditional morality, using a pragmatic or utilitarian approach, following the appropriate rules, using an intuitive approach, responding to self-interest, and being concerned about others. Plus, there are two more approaches that I found that people report using—creating their own rules and using a rational analysis to decide what to do.

As a result, instead of thinking of these major approaches as a list from which people choose one or more strategies, these eight approaches can be viewed as a matrix or map in which there are four pairs of alternative approaches that form a continuum that I call the Ethical Choices Map, a system I developed and described at length in *Making Ethical Choices, Resolving Ethical Dilemmas.*[2] I'll describe how this map can be used to understand the underlying attitudes that shape the way the different types of liars lie.

INTRODUCING THE ETHICAL CHOICES MAP

Think of this Ethical Choices Map as describing the approach people are likely to use when they encounter ethical dilemmas or make ethical choices to resolve problems, including deciding how and when to lie. People usually do not think about how and why they are making their choices. They choose something because it feels right; because there seem to be more benefits than disadvantages in doing so; because that's the way things are usually done; because they will benefit and it won't harm others; because they will help others; because they have learned it is the right thing—or a combination of these reasons. They usually don't have particular rules, guidelines, or language for describing how they choose and why. Often, because they see things from their own ethical perspective, they don't understand why others feel differently, not recognizing that we all inhabit different moral worlds—and in many cases, these different views may, though conflicting, both be right.

We can all agree that certain types of lies are clearly wrong—such as a lie to entice someone into a situation where they will be hurt (except in a war when the lie is used against an enemy). But in most areas of life, there are shades of gray, and from different viewpoints different things are "right."

I began to recognize these differences when I interviewed dozens of people from different backgrounds about how they made ethical choices, which eventually led me to develop this model that also frames the way people regard telling lies and responding to the lies of others. Depending on the situation, people may be likely to use different approaches or a combination of approaches at different times or settings—say, being less likely to lie with the people they were closest too and being more likely to fudge the truth or dissemble in a professional or work setting, when this was to their advantage, such as to claim undeserved credits to gain a promotion or make up an excuse to get extra vacation time.

The Four Key Dimensions in Making Choices

The four ethical choice factors—and the continuum of choices for each factor—are the following:

- Style of choosing—from rational (or logical/analytical) to intuitive
- Orientation—from other (more altruistic) to self (more self-interested)
- Philosophy—from moralist (or traditionalist) to pragmatic (what works)
- Attitude to rules—from follower (or team player) to innovator (rule breaker or maker)

Combining these factors together results in the Ethical Choices Map, illustrated in Figure 3.1.[3]

The T's and O's on the map indicate the difference between the individual who has a traditional religious perspective (the T's) and those who differ in

Figure 3.1
Ethical Choices Map

		Style of Choosing		Orientation	
		Rational	**Intuitive**	**Other**	**Self**
Philosophy or Values	**Pragmatist**	O			O
	Moralist		T	T	
Attitude to Rules	**Follower**		T	T	
	Innovator	O			O

other perspectives (the O's). The person from the traditional background is basically a person who follows the rules, intuitively knows the right thing to do because these traditional religious and ethical teachings are so ingrained, and is taught to be very concerned about others and the larger community. As indicated, the T person falls squarely in the center core of the Ethical Choices Map. This is the person who might be categorized as being a moralist and follower, and having an intuitive style and other-orientation. Such a person is most likely to follow the traditional admonition against lying and fall into the model of absolute integrity or real straight shooter side of the spectrum.

The complete opposite, indicated by the outer O's, is the person who makes ethical decisions by deciding what works best, perhaps evaluating things from a cost-benefit perspective, breaks the rules or makes his own when it suits him, thinks through what would be the best thing to do, and makes a choice based on what's best for him. In other words, this is a person who is a pragmatist and innovator, who has a rational style and a self orientation. Such a person is most likely to fall into the pragmatic fibber, real Pinocchio, or frequent liar end of the lying continuum.

You can see where you fall by taking the Ethical Choices Map assessment quiz in the next chapter.

Different Ways of Making Choices in Different Situations

Though people might have a characteristic approach, they may make choices in different ways under certain circumstances. For example, a person who practices the traditional core values of being a model of absolute integrity or straight shooter at home with his family and in personal relationships might often make decisions from a more pragmatic, rational, and innovative perspective to obtain the best career opportunities, and be more apt to lie for pragmatic reasons accordingly. A person may also be more or less consistent in how he or she uses an approach in different situations or changes his or her approach over time.

Also, it is important to recognize that these categories are themselves ideal types, representing the way people might be categorized as they approach lying and other ethical issues. So people might be placed along a continuum in each of these four dimensions, and depending on the situation, they vary in the degree to which they base their decision to lie or not lie on their self-interest or on the interest of others, and they may differ in the degree to which they follow traditional religious teachings about what is right versus working things out pragmatically, or the degree to which they act as followers or rule-breakers and rule-makers.

In turn, people with different ethical approaches may vary in the approaches they make under different circumstances, such as deciding to go along with the team in agreeing to lie—say, to conceal a mistake—even though they don't think the group choice is right. A business executive or company employee, for example, may be bothered by some of the things he has to do to conceal or change information, but he remains with the company anyway because of financial considerations. Only when the demands become too great and create too much ethical conflict does he finally decide to leave—or perhaps he does so only when he and others are caught in a lie. For instance, some executives in the financial world got caught up in lying about their company's performance before they got caught up in a crackdown by the Securities and Exchange Commission and other government agencies.

Sure, it may be ideal to be completely honest and always tell the truth. But under increasing degrees of pressure, individuals may choose to lie—some more easily than others based on their original ethical perspectives. But even if a normally truthful person thinks that the circumstances justify telling a lie, this is still making an ethical choice and it may have negative consequences for the person who chooses to respond this way, such as finding that other people don't want to be with him because they find him to be unethical. Or the other hand, the usually self-interested person may find that easily shaping and reshaping the truth produces gains in the short run but, in the long run, results in negative reactions as others recognize the lies and he or she finds his or her social life and job prospects narrowing.

In short, the Ethical Choices Map is designed to indicate how people actually make their ethical choices, including whether to lie or not, not to judge them. One can come to a better understanding of one's own choices and the choices others make by using the map, which shows how one reacts generally. And then one can further notice how one is apt to respond under different conditions (i.e., personal life versus professional/public life), under certain circumstances (i.e., in relating to one's parents versus relating to one's friends), and in responding to different types of people (i.e., in relating to a person who is very altruistic versus relating to a person you know is self-centered and will try to take every advantage if given the opportunity) or over time, influenced by the individual's age, stage of life, experiences, and current social environment.

For example, today we are in a culture where lying has become more widespread and accepted, as part of the emphasis on success and image, so people are more apt to lie when it is practical to do so, whereas several decades ago, through the 1940s and 1950s, the culture was much more influenced by traditional institutions, which considered lying a sin or wrong.

The Zones of Making Ethical Choices and Choosing to Lie or Not

A way to think about how we apply the ethical approaches we use is to consider the situations we face in daily life like a series of circles around us. We are in the center, surrounded by issues of decreasing closeness to us, like circles around a bull's-eye or locations increasingly distant from a central city. People have different priorities in what's important to them, but in general, as these circles of closeness grow more distant from us, they become less important, which affects the ethical approaches and techniques we use. These zones surrounding us are depicted in Figure 3.2.[4]

In general, if these zones are combined with the lying continuum or the Ethical Choices Map, the closer the zone is to oneself the more one is likely to fall on the absolute integrity/straight shooter side of the lying continuum or the core of the Ethical Choices Map. That's because we generally seek to be more honest and trustworthy with ourselves and those closest to us. It's part of the desire or pressure to be loyal and seek authenticity and integrity with oneself and one's closest friends and relationships. We have more emotional and psychic energy invested in them, because they have more of an effect on our personal sense of identity and well-being and because they involve the people we care about the most.

By contrast, there is less incentive to be loyal or authentic with those who are increasingly distant from us, such as with those at work, neighbors, or members of the wider community, unless of course we draw them into our inner circle. One major exception is the person who identifies very strongly with a social cause, making that an essential part of his or her being. Another

Figure 3.2
Zones of Making Ethical Choices

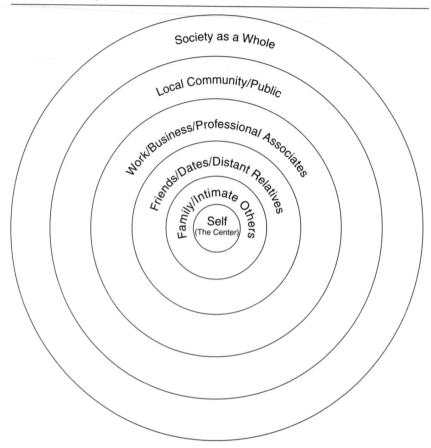

Society as a Whole

Local Community/Public

Work/Business/Professional Associates

Friends/Dates/Distant Relatives

Family/Intimate Others

Self
(The Center)

exception is the person whose very self is invested in his work, so that he invests it with much more emotional energy than family and mates.

Assessing Where You and Others Fall on the Ethical Choices Continuum

Now that you have a general idea of how the Ethical Choices Map works, you can think about where you and others fall in each dimension and how that influences how and when you are likely to lie under different circumstances in the different ethical choices zones.

The Style of Choice People Use

The style of choosing you use in making an ethical choice is whether you are more intuitive or rational in making your choice. While some people tend to be very intuitive in sensing, knowing, or spontaneously deciding what to do, others are more analytical in considering and weighing the options. Also, whether they are more intuitive or rational, some people are more intense and emotional, while others are more calm, cool, and collected.

Intriguingly, when I asked interviewees to describe their style, there was a clear split between the men and the women. Though this was only a small sampling and a somewhat larger majority were intuitives (about 60%), the differences conformed to traditional notions about how men and women think about things—the men were more likely to try to reach decisions logically, weighing alternatives in their mind, assessing costs and benefits, and thinking about priorities, and they were less apt to be emotional in going through the process. By contrast, the women were more likely to use intuitive processes, such as meditation, to think about what was going on in a more holistic way. The women were also more apt to report feeling more emotional intensity in reflecting on the problem, whether they did so more logically or intuitively, describing stronger feelings of guilt or suffering as they wrestled with what to do.

There also seemed to be a relationship between the kinds of jobs people had and whether they were more likely to be more logical or intuitive in their approach. In general, those who identified themselves with the creative, healing professions, or so-called people professions (e.g., writer, artist, nurse, therapist, social welfare worker, teacher, sales, and public relations) tended to be more intuitive, while those in the more scientific, analytical, or business management type of professions (e.g., computer writer, business manager, political consultant, architect, scientist, and academic) tended to approach ethical issues from a more rational perspective, or, as a few indicated, they tended to use a combination approach. In this combo style, they used logic to decide when it was appropriate to use one's intuition and when it was better to use reason, and they applied that style accordingly.

However, there didn't seem to be any connection in one's style of making choices and one's religious background, strength of religious involvement now, or political identification as a liberal, conservative, or moderate. Regardless of these factors, people seemed to differ in their approach. Rather, what seemed to be most closely connected with one's style of choice was gender and occupational choice—which are perhaps most closely related to personality characteristics and thus to one's style of making ethical decisions. The following sections briefly summarize the different styles.

The Rationalists

For the rationalists, an ethical dilemma is something to be weighed and considered. They look at the alternatives, think about the relative advantages and disadvantages of possibilities, consider the pros and cons, and examine the benefits and costs. Commonly, this is an internal process, and can happen very quickly, though some may consult with a partner or close friends or family members in assessing what to do.

The Intuitives

In contrast to the rationalists, who thought through and weighed their decisions, the intuitives came to their choices in a more holistic way, in which they got insights into what to do or had a gut level feeling about what was right. Although they might sometimes start off with some internal weighing of pros and cons or imagining possible consequences, they did so in a more haphazard way of now and then thinking about the issue. But then the decision came to them as more of a "Eureka" or "I feel it in my gut" response.

The Rational Intuitives and Intuitive Rationalists

Still others more equally combine resolving dilemmas both rationally and intuitively. Those who are more intuitive than rational might be called rational intuitives, while those who are more rational might be called intuitive rationalists.

What characterized both was their emphasis on having a variety of methods to draw on, so they could be alternatively rational or intuitive or a combination of both based on the particular situation. It was like they had a repertoire of approaches to draw on to find the best approach to fit the situation.

Determining Your Own Style of Making Choices

People thus vary widely in their style of making ethical choices—from the person who responds in a highly intuitive way to highly analytical rationalist. And in the middle is the person who combines both of these approaches as a rational-intuitive or intuitive-rationalist.

Still, there is a continuum in the way people generally respond, because we all have a bit of both in our makeup; we are all to varying degrees rational or intuitive. Additionally, we are all affected by the situation, our experiences over time, the person or group we are with, and different factors. This rational-intuitive dimension or scale looks something like this:

Intuitive	Rational-Intuitive	Intuitive-Rationalist	Rationalist

Where do you fall on the scale? If you are more intuitive in your approach, you may be able to sense this by visualizing where you might be and seeing yourself someplace on the scale. If you are more rational, you may feel more comfortable seeing where you fall after answering a questionnaire and scoring yourself. If so, you'll find the Ethical Choices Mapping Instrument in the Appendix, which includes questions on how intuitive or rational you tend to be and will give you a score on this dimension.

Assessing Your Self/Other-Orientation

The self/other-orientation reflects the contrast between acting out of self-interest or responding to others' concerns. In traditional moral thinking we are taught that this altruistic orientation is the ethical thing to do, however, choosing to act out of self-interest is also an ethical choice, though others may deem this particular choice to be unethical. I have sought to present these choices in a neutral way, without making a particular judgment about what I or others may think is ethical or unethical.

On the personal level, this orientation comes into play when we have to decide to do something for our kids or parents because we put their interests above our own or to do something for ourselves (such as taking an undesired job to support our kids versus pursuing a risky dream of becoming the artist we want to be).

Yet while we may teach the principle of putting other's needs first by being altruistic and doing for others, choosing to act in self-interest is still an ethical choice, and often it is necessary for personal survival. In fact, being too focused on others' needs can be self-destructive. For example, the codependent in an alcoholic relationship or the battered wife in an abusive relationship are cases of those who put others' needs first to an extreme.

The influence of these opposing influences on lying is that the more other-oriented person will be more likely to lie to protect others, while the self-oriented person will be more likely to lie to protect himself.

Though this dimension is presented as an either/or distinction on the Ethical Choices Map, it is really a continuum, and our position on this continuum can, just like how rational or intuitive we are, change in different situations and at different times. Also, the importance of this factor, relative to the other three factors involved in making ethical choices, depends on circumstances.

For example, when I interviewed people about their choices, the interviewees were more likely to think of themselves when it came to career and business/professional issues and more apt to think of others when personal relationships, particularly children, were involved. There also seemed to be a relationship between one's ability to think of others and one's economic situation. When one is in a more stable or higher-income financial situation, one is better able to consider others, whereas when one is in a lower-income financial status, one must be more self-oriented just to survive, before giving as much priority to others' concerns.

These self-other differences also reflect a difference between people who are more apt to be givers (other-oriented) or takers (self-oriented). And there are commonly gender differences in these approaches, since women have traditionally been taught to be supportive and nurturing, and men to be achievement oriented and competitive, as I found in my small survey. The women I spoke with were much more likely to be altruistic, accommodating, and to put others' needs first—and sometimes to think they were doing too much of this, particularly in personal relationships. By contrast, the men were more apt to put self-interest first, especially in making work choices.

Determining Your Own Orientation

In sum, people vary greatly in the degree to which they are self- or other-oriented in making ethical choices and resolving ethical dilemmas. So where do you fit? Again, think of this self-orientation as a continuum, in which the other/self-orientation dimension or scale looks something like this:

	Other/Self-Orientation	Self/Other-Orientation	
Other First			Self First

Where do you fall on the scale? If you have a strong intuitive style of perceiving qualities about yourself, you may be able to sense where you fall by visualizing how you are most likely to respond in most situations and imagining where you fit on the scale. Conversely, if you are more rational in your approach, you may feel more comfortable determining your orientation by answering questionnaires and scoring yourself.

Understanding Your Philosophy or Values

Another big split in our approach to ethical choices is between deciding based on practical, pragmatic, or utilitarian considerations and deciding based on what we have been taught is the right thing to do. Sometimes the choice is the same, but often it is not, because we have different priorities.

Often what's considered right is drummed into us through guilt, which is what the Catholics or formerly practicing Catholics I spoke with often experienced. But in a strongly secular society where guilt holds little sway and materialistic values reign, the power of practical and utilitarian thinking is strong, and that's how the majority of the people I interviewed made their choices.

In turn, this can have a strong influence on when and how much you lie—and if you feel guilty about it when you do.

There appear to be three major approaches based on this distinction of following traditional morality versus practical considerations, which is influenced by one's religious or spiritual upbringing or parents' teachings and one's current ties to a religious or spiritual tradition. These three basic philosophical approaches were the following:

- The moralist, who embraced the traditional notions of right and wrong, and rejected the utilitarian or pragmatic/practical approach as ethically objectionable, because it was contrary to their intuitive feeling of what was right and wrong.
- The pragmatist, who embraced practical considerations, often because he or she found traditional moral teachings not relevant to current concerns or was not currently religious.
- The moral pragmatist or practical moralist, who combined a mixture of both approaches.

There also seems to be a relationship between the philosophical approach one follows and one's primary other/self-orientation, in that those with an ori-

entation toward others are very likely to fall in the moralist category or second-
arily in the practical moralist or moral pragmatist category. By contrast, those
who are highly oriented toward serving their own interests (self-oriented) tend
to fall in the pragmatist category. Or, expressed another way, the moralists are
virtually all other-oriented, while the pragmatists are almost all self-oriented or
have a mixture of the other/self-orientation. As for those in the middle, they
tend to be split in their orientation—some slightly more other-oriented, others
a mixture of self- and other/self-perspectives.

Then, too, just as one's orientation is related to gender, so is philosophy,
in that women tend to generally be both other-oriented and more likely to
respond from a moral perspective. Conversely, men tend to be both more self-
oriented and more likely to make decisions based on utilitarian and practical
considerations.

In addition, there is a clear distinction between the philosophy or values one
uses in the personal and public spheres, just as there is in the case of applying
the self/other-orientation, because orientation and philosophy seem so closely
linked. In general, people are more likely to use practical and utilitarian considerations in a work and professional context and are more apt to turn to a
more moral perspective in deciding what to do in family matters or in thinking
about social issues and society as a whole.

So where do you fit? Again, think of your philosophical or values outlook
as a kind of continuum, in which the moralist-pragmatist dimension or scale
looks something like this:

Moralist	Practical Moralist	Moral Pragmatist	Pragmatist

Where do you fall on the scale? As in assessing where you fall on other
dimensions, if you have a strong intuitive style, you may be able to sense where
you fall by visualizing how you are most likely to respond in most situations
and seeing yourself someplace on the scale. Or if you are more rational in your
approach, you may feel more comfortable answering a questionnaire and scoring yourself.

Recognizing Your Approach to the Rules

The fourth major factor influencing our ethical choices is whether we follow
the rules we have learned are appropriate for a particular situation or whether
we break those rules and make our own. This is the difference between being
a follower or an innovator. Often, we may choose to innovate, creating new
rules because we feel that's the practical, sensible thing to do; so innovators
may tend to be pragmatists, as well. Additionally, since pragmatists often act
for their own benefit, that may result in a further link, with innovators tending
to be self-oriented, too. But this isn't always the case, because someone might
choose to create new rules because others are doing what he feels is not right,
so he acts innovatively to right the wrong. An example is the whistleblower

who pulls the plug on a seemingly corrupt and harmful way of doing business. Then, too, a person may take an innovative action to help others, so innovating can be for altruistic or other-oriented reasons, as well.

Normally, though, we are taught to conform, to go along with the group. Even though in the United States we place such a high value on individualism and independence, we still expect people to follow the rules to achieve and gain success. The idea is to win but play by the rules. That's why there's a strong pressure on people to be a team player, go along with the peer group, and fit in, and a powerful dislike of the person who goes too far in his or her own way. We make things hard for the whistleblower, the turncoat, the eccentric, the deviate, the spy. We want people to stand out and shine, but not too far or in certain undesirable ways. When that happens, we react by disparaging and rejecting the person who has crossed the line.

The way this influences lying is whether you are tempted to lie when others in the group do, such as when a team at work decides to cover up a mistake or refuse to go along, or whether you are likely to tell the truth because those are the rules or are willing to fudge or fabricate when it suits your purpose.

This pull in two directions can create ethical choices over what to do—should one follow the rules or not? This consideration in turn intersects with other factors affecting our choice: What's right and wrong? What's of most benefit to others or ourselves? That is when our style of choice—rational or intuitive—comes into play in deciding how to weigh these options or getting an overall sense of what feels right or good in a particular situation: going along with the rules or creating new ones we feel are better.

In some cases, the rules are very clear. And for some people in certain professions, there are formalized, often very detailed, rules of ethical conduct. For example, lawyers have an extensive book that reads like a law code with rules governing numerous situations, and additional books further interpret and expand upon these rules. And other professions—including doctors, therapists, police officers, and journalists—have well-developed codes of ethics, too.

In many other situations, especially in personal relationships and in the family, the rules are much less clear. Moreover, as times and technology change, the traditional rules change, too, and there are often heated debates about what the new ethical codes for behavior should be—such as in current controversies over prolonging death and euthanasia, and rules about privacy and revealing information in an information age. In response, new growing fields have arisen to deal with the ethical implications due to new technologies, such as medical ethics and bioethics.

Additionally, ethical principles about what's considered ethical differ from society to society, and within different social, cultural, racial, ethnic, and economic groups. Part of the confusion today is in deciding what rules apply when the codes of different groups come into conflict with each other. And there is confusion when individuals with different opinions about the appropriate rules to follow come into conflict, too.

Another source of confusion is that many times the applicable rules are unstated. They are not written down, and sometimes not even formally discussed or expressed. Rather, they are something that everyone seems to know or take for granted. Then, too, adding even further complications, there may be a distinction between the formal rules (what's written down or verbally agreed upon) and the informal rules (what everyone does in practice, such as in the office). It's like the laws against speeding. You're not supposed to drive over 55 or 65 on the freeway, but if the road is clear and straight, most people will go much faster.

Thus, when any ethical dilemma comes up, the question of what rules to follow always comes into play—although the applicable rules may be more or less formal, stated or unstated, outwardly agreed upon or quietly practiced. And while followers are more apt to go by the rules, whatever they are, if they can figure them out, innovators are more apt to improvise by applying or creating rules more spontaneously to suit the situation. Then again, one may tend to follow the rules in certain types of situations (such as at work, particularly if one is an employee with little power), while one may tend to be more of an innovator in other settings (such as in one's family and personal life).

The Three Major Approaches to the Rules

As in the case of orientation and philosophy, there are three major ways of relating to the rules:

1. Being a follower—determining the rules in a particular situation and going along with them.
2. Being an innovator—questioning the rules and being ready to create new ones.
3. Being a mixture of follower and innovator—seeking the middle way between following the rules and creating new ones when it seems necessary and sensible to do so.

Assessing Your Own Attitude to the Rules

Thus, as people vary greatly in style, orientation, and philosophy, so they vary in their attitude toward rules—from those who tend to follow them (followers) to those who tend to break them or make their own (innovators). People are also apt to make a distinction between how one acts in one's professional and personal life, being more likely to follow the rules in one's work, particularly if one is in a profession with a detailed ethical code, such as therapy or the law. By contrast, people are more apt to follow a more informal, spontaneous type of style in adapting and changing the rules to fit in family and personal situations.

Where do you fit? Again, think of your attitude toward the rules as a continuum, in which the follower-innovator dimension or scale looks something like this:

Follower	Innovative Follower	Follower Innovator	Innovator

Where do you fall on the scale? If you have a strong intuitive style of determining what's so, you may be able to sense this by visualizing how you are most likely to react to the rules in most situations and imagining yourself someplace on the scale. Or if you are more rational in your approach, you may feel more comfortable assessing your attitude by answering a questionnaire and scoring yourself.

The Relationship between Style, Orientation, Philosophy, and Attitude toward Rules

Whether you have a more intuitive or rational approach to making your choices, there appear to be some connections between your style and these other factors: orientation, philosophy, and attitude toward rules. The following patterns stood out from my interviews.

Style and Orientation

- The intuitives were more likely to be other-oriented.
- The rationalists were more likely to be a mixture of self- and other-oriented.

Style and Philosophy

- The intuitives were more likely to be moralists.
- The rationalists were more likely to be pragmatists or a mixture of moralist and pragmatist; none were strict moralists.

Style and Attitude toward Rules

- Both intuitives and rationalists varied greatly in their attitudes toward the rules; in each group, most tended to be a mixture of followers and innovators, though the intuitives were more often innovators.

Using the Four Different Dimensions in Resolving an Ethical Dilemma

Thus, as discussed in this chapter, you incorporate four different qualities in making ethical choices—style, orientation, philosophy, and your attitude toward rules—and these contribute to your approach to lying. In any given situation, these factors (also referred to as dimensions or categories) are joined together in different combinations, and you may be more or less likely to use a particular quality in that situation or generally. Also, you may differ in which qualities you are more apt to use in professional or personal situations, or in relating to different people in your life. You may change over time as well, as you enter different social situations at different stages of your life.

CHAPTER 4

Taking the Lie-Q Test: Learning Where You Fit

When I first wrote the earlier book I included the Lie-Q Test, which scored how you feel about lying or whether you would lie or not in different situations. This way you are more aware of your propensity not to tell the truth in different situations in your personal, social, and professional life, assuming you answered the questions honestly. Based on a scale of 0–285 (the highest possible score by adding up the numbers in the circles), you can fit into one of five categories (the last two categories have been combined, since relatively few people fall in those categories).

- The model of absolute integrity
- The real straight shooter
- The pragmatic fibber
- The real Pinocchio
- The frequent liar

Though this test was originally included as an afterthought—a fun way for people to think about how frequently they or others told lies, this turned out to be one of the highlights of the book—it was what interviewers typically asked me about. Everyone wanted to take the test and then post their results for all to see. It turned out to be a great ice-breaker and conversation starter, as people compared their propensity to lie.

The following test includes the original scoring key, though in the early to mid-1990s people were much less likely to lie—or admit it. So people would naturally get lower scores. But now that lying seems to have become more acceptable, as reflected by the increased examples of lying and cheating repeatedly reported in the news and discussed on popular TV shows—even promoted as a strategy for success in numerous reality shows—I suspect that more and more people will get higher scores. Accordingly, after you take the test yourself, we invite you to become part of our national survey. Just send in a copy of your test with the survey information to our address listed at the end of the book.

So now here's a copy of the test, with the original scoring key (though throughout the book I have combined the last two categories since relatively few people fall at the extremes). Where do you fit? And where do you think others you know might fit?

Be sure to answer the questions honestly. Then, add up the numbers in the spaces corresponding to your answers and look up your score (on a scale of 0–285) on the key at the end of the quiz.

What's Your Lie-Q?
(Lying Quotient)

This simple quiz does not aspire to provide a serious scientific evaluation of your character in matters of lying. It does try, though—in an entertaining way—to make you aware of your propensity not to tell the truth in different situations of your personal, social, and professional life. Answer the questions *honestly*. Then add up the numbers in the circles corresponding to your answers and look up your score (on a scale of 0–285) on the key at the end of the quiz.

1. Give yourself the number of points indicated for your response to the following statements about lying.

   a. It is always wrong to tell a lie. _____
      Yes (0)
      No (2)
      Not sure (1)

   b. It is all right to lie, as long as the lie doesn't harm anyone. _____
      Yes (2)
      No (0)
      Not sure (1)

   SUBTOTAL _____

   c. It is never right to tell a lie that will harm anyone. _____
      Yes (0)
      No (2)
      Not sure (1)

   d. It is all right to lie in order to protect oneself from harm. _____
      Yes (2)
      Yes, but only if it is really serious harm (1)
      No (0)
      Not sure (1)

   e. It is all right to lie to hurt someone else if that person has done something to hurt one. _____
      Yes (2)
      Yes, but only if that person has done one very serious harm (1)
      No (0)
      Not sure (1)

f. It is all right to lie in order to protect someone
else from being hurt. _____

Yes (2)

Yes, but only if that person will be hurt very seriously (1)

No (0)

Not sure (1)

g. It is all right to lie to become successful or gain an
advantage, as long as no one else will be hurt by that lie. _____

Yes (2)

No (0)

Not sure (1)

h. It is all right to lie to become successful or gain an
advantage, as long as no one else will be hurt by that lie. _____

Yes (2)

No (0)

Not sure (1)

i. It is all right to lie when the benefit to be gained
out-weighs the harm to result from that lie. _____

Yes (2)

No (0)

Not sure (1)

SUBTOTAL _____

2. What are the main reasons you would tell a lie? (Rate your biggest reasons with a 2; your occasional reasons with a 1; and reasons when you would never tell a lie with a 0.)

To protect someone from harm (_____ x 1 =) _____

To cover up an embarrassing situation (_____ x 2 =) _____

To avoid punishment (_____ x 2 =) _____

To make someone feel good (_____ x 1 =) _____

To get revenge (_____ x 3 =) _____

To get a job (_____ x 1 =) _____

To get a promotion (_____ x 2 =) _____

To get more money (_____ x 2 =) _____

To get out of an undesired social obligation (_____ x 1 =) _____

To further your reputation (_____ x 1 =) _____

To escape blame for a mistake (_____ x 2 =) _____

To put the blame on someone else	(____ x 3 =) _____
To conceal your age	(____ x 1 =) _____
To seem more successful	(____ x 1 =) _____
To do better on a test	(____ x 2 =) _____
To obtain a contract	(____ x 2 =) _____
To make a better deal in business	(____ x 2 =) _____
To sell something to someone	(____ x 2 =) _____
To pay less for something	(____ x 2 =) _____
To have or cover up an affair	(____ x 3 =) _____
To protect a member of your family	(____ x 1 =) _____
To make someone you don't like look bad	(____ x 3 =) _____
To hide an unpleasant truth about yourself	(____ x 2 =) _____
To get out of paying a ticket	(____ x 2 =) _____
To avoid being accused of something you did	(____ x 3 =) _____
To cut through some bureaucracy more quickly	(____ x 1 =) _____
To seem younger than you are	(____ x 1 =) _____
To get ahead in line	(____ x 2 =) _____
To get into someplace without paying	(____ x 2 =) _____
To keep someone from knowing information they shouldn't know	(____ x 2 =) _____
To get a date	(____ x 1 =) _____
To make the results of a project come out as desired	(____ x 2 =) _____
To keep someone from knowing something bad (e.g., an illness)	(____ x 1 =) _____
To let someone think you like something when you don't	(____ x 1 =) _____
To have a better sexual relationship (or to get sex)	(____ x 2 =) _____
To get out of doing something with someone you don't want to do something with	(____ x 2 =) _____
To convince someone that your position is right	(____ x 2 =) _____

3. Indicate on a scale of 0–3 how often you might lie to each of the following types of people (0 = never; 1 = rarely; 2 = occasionally; 3 = often).

Salesmen	(____ x 1 =) _____
Customers or clients	(____ x 2 =) _____
Police officers	(____ x 1 =) _____
Clerks	(____ x 1 =) _____
Business associates	(____ x 2 =) _____
Employers	(____ x 2 =) _____
Employees	(____ x 2 =) _____
Friends	(____ x 2 =) _____
Relatives	(____ x 2 =) _____
Parents	(____ x 3 =) _____
Children	(____ x 3 =) _____
Neighbors	(____ x 1 =) _____
Priest/minister/rabbi	(____ x 3 =) _____
Lovers	(____ x 3 =) _____
Spouse	(____ x 3 =) _____
Pollsters	(____ x 1 =) _____
Reporters	(____ x 1 =) _____
Therapist/counselor	(____ x 3 =) _____
Teachers	(____ x 2 =) _____
Students	(____ x 2 =) _____
Business partners	(____ x 3 =) _____

SUBTOTAL _____

4. How many lies have you told in the last week?

None	(0)
1–4	(1)
5–9	(2)
10 or more	(3)

_____

5. How may lies have you told in the past day (or yesterday, if it's still early)?

None	(0)
1–4	(1)
3–4	(2)
5 or more	(3)

_____

Now, total up your points from the five sections to get your Lie-Q!   _____

Scoring Key

0–24	A Model of Absolute Integrity—but are you for real? You seem too honest to be believed.
25–49	A Real Straight Shooter—most of the time. Flexibly honest.
50–99	A Pragmatic Fibber
100–149	A Real Pinocchio
150–199	A Compulsive Liar—you probably cheated on this test.
200+	Someone Who Will Lie about Almost Everything—are you reading this in prison or on *Primetime*?*

*In discussing the Lie-Q Test, I have combined the last two categories into what I call the "Frequent Liar," because of the relatively small number of people in these categories.

PART III

Lying in Public and Professional Life

In Chapter 3, I described the zones of making ethical choices, which similarly affect whether you are likely to lie or not. As I noted there, these zones are like a series of circles, with us in the center, and the surrounding circles reflecting our social connections, which are of decreasing closeness to us. As the zones are further and further away from us, they are less important to us personally, so we may be more likely to lie for pragmatic or strategic reasons, whereas when the zones are closer to us, we are more likely to be concerned with the demands of personal loyalty and trust, and are therefore less likely to lie.

The three outer zones include society as a whole, the local community and public, and work, business, and professional associates.

The chapters in this section look at a variety of situations in which different types of people make different choices and employ varying styles of lying in their public and professional lives. The section illustrates how people may be guided by the different lying styles of their work and professional peers in different types of organizations and occupations.

More specifically, the major types of situations discussed include: (1) everyday social lies, (2) lying in public, (3) lying at work, and (4) lying in business. Each chapter will include suggestions on how to deal with the lying styles of different types of people more effectively in these four public and professional arenas.

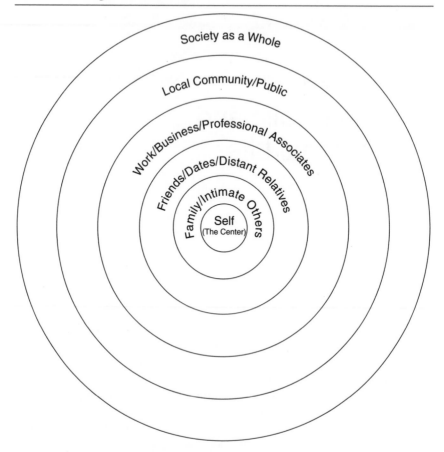

CHAPTER 5

Everyday Social Lies

Some lies are so common that many people don't even consider them lies. They have become more like social conventions whereby people offer comments and opinions, make agreements about little things like plans to meet, and give excuses that aren't exactly true. In turn, many others don't take such statements seriously—maybe the person means them when saying them, or maybe not; such statements are more like social glue to many people.

However, there are still some people who really do care and want to apply strict standards. They see such sloppy habits and imprecisions about the truth as a decline in manners and trust, and they distrust such people who are loose with the truth, even in everyday social situations.

In other words, the people who tend to see these everyday social lies as not really lies or just as common social conventions tend to be the pragmatic fibbers, real Pinocchios, and frequent liars, whereas those who seek to avoid such lies are the real straight shooters and models of absolute integrity.

These social lies fall into six main categories:

- The lies that cover up feelings and opinions;
- The lies to create a better image or appearance;
- The little misrepresentations made to avoid or shorten undesired contacts.
- The agreements made because it's easier to say "yes" when the real answer is "no";
- The excuses given to avoid activities;
- The lies told to cover up forgetfulness and tardiness; and

COVERING UP REAL FEELINGS AND OPINIONS

Perhaps one of the biggest uses for these common social lies is to cover up how we really feel or think when we believe that our opinions or beliefs may hurt or offend someone. People ask: "How are you?" or "How do you feel?" They don't really expect you to say how you really are. The usual responses expected are "Fine" or "I'm feeling great." Quite often, people don't even pay much attention to the response.

What if a person who gives the expected response really isn't feeling fine? Is it a lie to say he is? Perhaps. But this is the classic "white" or harmless lie, because the person who asks this question generally doesn't want to know the truth if the person isn't feeling fine or great; he's not interested in the details, he's just making a passing comment.

Most of the people I interviewed and, I suspect, most other people, go along with this convention. But some people choose to break this convention and say how they really feel when they don't feel fine. These are the real straight shooters and models of absolute integrity, who are determined to tell the truth, even when others would be more comfortable with a social lie. What happens then?

One of the people I interviewed, Roger the philosophy teacher, had tried this from time to time as an experiment, and he found this broke open new doors to communication. He did the unexpected, and generally people seemed to respond favorably. As he explained:

Usually, when people ask you: "How are you?" they don't expect you to say how you really are. But I do generally. I feel I want to tell the truth if I'm asked, even if I'm not feeling particularly good at the time, so I do. So a lot of times I do tell people how I'm feeling.

But if I'm not feeling particularly good, I'll try to say that in a comfortable way. For example, say I'm feeling depressed about something, and people say: "How are you?" Sometimes I'll make a joke about it and say, "Well, on a scale of ten, it's about a three." Or I might mention something that's recently been going on in my life, if this is someone I know.

I have found that people do seem to appreciate the honesty. And it creates a new possibility for communication, because I've broken out of the conventional. So much conversation is conventional. People think and respond in routine ways. But then, when you break the mold, that sometimes gets people thinking and reacting. I've found it has helped to make some of the people I've used this with more open and straightforward with me in return.

However, unexpected candor can make some people uncomfortable. Sandy, a marketing consultant, noted this had happened to her at social gatherings. In response to her comment, "Oh, how are you?" the person had started to tell her. "I didn't like it, and I wasn't sure how to get the person to stop diplomatically, so I felt a little trapped into having to listen." But then Sandy became trapped because she was lying with her question and expecting a routine social lie in return.

Storm, the writer, often felt that friends who asked him for an opinion were really looking for reassurance. As Storm commented:

I sometimes tell lies that don't hurt people or ones that will make them feel better about themselves in everyday social situations, where the real truth is not that important.

For example, sometimes a friend will come to me and ask for my comments on some writing or other work they have done, and I sense what they really want is some kind of stamp of approval. They seem insecure and they want to feel what they have done is okay.

Well, when they come to me like this, I won't say this is terrible or awful, even though sometimes it is. Instead, I always try to put a prettier picture on it. In some cases, the work may be absolutely irredeemable, and in that case I might try to tactfully make some suggestions, though without putting their work down. For instance, I might say, "I don't do it this way. This is how I do it." And then usually, they take my advice.

On the other hand, when these social lies about feelings and opinions might have some consequences in the relationship, people might tell the truth.

For example, to save her feelings, Don, the engineer, would often tell a casual girlfriend that he liked something she had cooked when he actually didn't. But if this were someone he was going to see for a while and she might cook what he didn't like again, then he would say something so he would not have to experience it again.

In conversations, people might avoid saying their real opinions or even state false opinions to help maintain the social peace. It was, as Blanche, the public relations specialist, expressed it, a way of being safe.

I think people tend to be safe. They are careful, particularly when it comes to talking about sensitive subjects, such as religion and politics. A lot of people I know, for whatever reason, are careful people. And I find that they're very sensitive to other people's feelings and don't want to hurt their feelings. Also, they want to avoid saying things that could be controversial. A lot of people I know feel safer that way.

In fact, Blanche had a memorable experience at a prestigious dinner party. Her mother-in-law had reminded her not to talk about politics, because Blanche tended to be a fairly outspoken liberal, and this was to be a conservative gathering. Blanche found a way to break the taboo safely. As she described it:

It was a big society dinner sponsored by a conservative local newspaper publisher. My mother-in-law, who is very conservative, invited me, though I'm a liberal Democrat. So before the dinner, my mother-in-law said: "I don't want you to talk about politics." And when I asked her what I could talk about, she said horticulture. I told her, "It's fine for you to talk about horticulture, you raise cymbidiums. But I have very little to talk about if we talk about horticulture. But I will do my best."

Well, I remember wearing white gloves to this dinner, because it was that kind of event. And I also remember trying not to talk with my hands, because my father had told me that was always a dead giveaway as to my ethnicity and past. So I was trying to conceal that, too.

Anyway, I met the daughter-in-law of this publisher and her two friends at our table, and we got along famously. Then we were talking about cymbidiums, and I had very little to contribute to the conversation, and she looks at me, and she asks me why I'm not saying anything. Then she says there are only four of us, why don't we talk about something more serious? When I explained about what my mother-in-law had asked, she said: "Well, it's all right if I initiate it. Then, it will look like you are being responsive and polite." And so she started. And the two of us had a grand old time.

CREATING A BETTER IMAGE OR APPEARANCE

Creating a better image or appearance for the self can be fertile ground for social lying. In the classic *The Presentation of Self in Everyday Life*, social scientist Ervin Goffman points out how all of us have public and private personas, and he says that we create and play out our various roles on a kind of dramatic stage.[1]

Some of the people I spoke to described trying out different roles or experiencing others doing this. In some cases, they found it enjoyable, like a kind of game, or a way of feeling more confident and successful by adopting such an image. But in other cases, they felt bothered by the deceptions involved in elaborating on what they saw as the underlying or real persona.

On the other hand, Sandy, the marketing consultant, emphasized the fun of role playing. As she explained:

I sometimes like to imagine I'm someone else. So I'll go to a social event, and I won't tell people what I really do. I'll just be another personality for a while. I'll use another name. And I'll take on different traits to go with it. But then the other people I'm with will be aware that I'm engaging in this kind of pretense and they may adopt their own other self, too. It's like stepping into another role on Halloween, though I might do this at an everyday party. Afterwards, I step back into being myself again.

Others spoke of getting advice on image building from consultants, so they would dress differently or change their speech patterns to attain a desired image. "And why not do that?" asked Barry, a management consultant I spoke with. "After all, if you create a certain image of success, people will tend to relate to you in the way you appear. And that will help you to become successful."

On the other hand, Roger, the philosophy teacher, and Raphael, the counselor and healer, had reservations about playing a part. Roger described his own discomfort in trying to misrepresent himself:

It happened when I was at a dinner party, and somebody asked me who I was, and I misrepresented myself. I was going to see if I could take this person in when he asked me if I was a member of some sort of debate group, so I said I was. I started out thinking it was a kind of game. But then, as we kept on talking and he asked me more questions about myself and the group, I just didn't feel very good about doing this. I felt bothered that maybe I might slip up, and I felt like it wasn't right to be trying to take him in. So it started to feel like a stupid game I was playing.

Raphael was bothered by the adoption of personas by others, although he enjoyed creating a looser, more freewheeling persona for himself, considering this more in the nature of having fun for himself than an actual lie, though some might view this as having a different standard of lying for himself. As he commented:

There's so much posturing going on. There's men trying to assume a tough, machismo, I-can-do-anything role, and then there's people trying to look their best. There's so much secrecy. So many people not telling the truth of what's really going on. You say, "How are you?" "Fine. How are you?" "Fine." There's just so much superficiality in relationships. So much make-up and posturing.

It's like making up a résumé in a job search. You don't put on a résumé that you have a real weakness, such as getting unfocused, becoming really scattered at times, or getting very anxious. You want to look good and secure on your résumé. Just like you want to look good in social situations.

AVOIDING UNPLEASANT OR UNDESIRABLE CONTACTS

People may also use these little misrepresentations to avoid unpleasant or undesirable activities or contacts. For instance, people at a party use familiar getaway lines such as: "I just want to get another drink," or "Excuse me, I just saw someone I need to talk to." They cover up what could be the real reason for leaving—the person is a bore and they just don't want to talk to him. They might also use such lies to get out of going to some event in the first place, canceling out, or leaving early.

People also may use such getaway lines and excuses with strangers. Roger, the philosophy teacher, often did this to get away from panhandlers.

Say a panhandler comes up to ask me for money. The truth is that I'm unwilling to give them money. But I say: "I can't spare any," which means I can't afford to give, which is not true. But I'm afraid if I say I'm unwilling to give them money, they'll take that as a hostile response, and maybe they'll attack me, yell at me, or something. So it's just easier to say I can't and get away.

And others reported coming up with their own excuses to evade religious proselytizers, political promoters, and others who approached them on the street.

LITTLE LIES

These social lies are really quite common. Their purpose is to make it easier for us to function and at times save face or help us to make a better appearance. If there's something we don't want to do, someone we don't want to see, a minor error we have made, an appointment we have forgotten, a lie is often a handy way to escape the consequences or give us an easy out. In turn, people generally just accept these little excuses—even if they know or suspect they aren't true. The situation just isn't that important, and there isn't that much energy to confront everyone on all these little lies.

But while these social fictions may not be that important, they do raise questions about how they might contribute to a larger pattern of lying about more serious things and to people with whom one has a closer, more enduring relationship.

DEALING WITH EVERYDAY LIES YOURSELF

If you can distinguish between the attitudes of different types of people toward lying, you can better manage how you deal with what they tell you and what you tell them.

For example, with most people, who are likely to be pragmatic fibbers, real Pinocchios, and frequent liars, you can commonly take any of these everyday lies they tell you with a grain of salt—maybe they are true, maybe not, but don't give them a great importance. Conversely, you can similarly feel free to fudge opinions and comments to smooth over your social relationship. However, when something matters; when it's important that you have a firm commitment or understanding, like an agreement to share leads and commissions with a recent acquaintance, then make it very clear that this is an understanding in which you expect a firm agreement—and even insist on getting any agreement in writing. Just a handshake is often not enough with people in these categories, whereas it might be fine with the model of absolute integrity or real straight shooter.

Conversely, if you are with someone who is a model of absolute integrity or a real straight shooter, then you can expect that they will normally tell you what they really think, and, in turn, you should be sure to be straightforward and forthright with them. Don't just tell them what you think they want to hear.

CHAPTER 6

Lying in Public

Beyond these everyday social lies, the next arena for lying is everyday public encounters—in stores, with salespeople and service people, with public officials and authorities, with neighbors, with landlords and tenants, with lawyers and politicians, and the like. In such situations, because people don't have intimate bonds, people may feel freer to lie. Moreover, many people already think the other person may be likely to lie to them. In that case, lying becomes like a game, a war, or a battle of wits.

WHO IS MOST LIKELY TO LIE?

As with everyday lies, you will find the pragmatic fibbers, Pinocchios, and frequent liars far more likely to lie when it's practical, with the frequent liars even less likely to be trusted. In this arena, the models of absolute integrity and real straight shooters may be more willing to bend the rules and be more open to lying, though they are more likely to lie less or to feel some guilt about lying. And again, you can expect the models of absolute integrity to do all they can to frame what they say to avoid actually stating a lie and to be more comfortable simply omitting information. The result is still a lie, since the listener thinks one thing, based on the omitted information, which isn't true, but it feels less like a lie since the individual hasn't actually stated a lie.

Aside from these categories of liars, social categories can also be useful in suggesting when people are more likely to lie, since people in different social groups partake of different cultures, norms, and expectations. For example, among healing professionals, including doctors, nurses, and psychologists, there is a strong ethical code that promotes honesty with both patients and colleagues, except in certain situations, such as when trying to temper the news of a terminal diagnosis to help the person feel better by offering hope. By contrast, for many people in sales, there is more of a priority on making the sale, even if it becomes necessary to shade the information given to persuade the client to buy. Certainly, many sales people urge transparency and forthrightness in certain types of selling—but generally, there is this cultural difference that places the bottom line at a higher value than it would be to healing professionals. So lying, evasion, and fudging may go with the territory.

In turn, these differences in cultural values about lying and honesty have given rise to common perceptions about the members of different groups. Such perceptions are essentially stereotypes which are often true, though not always, and being aware of these patterns can help you in knowing how to generally deal with members of these different groups. This way you have a different mind set when you speak with them based on general perceptions of that group, while being ready to modify your perceptions to take into account individual differences.

For example, one common suspicion is that people in a position of power and influence can use that power and influence deceptively and unethically, such as to close a deal or persuade someone to give them a better deal. Another suspicion is that disadvantaged people will use lying to get ahead, while members of the middle class tend to be more likely to be responsible and follow the rules.

In fact, when I was growing up, my parents used to impress upon me the notion that we were part of the "respectable and responsible middle class who formed the backbone of this country"—or any other developed country for that matter. They also warned me about the wealthier and more powerful people "up there" who were quick to take advantage to acquire more wealth and power, while the people "down there" in the lower classes could be difficult to trust, since they were driven by concerns to survive and would do whatever necessary to that end. And these images of the upper, middle, and lower classes are still with us.

In turn, those class distinctions were repeatedly confirmed in my interviews when I asked about who was more likely to lie—those on the top or those on the bottom? The groups I heard mentioned again and again as those who might be more likely to lie were salespeople, lawyers, public relations people, and politicians—all people who use persuasion. It's no wonder such people tend to be associated with lying; they make their living by trying to outmaneuver and manipulate others, and maneuvering and manipulation are key reasons for crafting a lie. This doesn't mean these people necessarily lie. Indeed, lawyers have codes of professional responsibility, and others have codes of ethics. But they may be more likely to do so—more likely to be the pragmatic fibbers, Pinocchios, and frequent liars of this world.

Comments from the people I interviewed reflected these suspicions. Roger, the philosophy teacher, had this to say:

I usually expect salesmen to lie. Especially when I'm a customer for the first time. I feel that they may not tell me the full truth. They may not lie directly, but they may hold some things back. So generally, I try to be pretty wary when I'm first meeting a salesman.

Alison, a counselor on personal growth, said this:

For me, it's salespeople, people in real estate. You can't generalize. I work with some sales and real-estate people who are very spiritual and concerned about having integrity. But commonly, these people are into persuasion and manipulation, and that can lead to lies.

A man I encountered, a former lawyer now in real estate sales, helped to confirm this impression at a cocktail party:

I have a boss who told me and tells all his salesmen to say anything you have to to make the sale. That's the way to succeed in this business.

However, Dick, the sales manager, believed that "in the long run, honesty and integrity pay." He believed there was a good reason for associating the salesperson with this image of deception. "I think the closer you get to a money motive, the closer you get to people lying." It's an observation that has been echoed repeatedly during the recent economic meltdown, where a growing list of financial people, from financial planners to stock brokers to investment bankers, have been caught up in assorted financial scandals.

As for public relations people, Storm, the writer who frequently worked with them, had this to say:

PR people, I think they lie all the time. It's an ingredient of the profession. They're always coloring or not saying things to manipulate the truth a little to present an image. I just think when you're dealing with a PR person, you have about a 90 percent chance they're going to be doing some kind of deceptive thing to some degree. Some are less hurtful than others; some want to lie less; some may not lie at all, though in my experience it's very few.

What about lawyers? Joanna, a business consultant, and Jerry, a psychologist, expressed some of the common reservations.

Joanna: "I think lawyers are taught to be misleading. Even if they may not lie outwardly, lawyers still have to be an advocate, which means presenting their client in the best light. So they may not say something unless someone asks them directly. Or they will leave things out to give an incorrect impression. And often it's like they are playing a game, where the truth doesn't really matter, just who wins or makes the best point. And maybe that's their job; they're supposed to do this for their client. But it bothers me, and I think lawyers with their abilities to twist and shade the truth in creative ways are doing major damage to our country. They're undermining the basic principles of honesty and integrity, and I think in the long run we will pay for it."

Jerry: "The way I see it, attorneys have a relativistic ethic. They don't see lying as being an absolute wrong. Rather, the truth becomes relative. Maybe it's a gross generalization, but I would say generally, any attorney is paid to shape the truth by presenting one side of an argument. Maybe it's not a lie exactly, but it comes pretty close."

And politicians too were perceived with some skepticism, since they were commonly expected to lie to get ahead or to win support for their policies or programs. Stan, the high school teacher, expressed a commonly held view:

Politicians and lying! How can they not? That's part of the territory. I can't think of a president who didn't lie—for sometimes good and sometimes not so good reasons. And I teach civics! Even with the cherry-tree story, Washington certainly told a few good ones in his lifetime. And we all know about the lies of Nixon, of Johnson, just about every president we've ever had. It all comes out.

Beyond the big four, there were many other groups that got a mention, including doctors and physicians ("They're reinforced, if not to lie, at least to conceal bad truths"), government officials ("Part of their job involves maintaining a good front"), and spies and CIA agents ("They're actually paid to lie and spread misinformation").

And people out of the mainstream or in disadvantaged or minority groups were perceived as likely to be liars, too, because they had more of a struggle to survive. For example, some frequent comments that came up in the interviews were that people who were "poor and desperate for money," "on drugs or suffering from a chemical-abuse problem," "alcoholics," "insecure," or "irresponsible" might be most likely to lie.

Generally, such lying was regarded negatively, though there were some lies that were commonly felt to be justified, for example, if one was cheated by a large organization and the lie was used to gain personal justice, such as in dealing with a phone or telecommunications company or an insurance company. If people think the company has done them wrong, or if they think they might be hit with extra charges otherwise, lying might be a way out for anyone, regardless of their place on the continuum of lying, though the pragmatic fibbers, real Pinocchios, and frequent liars might be especially likely to use a lie; the models of absolute integrity and the straight shooters, on the other hand, might be more likely to try to work things out through the system.

Following are some examples of how and when the interviewees used lying themselves or experienced deception from others. For instance, Dee, a real-estate investor, used subterfuge to get the phone company to adjust a bill she didn't think she deserved. As she described it:

I ended up with a large phone bill because someone had called me from Europe, and for some reason it got put on my bill, though it wasn't supposed to, because this person had called me. But the phone company didn't want to take it off.

So I told the person I was discussing the bill with that I was in law school, and I was planning to make this a test case for the phone company, if they didn't take it off the bill. And when I said that the company finally did take it off the bill.

So I lied, and I wish I didn't have to do it. But I felt I had to, because I felt I was right. The operator hadn't told me this was going to be a collect phone call, and then they put it on my bill. It was for $90, and I didn't feel like I should pay.

Raphael, the counselor and healer who sometimes works with social services, noted how he often encountered client deception to avoid actions they felt would be unjust. As he explained:

My clients see me as aligned with the authority, so they don't tell me things, to protect themselves. Such as about child abuse, drug use, alcoholism, domestic violence, things like that, because if they tell me something, then it may get to the authorities, and they may risk having their children taken away from them. Or they might fear other penalties from the law.

LYING TO NEIGHBORS

Probably the one area where people didn't experience much lying was with neighbors, generally because people had little contact with them. If they had contact, it was usually of the nodding-acquaintance variety.

Blanche, the public relations executive, expressed what seemed to be the most common feeling:

You know the old expression: Fences make good neighbors. So I don't know my neighbors very well, and I have fortunately never had a situation where any issue involving lying has ever come up. And besides, why would one lie to one's neighbor? There just doesn't seem any point.

But should there be a neighborhood problem or dispute, lying might occur. For example, I heard accusations of lying when I was a member of neighborhood community board conflict-resolution panels. This was a San Francisco community-service program in which a panel of three or four volunteers would help people mediate a problem. Typically, these were things such as disputes between neighbors over trees and noise.

One of the people I interviewed, Susannah, the financial planner, described a byzantine saga of deception, revenge, and legal wrangling involving a neighbor who claimed that one of her beautiful trees blocked his view. After she tried to work out an understanding by reasonably trimming the tree, he apparently decided to "trim" her tree himself while she was out of town. Let Susannah explained what happened:

My neighbor lied after he vandalized my tree, because when I went and confronted him, he denied it. And I know he did it, although I have no proof, because we have been battling about this tree for years. And I'm sure he lied, to escape possibly serious consequences for damaging my tree.

But in her own quiet way, Susannah took steps to deal with the lie, though she was normally a model of absolute integrity. First, she fantasized that a large gorilla like King Kong stepped out from behind her tree, patted the top back into shape, and then went over to ravage the garden of her neighbor. Then one night Susannah quietly stopped by her neighbor's garden and carried out some of the things she saw the imagined gorilla doing, such as pulling up some of her neighbor's just-planted greenery. It was her way to quietly counter her neighbor's deception by being deceptive herself, although otherwise Susannah would consider herself a generally righteous, upright, moral, and ethical person—a perfect model of absolute integrity ready to lie only in a special circumstance to overcome an injustice and thereby restore moral balance in the world.

CHAPTER 7

Lying at Work

Work lies run the gamut: employees lying to employers; employers lying to employees; coworkers and colleagues lying to each other. And there may even be institutional, company-wide lies in which certain procedures become a form of lying, such as the fiction of filling out forms and time sheets a certain way when in fact people in the organization are doing something else. Indeed, the work environment can often be especially conducive to lying because there is so much at stake. The need to keep jobs, earn more money, get a promotion, find excuses for problems with work, and jockey for position, prestige, power, and money can be an ideal germinator for lies.

For example, a company tends to lie in the name of efficiency to spur productivity, keep employees working, pass the buck, or evade revealing negative findings, because it fears liability. Employees tend to lie to advance their careers, to protect themselves against mistakes, and to put down the competition. Coworkers often lie to shift blame or out of petty jealousy.

In turn, such a climate can encourage some people to form a series of temporary—or ongoing—and ever-changing alliances to gain support against the possible forays of others or to help in the attack or both.

But in certain work settings, such as when the company or employer tries to create a more open, supportive climate, such lying is apt to decline—because people have less to attack or defend.

These pressures affect individuals all along the continuum of lying, though the models of absolute integrity and the straight shooters may be more likely to try to do the forthright thing, while pragmatic fibbers, Pinocchios, and frequent liars may be more likely to do what is most strategic at the time without any qualms about it. However, it is here in the workplace where the models integrity and straight shooters are more apt to be more pragmatic themselves, especially in recessionary times, because their economic survival or thriving may depend on it. Still, if they are dissembling or holding back information, they may be more likely to give off body cues that they are telling a lie, because they are not used to doing this and more likely to feel some guilt for feeling compelled to lie.

For example, take the difference between Fred and Ella. Fred, who would most likely be categorized as a frequent liar, was something of a charming rogue who could convince Eskimos to buy refrigerators, to cite an old canard. He was a frequent speaker at business and marketing groups, where he talked about improving market performance, and he commonly used free speaking engagements to feed newcomers into high-priced workshops and seminars he was giving. He used assorted ploys to get attendees to quickly buy, such as putting a high price on a workshop, and then slicing it in half—but only if the attendee was willing to buy within 10 hours. Otherwise, the offer would go away forever. And then, at events, he fleshed out basic marketing info with stories about how he had helped a variety of clients achieve breakthrough success—although he danced around exactly what he did. For that, you would have to pay even more for a more exclusive seminar or personal coaching by him. And he was quite successful at getting newcomers to pay this way—though then he often did not follow through on his promises to provide even more high-valued information or promote the work of attendees, despite lavish praises and claims of very strong interest. So he left a lot of people feeling disappointed or burned. His technique was a little like that of a strip miner, who tears through an area, takes out the easiest pickings on the surface, and then moves on.

Enter Ella, a model of absolute integrity. She had signed up for one of Fred's seminars, drawn in by his convincing pitch to provide hard-to-get information that would help her break through in giving workshops and seminars herself. Though she felt much of his seminar information was fairly basic, since she had been to other marketing programs, including university classes, she didn't immediately take Fred up on his guarantee of a full refund at the end of the program, because he promised to send everyone in the workshop some high-priced workbooks for free—his "gift" to everyone in the class, as he put it. But then weeks went by, and though Ella sent Fred repeated e-mails she received nothing, and she became more and more steamed. When I spoke to her about five weeks after the seminar, she was livid—determined to either get her several hundred dollars back for the program or expose Fred to the world for being a cheat and a liar. As she put it:

Fred sucked me in with his claims of being privy to highly secret and powerful information and his claims of who he knows. He made all kinds of claims about sales and successes he had, which led me to think he knew much more than he did. And so I was willing to scrape together $300, money I need for the rent, because he made it sound like he had a way for me to make thousands of dollars very quickly. But then, when I attended his workshop, I felt a lot of the information was old. And then I was sucked in again by his claims that he would be sending us workbooks with a lot of very valuable information, so I didn't immediately ask for a refund, and then he never sent the money.

So I realized he's really a con—and if I don't get my money back, I'll expose him to the world. And if anyone I know wants to still work with him after I've told them what happened to me, well, I don't want to have anything to do with him either. I just don't want anyone like that in my life anymore.

So sometimes people with opposing lying styles can prove very combustible when they get together—and it can be hard for someone who is a model of absolute integrity or a real straight shooter to work in an environment filled with pragmatic fibbers, Pinocchios, and frequent liars, especially when they have a boss in that category who sets that tone. Conversely, the pragmatic fibber, Pinocchio, and frequent liar types may find working in an environment filled with models of integrity and straight shooters too constricting, because they are always coming up against rules and restrictions of moral and ethical behavior that they want to break to quickly achieve the results they want.

It's the difference between process and results thinking. While the models of integrity and straight shooters tend to be concerned about doing whatever they are doing in the right way, the pragmatic fibbers, Pinocchios, and frequent liars are more interested in getting to the right result in whatever way works best.

These different attitudes affect the propensity of these different types for telling different types of lies in the workplace.

ORGANIZATIONAL LIES

Organizational lies usually occur when the usual rules or channels of an organization aren't working, so people go outside the system, which can create a lie when people cover up doing this. What makes it an organizational lie is that management knows about it and goes along, perhaps because it agrees with what people are doing or doesn't want to rock the boat.

Frances, a computer systems supervisor, described how this often occurred in her own very large company in a few key areas—keeping time sheets, testing systems, reviewing employee performance, and dealing with promotions. Note that she sounds much like a model of absolute integrity working in a more pragmatic type of environment. She began with the time sheets:

There's all kinds of fudging that goes on, and the company knows about it. This is the way it's done.

Basically what happens is we work 37 and a half hours a week. But on the time sheet, we are supposed to show that we worked 40 hours a week. So what the company is doing is teaching its people to lie. Someone starts working for the company, and almost immediately they've got to fudge their time.

I don't really feel comfortable doing that, so I put down what I really work. Normally, it's 40 hours or more. But if I work less than 40 hours, which we may do, say because of a doctor's appointment, I put down what I did and any explanation.

But, then the others just go along with the usual procedures. Why not put down 37 and a half hours and be accurate? We have quizzed our bosses. We have wondered why. We have guessed that maybe they're lying to upper management about how much everyone works, so it seems like people are doing more or getting paid less per hour. But they don't tell us anything—just to keep filling out the time sheets this way, which is a lie.

In some cases, this fluid approach to keeping time actually worked to Frances's advantage, such as when she was out for about a week, and her supervisor gave her some extra days' credit. Even so, she felt bad about it—as if she were collaborating in a secret company lie. As she told me:

One time I had to have some tests at the hospital, and I thought I was just going to be there for two days, so I worked some extra hours before I did this to make up for this. But then it ended up that I had to take the whole week off, although I had expected to work it.

Then, when I got back, I said to my boss that I probably only worked a total of twelve hours that week, including the time I worked on the previous weekend. However, he said, Don't worry about it," and he put me down as sick for three days, so I could get paid for the whole week.

The whole thing made me feel a little funny, because I find it hard to live with a lie. But then my boss thought it was okay, because that's the way things are done.

EMPLOYER LIES

When employers lie to employees, they may do it to protect the organization from a disgruntled employee, prospective employee, or former employee when the employer has to do something that person might not like—such as not hire or promote him, transfer him, or fire him. So sometimes it is easier to give another, more gentle or diplomatic reason than to tell the blunt truth. Sometimes the lie involves liability. An employer might hesitate to reveal what's really going on because it might be used against him later in a suit. Another common lie is the lie to avoid embarrassment or save face when the employer has made a mistake and he doesn't want to lower himself in the eyes of his employee or employees. And sometimes employers may lie to suggest there is an opportunity ahead, knowing there is not, in order to get the employee to work harder or accomplish some task. In turn, since employers have the power, employees don't typically confront them over the lie.

But when employer lies get serious or pervasive, not only are employees more apt to provoke an angry confrontation and perhaps leave the organization, but such lies also are often what trigger employment discrimination or unfair practices suits. The employee who can't effectively confront the lie feels upset or angry about what happened and brings in the big guns to help fight the battle for him.

This is what happened when Roger, the philosophy teacher, applied for a job. The department chairman gave him some administrative reason for not hiring him, when, in fact, Roger believed that the chairman liked someone else better, perhaps because Roger was something of a maverick. As Roger commented:

I've been teaching in about a dozen different places for seven years, and I guess you could say I've sometimes ruffled some feathers, because I'm a pretty outspoken person. So it's true—sometimes people don't like me because I say what I think.

So that may be why I've had some experiences where my position has not been renewed after a year or where someone has decided not to hire me. But I don't always feel they really tell me why. I've asked, but often my experience has been that the person may not tell me what's so and I felt that he is withholding the truth, maybe because he'd rather say something safer to avoid hurting my feelings or provoking some kind of confrontation.

For example, a classic case of this type happened to me recently when I went to an interview at a university in a city near San Francisco. The man claimed he couldn't hire me after the interview because of some kind of administrative problem with the university—there were some limits on the number of part-time people he could hire.

Well, if that was so, why even interview me for a part-time position? I suspected that he just didn't like me as much as someone else. Finally, I cornered him and asked for the real truth—didn't he prefer these other people to me? Finally he told me the truth that this was so. There were some limits on the number of people he could hire, so that part of his statement was true. However, he had also rated the people he interviewed. I rated lowest in the group. I imagine he tried to avoid telling me this to save my feelings or to avoid legal hassles later, but I preferred knowing the truth. And I think it's his right to not hire me because of not liking me. I just wanted to know.

Similarly, Dick, the sales manager, found it easier to give a phony reason for not paying an employee than to tell her he wasn't satisfied with her work. That way he could avoid confronting the situation. As he told me:

A few years ago, I used to give my support staff part of my commission for doing a good job, and when this woman suddenly quit on me, she wanted her commission. Well, I was outraged that she would just quit without any notice, and then on top of this I thought it outrageous that she would expect a commission, too.

However, I didn't tell her this. I just told her that I didn't have the money now, and so I wasn't going to pay her. Of course, I had the money, but it was easier to say that I didn't have the money rather than confront her and tell her how dissatisfied I was with her work.

Because Dick didn't tell her the real reason, the woman broke into his office to get the money. Looking back, Dick felt bad because he hadn't been honest with her in the first place.

It was just a real embarrassing situation all around. A couple of weeks after I turned her down, she broke into the office, and no one knew why she was there. So when a couple of people saw her in my office, it got very emotional. She started screaming, saying that I ripped her off and stole from her and I owed her money. And then, when they called me, I just told them to let her go, so they just got her out of the office and we hushed the whole thing over.

However, I felt very badly about the whole incident. I didn't feel good that she was leaving. I didn't feel good that I had been subsidizing her out of my own pocket to keep her there and then she left. And then I felt especially bad about the lying, telling her I didn't have the money, rather than telling her the real reason I wasn't going to pay her. I think if I had shared my real outrage with her in the first place that might have avoided her trying to come back to get the money afterwards. So her coming back made me feel even worse about the whole thing, and I wish I had just told the truth.

SETTING THE TONE

Besides lying directly to employees, employers can play a part in creating a tone or culture in the organization that can encourage or discourage lying.

For example, if employers create a competitive, closed, nonsupportive environment, it can contribute to lying by employees to each other and to the employers, because such a setting leads people to feel self-protective and defensive. So the lie becomes a shield to fend off threats and attacks and advance against others. In effect, employees are led to adopt more pragmatic approaches to protect themselves.

By contrast, if employers set the tone for a warm, open, supportive environment, it tends to discourage lying, because people don't feel the need to protect themselves and they can share their flaws, mistakes, and fears openly and get support. They can be more honest about themselves, so they are better able to use a more high-integrity approach.

Judith Briles, who has written about corporate ethics, noted this important role of employers in setting the tone when I spoke to her. As she commented:

My experience is that when lies are going on, especially from the employer or person in charge, it contributes to regarding lies as an acceptable option, since the person we look up to, the person who we might want to be, does it.

LYING BY EMPLOYEES

Common employee lies revolve around exaggerating ability, experience, or power or making false claims about plans and intentions to get a job; using excuses or falsehoods to explain away delays and cover up mistakes, being late, or not working as hard as one should; and shifting the blame or getting revenge against someone else. Then, too, employees may lie because they have different values and priorities than their bosses, and the lie is a way to get what they want.

To Get a Job or Promotion

One of the most common and most socially acceptable employee lies is exaggerating past accomplishments to get the job or promotion in the first place. Then if you get it and carry out the task successfully, the lie becomes a fait accompli—no one discovers it or cares about it, or all is forgiven after the fact. Sometimes the successful liar is even praised for his initiative and cleverness, except in certain fields where the discovery of the lie can destroy careers because of regulations and certifications required in those fields.

For example, Stephen, the writer, described a typical use of this approach, which he diplomatically calls "fudging":

I may fudge a little bit when a prospective client asks me if I've had any experience in something that I haven't, say, insurance writing. I might say I have or talk about how I've written things in a related field that suggest I'm experienced in this area. So I try to get as close as I can.

To Make Excuses or Cover Up Delays, Lack of Work, and Mistakes

Perhaps the biggest reason for lying is to excuse or cover up for something done wrong, at the wrong time, in the wrong way, or not at all. One person may do this to cover his or her own neck—or a whole team of people or even a whole division in a large company may get involved in the classic pass the buck, stonewall, or "I didn't do it, shift the responsibility" charade.

Judith Briles, whose books include *Women to Women: From Sabotage to Support* and *The Confidence Factor*, describes this as quite common. "When people don't deliver what they say they were going to, they will often make up all sorts of stories covering up," she said. However, such lies, while common and unlike the lie told to achieve success, can be quite damaging to the employer or company. Not only may they damage quality of work, but they also can lead to more and more layers of lies, compounding the original problem. As Briles commented:

As an employer, such cover-ups are not acceptable. If there's a delay, a mistake, a slip-up, I would want the employee to tell me what really happened. The problem is that excuses contribute to confusion and shoddy workmanship. For if you have this one excuse here, this other excuse there, another excuse over there, as an employer, you can keep entrusting getting the work done to whoever is supposed to do the work. But meanwhile, as the layer of excuses builds up, the slippage in production can continue and get worse.

And then, of course, there are those who lie to get out of going to work now and then entirely—lies of the "I'm sick" or "There's been a family emergency" variety when nothing is wrong. A local newsworthy problem may provide a convenient excuse for a way out, such as the San Francisco earthquake did for many people who weren't really harmed but claimed to be in order to get out of doing something.

Other lies are designed to pass the buck or escape responsibility. Such lies are rooted in people's insecurities and fear of losing face or being punished. When I spoke to therapist Sylvia Mills, she described lies of this type this way:

Many people lie because they are frightened of authority. They lie to cover up. A lot of people have problems dealing with authority and being up-front, because they may feel insecure or scared of losing their jobs. Or they may cover up because they don't want to lose face or they don't want to cause the loss of face for someone else. In other cases they want to pass the buck, which is very common. They deny responsibility, saying: "It wasn't me. It must have been someone in some other department." Blaming can sometimes facilitate their own work, because then someone else has to deal with the paperwork or problem. There's a lot of escapist lying in large companies or bureaucracies.

To Obtain a Forbidden Goal or Take Advantage

Employees also might lie to get something they shouldn't have. The classic example, of course, is the employee who embezzles and tries to cover up, which is a serious felony. Often, employees lie and cover up to get other things too small to notice or make a big deal about, such as the employee who makes personal calls on work time, spirits away small quantities of office supplies, or uses the copy machine for his own work and then tries to hide his use. Or there may be somewhat more serious deceptions to gain something that the employer has expressly forbidden or which the employee knows is disloyal, hurtful to the employer, or otherwise wrong.

Alison, the counselor and workshop leader, described such a situation where a trusted employee violated an agreement that no staff member would date clients. But he did, causing her to lose some clients; then when she found out about this and told him expressly not to, he did it again and tried to cover up, though she eventually found out and fired him. The lie and the act it covered up not only damaged her business, but Alison also saw them as a betrayal of a long-term friendship she had had with her assistant. As she explained:

I had an agreement with a male assistant that he would not date any female clients who showed up at my workshops. I made this agreement after I lost four or five clients who he dated. This happened because he would go out with them a couple of times, have a short romp with them, and then they'd be too embarrassed to come back after it ended, because they'd have to see him. So finally, after this happened four or five times, I made him make an agreement that if he wanted to be assistant for me, he couldn't date them. But he broke the agreement. And when I confronted him, he claimed he had totally forgotten that we had that agreement. But at the time we made the agreement, I made such a big deal about it that it's hard to believe he couldn't remember.

I didn't believe him and I fired him. I think if he had admitted or confessed what he had done, it might have been different. I might have forgiven him and given him another chance. But I felt not only did he break our agreement, but here he was trying to cover up and lie about it, too.

And this lie hurt so much, because this is somebody I had trusted so much in the past. He was someone who always had kept every agreement. He had always followed through and done everything he said he would do. I would literally trust my life with this guy.

As we spoke, I tried to stay calm, and immediately he offered to dump the woman, which made me feel even worse about the whole thing, because I thought: "Here he has lied to me about doing this, and this woman isn't even that important to him."

Though later I found out he was still seeing her six months after he left me, so maybe he would have kept seeing her anyway and tried to lie about that.

In any case, that one lie was just so devastating for me that I had to fire him. And since then we've barely spoken. So it's very sad, and I feel this tremendous loss.

To Gain Alternate Goals or Priorities

Employees may lie when they have different ideas or priorities than their employers. For example, Raphael, the counselor and healer, experienced this situation in his part-time employment at a social welfare agency. The organization had policies about limiting treatment for clients after a certain number of visits. But Raphael thought a particular client needed additional treatment, and he felt it more important to fudge a little to provide that treatment than follow agency guidelines. Then he did some fast maneuvering to "cover his ass" when his boss had questions about what he did. As Raphael told me:

I've been having some problems with my current boss at the agency, because she hasn't let me get away with some things. She has been calling me on everything, including some things I have been doing to try to better help my clients. I've been going ahead with these extra services, because I feel the clients need them. As I learned on an earlier job, if you think you can get away with something you believe in, do it, because it's easier to get forgiveness than to get permission sometimes in a bureaucracy. So I've done that, though it has created some tense times.

LYING BY COWORKERS AND COLLEAGUES

Just about any situation that evokes a cover-up or a desire for extra advantage can trigger a lie between workers and colleagues. However, when coworkers work independently, have little interaction, or are in equal position without any reason to compete, there is little reason to lie.

In the interviews, some of the most common reasons for lies were: to conceal ignorance; to get others to front for someone who wanted to take some time off or who wasn't able to do some work; to compete for positions and promotions; to claim credit for something someone else had done; and to get even for petty jealousies.

Gaining a Competitive Advantage

The desire to get ahead or outdo another person can be another powerful motivator to lie. An employee can conceal his or her real interest in a position or promotion and secretly disparage other hopefuls behind their backs while professing complete support and loyalty on the surface.

However, what is especially interesting about this competition is the way, according to Briles, that men and women do it differently. Both may lie or conceal the truth in the pursuit of a benefit. But more commonly, women will conceal their real interest from each other. By contrast, male rivals are more apt to declare themselves openly. As Briles told me:

Men tend to be much more overt about what they do; women more covert. For example, women tend to try to develop closer relationships and friendships at work, but they don't recognize that everyone is not friend material. So in wanting to develop this relationship and the rapport, one woman can give another the benefit of the doubt. But this can open up the women to being sucked in and taken for a ride by someone who is not really a friend, and it can leave her feeling more devastated and betrayed.

A good reason for this is that as women we grew up not only being taught to be nice and be pleasers, but we were taught to be friends with everybody. Also, we were taught that you don't compete with friends. So that leads women to tend to deny their attempts to compete with each other, such as when one woman announces she is interested in competing for something. Another woman who feels she is supposed to be her friend thinks she isn't supposed to compete. But then if she really wants something, she may compete actively anyway. But she just won't tell the woman who has announced her intentions about it.

By contrast, men tend to have the view that it's okay to compete with friends, and if you lose or you win, you can still be friends and go play racquetball or whatever after the game is over.

The result of this, as Briles explained, is that after the competition is over, the women who previously thought they were friends are likely not to be friends anymore, because the woman who announced herself openly will feel betrayed.

Undermining Other Employees

Still another source of lying between coworkers is the effort to undermine, put down, or "get" someone else out of jealousy, revenge, in battles for power, or for other reasons. Such behind-the-scenes battles are the everyday stuff of office backstabbing or office politics, as this is sometimes more gently and diplomatically known. And in some office settings, particularly where communication is closed and people conceal what they are thinking and feeling, these battles to look good by making others look bad can be rampant. But they tend to be less common where the office culture is more open and supportive.

In any event, such lies can be used as a web or trap to make the unwary victim look foolish, mistaken, or otherwise slip up. But those lies can also backfire, leaving the liar looking worse. Briles gave me an example of using lying to discredit another coworker, based on her research for her book on business ethics. As she described it, one woman tried to make it appear as if another woman wasn't following through on her calls, so she would appear irresponsible. As Briles told me:

A secretary to the head of sales in a major high-tech company—let's call her Sharon— was pregnant and ready to go on a maternity leave. Shortly before she was to leave, her boss called her on the carpet for not following the company's policy that whenever an employee went on a break or to lunch, she was supposed to arrange to have her calls transferred to the receptionist, who would take them and then put any message on the company's voice mail.

At the time her boss called her in, there had been a two-week period when Sharon hadn't gotten any calls, and Sharon had been surprised by this. Normally she expected to have a few messages waiting for her when she returned from a break or lunch. And now her boss was telling her that the company couldn't tolerate her laxness in having calls referred anymore, and if she didn't check out with the receptionist and stop leaving her desk and phone lines unattended, they would terminate her.

Sharon was stunned, because she had been telling the receptionist to take messages and forward her calls when she left. After a little investigation, Sharon discovered what was going on. It turned out that another woman, who was after Sharon's job, would call the operator as soon as Sharon left and tell the operator to have all calls revert back to Sharon's desk, claiming that Sharon had asked her to pick up her calls. Then this woman would pick up these calls herself and go in to Sharon's boss and say: "Sharon is never at her desk, and I'm having to answer her phone all the time." So the woman was setting Sharon up and then telling her boss that Sharon wasn't doing her job.

How did Sharon deal with this?

Basically, Sharon dealt with it by confronting the woman. She told her that she had checked every day with the receptionist, which she had, and that she knew something funny was going on—essentially she told the woman she knew she was lying. And then she told her: "I'm not going to tolerate it any more." Then she handled it with her boss by suggesting there was some misunderstanding about the way her calls were to be handled. So she did handle this with some finesse and so as not to discredit the other woman, which might have made office relations even worse and backfired on her. But the woman knew Sharon knew what she was doing, and so, as Sharon told her, she stopped doing it.

As for her boss, he figured out what was going on and eased up on her.

And the other woman? What happened to her? Apparently, Briles indicated, the boss just let it go, glad that the problem had been papered over, although this incident might have tarnished the reputation of the woman who lied.

CHAPTER 8

Lying in Business

Business is one of the most common arenas for lying, perhaps because so much is based on the art of the deal, where doing well often encourages manipulation, posturing, managing impressions, and yes, deception to get ahead. In turn, much of this jostling to gain the advantage is considered part of the business game, permitted or encouraged by the rules, so often it becomes hard to draw the line between what behavior is perfectly acceptable and what behavior crosses the line.

In turn, the models of absolute integrity and straight shooters are more likely to stay on the acceptable side of the line, while the pragmatic fibbers, Pinocchios, and frequent liars are more likely to cross over easily and without any guilt pangs. While the former are more likely to be the ones who leave questionable deals on the table or blow the whistle on such deals, the latter are more apt to stay aboard as long as it seems practical to do so and then quietly leave the sinking ship before it goes down.

Given this wide range for lying and this uncertainty about what is a lie, what are the major types of lies in business, and how do people feel about them?

There seemed to be major categories of reasons—lies because of:

- Money (to get out of paying, to postpone paying, to pay less, to get more, to conceal a cash flow problem),
- Obligations (to get out of undesired ones or postpone them),
- Information (to get it, to conceal it, or to cover up a lack of it), and
- Mistakes (to cover up making them).

Other key reasons for lying were to look better, gain prestige or power, or get business (say by showing off) with an ersatz self-image, exaggerating to appear in a better light, taking credit for something undeserved, and claiming an ability to do something and then not being able to do it (or not following through). There might be revenge lies for a business deal gone sour.

LIES TO LOOK GOOD

People like to present themselves in the best light, and if a little lying will help—including taking credit where credit isn't due–some people will do this, particularly in business situations where the stakes are high.

These kinds of lies might be considered, as Owen Edwards calls them, "less as lies than as the truth improved."[1] It is probably in this one area that people in business have the most trouble in deciding whether something is a lie or whether it is a positive shift of emphasis to show oneself off to the best advantage. As Edwards observes:

Perhaps this penchant for counterfeit self-improvement is a universal trait. Psychologists have begun to suspect that some illusions about our worth may be essential to maintaining mental health.[2]

Indeed, as Edwards comments, this self-puffery is learned early in life, because "we learn that being seen in a favorable light has its rewards. People are impressed, attention is paid, and we are well liked."[3]

The business consultants and therapists I spoke to agreed that, within limits, this "spin" is fine from various perspectives–as an accepted practice in the business world, as a moral way of elevating the self as long as one's intentions and underlying purpose are good, and as a psychologically healthful thing to do.

From the psychological point of view, therapist Sylvia Mills seemed to think that such positive presentation of self was quite healthy as long as a sincere intention was there and the claims were in keeping with reality. As she commented:

What's the line between out-and-out lying and talking "as if," which is one way to program yourself for success? According to this principle, for example, you talk as if you are confident or successful. Sometimes I use these positive affirmations.

I think the key distinction between this "as if" talk and a lie is the person's intention. If he is presenting himself in a certain way to cover up something or mislead somebody in some way, then that would be called a lie. But if a person is doing it for himself, such as to improve himself, by saying "I'm very successful," or "My book is doing fantastically well," I don't think they're lying. Rather, they're living in expectation—which is fine.

In fact, some psychologists make tapes for people to help them build self-esteem, and these tapes encourage them to present themselves in a very positive way. For instance, they may be asked to repeat and keep thinking to themselves: "I am confident." They're not confident in the beginning, but when they play the tape over and over and keep asserting that thought, they'll believe and therefore become more confident. So I think this kind of self-presentation or affirmation can be used for reprogramming, which is a positive.

There is a point, Mills agreed, when such self-presentation becomes a lie. That point was elusive, but it seemed to hinge on the intentions behind the image—combined with a dose of reality. If the person wanted to make a certain impression that was misleading and he wasn't working on his own internal programming to make that impression a reality, then this presentation would be a kind of lying, because, as Mills put it, this person would be "living in fantasy." Then, too, if the person always knew his goal was impossible, that would be a lie. As Mills put it:

If a person truly believes he can achieve it, even if he can't, then that's not a lie. But if he pretends to be someone he has no intention of becoming, then there's deceit on purpose, and that's a lie.

Between these two extremes, it's a matter of degree when something becomes a lie. It's a matter of quality and quantity.

For example, I regard myself as an honest person. Yet sometimes I get involved in this kind of behavior—it's certainly not daily or even weekly. Its quantity is small, so is the quality. There's not an enormous discrepancy between the person I really believe I am and the person I'm trying to be.

It's a little like if I'm late; I'm likely to be just five or ten minutes late, not three hours. Similarly, when it comes to the presentation of self. I'm basically the person I say I am, and if I exaggerate, it's by very little. But if somebody tells big whoppers to brag, then that's another situation. The farther you actually get from reality, the more likely something will be judged to be a lie or deceit.

Because this potential for "legitimate" and "illegitimate" posing exists, it is always a good idea to check things out before buying any kind of service or dealing with anyone who claims to be a professional. Look for inconsistencies between actions and claims, and listen to intuition or gut feeling.

TAKING THE CREDIT AND MAKING CAN-DO-IT CLAIMS WHEN ONE CAN'T

Other common lies involve a person taking the credit due to someone else or claiming he can do something when he can't or when he doesn't follow through.

In some cases, these "take credit" lies are accepted—such as when a boss gets the credit but the underlings do the work. I think we would have to call them institutionalized lies—socially accepted and endorsed perhaps. But they're still lies.

On the other hand, there are some areas where "take credit" lies do become viewed as harmful. When they involved writing or art or people's ideas, these lies can turn into plagiarism, which is punishable by law. Such lies might occur in an office where, in the course of jostling for position and promotion, one person takes the credit or the glory for another's work, while someone who should get credit does not.

LIES FOR REVENGE

Lies committed for revenge when a business deal goes sour or other personality conflicts surface are definitely beyond the pale. These are clearly malicious, evil-minded, hurtful lies, ethically acceptable to no one. A person may use such lies against another, intending to hurt, yet at the same time concealing the lies, because he knows there could be serious legal consequences. There may be one exception: After the lie succeeds, the person seeking revenge may want the victim to know that he is responsible.

THE CASE FOR HONESTY AND ETHICS IN BUSINESS

While lies may lead to success in the short run, honesty and ethical dealings can contribute to long-term success based on trust and fair dealing, as well as contributing to the social fabric as a whole. Many of the people I spoke to, for example, commented on the way honesty in business was simply the pragmatic thing to do.

For instance, Dee, the real estate investor, told me she would never lie in a business deal. Why?

Because I don't see the advantage in lying. It will only backfire eventually when the truth comes out. And if you enter into a business relationship with someone, that's likely to happen. Maybe not immediately. But sometime. And then that cannot only damage the business, but people who lie in one deal create a trail that can follow them to hurt them in business deals in the future. They may even end up injured or in jail. So there's really no pay-off in the long run. It's better to be straight with people in dealings up front.

By the same token, being honest can be a way of getting the help one needs in business. Robert Middleton, a small-business consultant, found this in his own practice. Business people often would try to posture to make it seem as if their business was going better than it was. But to get help they would have to be open about what was going wrong. As Middleton commented:

When someone comes to me as a client, at that point I find that people are ready to tell the truth because it's not working. Their survival is at stake. They realize that they have to trust someone, and so then they open up quite a lot and will answer just about any question about what they're doing, how much money they are making, and the like.

Another business consultant, Dave, found that being open and honest about his own needs attracted people who could support him. He had tried to play the expert who didn't need people, because he felt that helped to increase his own stature. But that tended only to isolate him and make him more vulnerable, and he actually gained strength by admitting his own vulnerability and need for help. As Dave told me:

I had a real breakthrough when I decided to open up and let people contribute to me and support me. I had pushed people away before, because I had this conception of myself as the expert, and so I felt that people couldn't contribute to me, because I was supposed to be the one contributing to others because I was the consultant.

But once I started telling the truth about that to myself and opening myself up to others, a lot of contributions started to come in. Before I had been saying "I don't really need anything from anybody," which was absolutely untrue.

Some of the things they contributed to me were ideas. For example, they gave me ideas on ways of conducting my business and how I can charge for my services. Then, too, I had been trying to deny that I needed any help financially, and once I was willing to recognize this, I got some help from my father. I wrote to him, telling him that I needed some financing and gave him a plan of what I was going to do to extend my business, such as advertising and putting on workshops for larger companies. And I told him that "I would love to be supported by you," and he gave me the money I needed.

So as a result, I've been able to take my business in a new direction. Instead of doing so much one-on-one consulting and working on particular small projects with businesses, I've been doing more workshops, which have also been very successful. I've been able to contact and work with the larger companies. So, without all this financial help and these new ideas, this may not have been possible.

Additionally there is that need for ethics, because it helps to make one feel better about oneself. It's a source of self-respect, a point that Michael Josephson, the president of the Joseph and Edna Josephson Institute for the Advancement of Ethics, made in a speech in San Francisco on making ethical decisions in business. As he stressed in his talk: "Ethics is not entirely personal. Ideals of ethics are universal, they are timeless, they have existed forever." He said one of the first qualities essential to ethics is honesty, which means being trustworthy, and that is different from being truthful, because truly honest people don't deceive, while professionals might mislead people without ever lying.

It's a nice sentiment to be left with as we contemplate the potential for lying and cheating in business today. But is a more ethical, honest approach possible? Josephson observed in his talk: "In an immoral world, doing the right thing is not rewarded. But do we live in an immoral world? Is the business world based solely on a Wild West, survival-of-the-fittest, to-hell-with-morality ethic? Or is there really an underlying code as well as a pragmatic value in being honest, trustworthy, and sincere? I'd like to think there is."

In fact, after several decades of excess capped by a recession, there seems to be a shift back to increasingly seeking honesty and fair dealing in business. The big get-ahead scramble driven by greed led to inflated earnings and prices, a high-tech bubble followed by a real estate bubble, and the revelation of numerous stock and business deal scandals. Bernie Madoff was only the tip of the iceberg. But now that the iceberg has risen even higher and the tip has been sheared off, there seems to be a renewed interest on steadying the economic ship—and that includes getting back to the fundamentals of trust that build bonds between people and knit together the fabric of society.

PART IV

Lying in Personal and Private Life

CHAPTER 9

Lying to Friends and Relatives

When we look at lying to friends and relatives, we move from the arena of public life to the more personal and private sphere of life. To a great extent, the rules about lying change; it becomes more taboo. The closer the relationship, the greater the sense of betrayal when a lie occurs, although many lies may be excused or forgiven because they were designed to protect or help another person.

It is also here that both those less or more prone to lying are more driven to be forthright and honest, though their motivations may differ. Those who generally lie less are more likely to want to be forthright and honest out of principle and to feel guilty when they have to keep a lie secret. By contrast, those who generally lie more are more likely to be honest and open when it is most practical to do so or when there is a greater risk of getting caught.

This initial chapter in this section focuses on lying among friends and relatives. Future chapters deal with closer types of relationships—between single men and women; between spouses or partners in committed, live-in relationships; and between parents and children. These chapters illustrate this pattern or correlation between closeness and lying and point out the loss of the relationship and trust that a lie can bring about.

LYING TO FRIENDS

The people I spoke to had little experience with friends lying to them or lying to friends themselves, because friends, by their very nature, are people with whom one voluntarily chooses to have a relationship. Indeed, some people select others as friends because they feel they can be open and honest with them and trust them.

The lies committed were usually of the helpful, supportive, white lie variety, such as telling a friend he had made a good choice or had good taste about something when one couldn't agree less. Storm, the writer, made this point when he told me:

Sometimes my friends have engaged in some lies to help me. For example, when I had a drinking problem, some of my friends who knew helped me out by covering up for me from time to time. Or they may have lied to protect me from knowing something that would hurt me.

But if someone engaged in any lies to hurt me, he wouldn't be my friend for very long. For instance, if I thought a friend was trying to steal from me or was doing something out of revenge, I wouldn't continue to consider him my friend.

And, yes, that sort of thing has happened to me a couple of times. Someone I trusted who blew that trust. But then once someone does something like that, then that can break the friendship forever. It's hard to restore that trust which is the basis for friendship, and you just write that person off your list.

As Storm made it clear, he didn't want to have people he couldn't trust as friends. Similarly, Blanche, the publicist, characterized friendships much the same way. As she put it:

There are all kinds of friends in the world, from the social friends to the deep, close friends. Well, with social friends, you might expect some of the usual trivial lies, like excuses when someone can't make some event, and those are no big deal. But then, with deep, close friends, I think a lie would be terribly hurtful. You don't expect it from them. You expect them to be honest, trustworthy, and sincere.

Some people even thought that the basis of a good friendship was the ability to tell a good friend everything, the bad along with the good. For example, Sarah, an educator, voted for complete honesty. As she commented:

I just don't want to have someone in my environment personally or professionally who can't be straight and up-front and live their life honestly. I just feel if people are friends, they should have integrity in their total relationship, in every moment.

I know many people feel that the white lie between friends is okay, such as concealing some information so someone's feelings don't get hurt. Well, I have a hard time with that. I think that puts up barriers in the friendship. It's like keeping secrets from a friend, when I think the essence of true friendship is to share.

For example, say you learn that a friend's husband is fooling around with someone. Some people I know would say: "Why should you tell them? Why is that your responsibility? Why should you hurt their feelings?" Or say you learn something about their job that might make them feel bad. They would say to keep this from them to save their feelings as well.

But I think that's baloney. I think you should feel free to tell friends what you really know or think. I think good friends do this for each other, and that's what makes a true, real friend.

While lies among friends may be less common, friends do lie, and there tend to be certain types of lies that are most likely to occur. First and most common, there are the benign and supportive lies of help and protection. Second, there are the little lies that are more like humorous or entertaining exaggerations, and which add vitality to the friendship.

But then there are those that threaten it, such as lies that occur when a person is undependable, or the lies that occur when a person violates some basic rule of the friendship (such as breaking an agreement in order to do something else that sounds better and making an excuse to avoid revealing this to the friend). Perhaps the most damaging lies that involve friends are those that arise over money.

Also, lies are often told in breaking up the relationship to reduce the pain of the break-up or sometimes to increase it with a lie to make the person who is leaving feel bad.

And finally, for people who have a higher level of expectation for the amount of openness and revelation a close friend should share, there may be lies when the other person is more concealing than expected. For instance, Raphael the healer, who was more sensitive to such things, had this to say.

I think it's pretty common for people to hold their real feelings back and not say things sometimes, which I see as a kind of a lie. For example, friends may not call me when they are hurting, or people may not call me when they are angry with me, or they may not write to me and let me know what's really going on, such as any judgments that they have about me, if they have judgments. I think that happens because people want to stay more removed. They don't want to get into a discussion about such things. They don't care enough to go through with it. Yet I think that's an important part of a real friendship.

I have a male friend who's a dancer I respect. He's been very honest and friendly to me, and usually he's a very warm person. But also I have sometimes gotten this feeling of distance. And sometimes I have wanted to say to him: "Jack, I would really like to know what's going on. Are you feeling withdrawn from people generally? Is there some reason you feel like pulling away from me?" But it's scary for me to do that. It's like maybe making an issue of something where maybe there wasn't an issue. Or maybe just bringing this up might make him uncomfortable, so, instead of relaxing the relationship, it might put more stress into the relationship. I did this once and it helped to clear the air, but it's still a scary thing to do, because there is the potential for making things worse instead of better.

Lies to Help and Protect

To make a friend feel better you might say, "You look good," when the friend really does not. Or you might lie because the knowledge would be worse than the lie or because you feel you have no right to interfere, such as when the friend is unaware that his person's lover or mate is cheating on him.

While some people may feel that friends should be completely, even brutally honest, many others would temper that honesty with a dose of caring.

Storm, the writer, described how he appreciates the deceptions of his friends.

Normally, I don't lie to my friends and my friends don't lie to me. We wouldn't be friends if that were true. And there are certainly types of lies that people I call friends wouldn't tell to me or I to them. For example, in the writing game, some writers might stab you in the back, because they want to get a story or cover their own ass about something. But I don't operate that way with my friends, and none of my friends do with me either.

In fact, there was one time when some of my friends lied to me to help me with my alcoholism, and later on, I was glad they did this. Basically what they did was conspire secretly behind my back to get me to go to this treatment center, including talking to my dad and getting him to agree to come out and take me down there. I didn't know they were doing this at the time, and later I decided I needed to go there myself. But when I heard about what they had tried to do, I really appreciated it. I felt they were really showing love and trust and faith in what they were trying to do.

Lies to Embellish and Entertain

Other lies that are okay among friends are those that are done within limits to exaggerate and embellish in the name of amusement and entertainment. Such lies are harmless and benevolent. Perhaps the other person is aware that this is a lie—really a tall story or an exaggeration—and goes along with it because he enjoys it.

Blanche, the public relations executive, said that she frequently used this kind of lying with her friends, and that whether they knew the truth or not, they enjoyed going along with her stories. As Blanche commented:

I do embellish. I tend to hyperbole, to exaggeration. I once had a client who called me a dissembler when I said something to make him look less silly by turning a situation around to make him look better. Now a dissembler is a term for a liar, but the way he said this, I could tell he was saying this in a friendly, kind of kidding or teasing way, because he knew I was doing this to try and help him.

Also, some of my friends have called me "dramatic" because I tend to build things up. I take things that from their eyes are very undramatic and make them bigger, because I don't see the world in this flat way. For example, I might tend to say something like: "It was really wonderful!" or "She's so awful," when I don't really mean it was all that wonderful or that she was that awful. It's just an overstatement to dramatize, to make things seem more exciting.

Why do I do this? Because I tend to want to be amusing. It's almost the same thing that a comic does. For example, I'll embellish by turning a story around to have a funnier ending. Or I'll exaggerate to make things more interesting. For example, say somebody doesn't look that good, I might say something like: "Oh, you should have seen what she wore. She really looked like the Medusa with her new perm and all her gold jewelry."

Such lies are normally viewed as acceptable, because Blanche kept them within acceptable limits. But when a friend's exaggerations become even more extreme, others might see that person as a pathological liar who exaggerates and distorts everything and whom no one can trust. And should that become a pattern, the friend might be likely to become a former friend who has burned his or her one-time friend too many times.

Lack of Dependability and Follow-up Lies

While these helpful, benevolent, and fun lies may generally be okay, there are other lies that threaten the trust so central to the friendship.

One common type is the lies or promises friends tell about things they are going to do, but then they don't follow up. The lack of certainty, dashed agreements, and wasted time and effort that result can seriously damage the friendship.

Some friends may seek to compensate when a friend is undependable but there are other things they value in the friendship. Yet even here, the lack of dependability may place barriers on the depth of the friendship. This happened to Alison, the counselor and workshop leader. As she told me:

I have this friend—I'll call her Francine—who has trouble keeping her commitments or being on time for things. For example, once in a while she'll say: "I'll call you real soon, and we'll make a date for lunch." But then it will turn out that it won't be real soon because she gets hung up with other things sometimes.

My other problem with her is that she is always late, so I can't depend on her. But I have found a way to compensate for this by either setting the time we get together earlier so she'll meet me when I really want. Or I'll use humor when we talk about this to try to give her the message to correct this.

But then, because of this problem, I don't do as much with her as I would do otherwise. For instance, different things will come up and I know that we'd have a good time together. But I'll ask a different friend or I'll go alone because I don't want to hassle with the time problem.

Money Lies

Among the most damaging lies to any friendship are lies about money—to get it, to avoid giving it up, to pay less, and the like. When a friendship is linked to these money issues, the conflicts that arise over money can destroy the friendship.

In some cases, of course, money can help a friendship—such as when one friend loans money to support another—as long as nothing goes wrong (the money is returned) and there are no unfulfilled expectations (such as when a friend loans money, hoping, but not expecting, that it will be repaid). But most money lies and the conflicts that result are destructive.

Alison, the counselor and workshop leader, for example, had a friend who continually "forgot" her wallet, so that Alison had to pay for everything, and her friend never paid her back. Though Alison continued to go along with this for some time, because she enjoyed these evenings with the friend who had little money, the ploy made her feel resentful. As Alison commented:

It bothers me that people sometimes take advantage and manipulate you through lies. There was one time when I was about thirty and a single parent, and I was in a needy space that a friend took advantage of. This woman and I would go out together about once a week, and that was my salvation. This was a chance to go out and have fun, let loose, and maybe meet some guys. Well, the way she took advantage of me is that every single time we'd go out, she'd always forget her wallet. Every time. And I would have to pay for her. After about sixteen times, I realized I was being taken.

I would overlook it. Why? Because if I didn't pay, it would crimp my good time, and I didn't want to do this, because I had a baby sitter, and this was like my big night out. So it was worth it to me at the time just to come up with the extra money to cover her. Then, too, I guess I went along with this, because I knew she didn't have a lot of money, and this is how she survived.

Roger, the philosophy teacher, described how a friend, who worked as a fireman and became wealthy as a real estate investor, lost friends over debts.

Once he gained his money, Bob had a lot of friends come to him for help, and they promised to repay it. But then they didn't, and he lost friends that way.

Maybe they felt that because he had money they didn't have to pay him back. But he didn't think that was right. He told me that since he has a lot of resources, he's willing to share a certain amount of them, and so was willing to loan small amounts of money to people on an interest-free basis. But he has insisted on being paid back on time.

Otherwise, he feels that people are trying to take advantage of him, and get out of an agreement they made. So he's lost friends as a result. But then, I think that's right, too. People shouldn't think that just because a friend has more money that they have a right to that money because they're a friend. That's when a friendship can run into trouble. The person who borrows the money starts to think he shouldn't really have to pay it back because his friend has more. But the person who loaned the money did so because he both wanted to help his friend and the friend agreed to pay it back. So no wonder he might be angry when the friend doesn't do this. He feels the friend broke the agreement intentionally, and he feels ripped off.

Lies to End the Friendship

Finally, there are lies used when people feel angry with a friend or uncomfortable about ending the relationship, want it to be over or less intense, and don't want to reveal these feelings to their friend. So there are excuses, postponed meetings, unreturned or delayed calls—anything to avoid a confrontation and help the relationship slip away without a messy end. Frances described this process with one long-term friend she wanted to break away from. As she told me:

I have a friend that I have a real difficult time being with, because I feel we live in a lie. Nothing has ever been straightforward with us, and I just want to be out. We've known each other for about fifteen years. And during this time, she has always had a lot of money problems and I find myself very frustrated about this because she'll approach me to get help. But then I also don't want to run her life or tell her how to run her life. But she always seems so needy that I have felt like I should give her some guidance; so I find the situation draining and I feel pulled in two directions.

That's why I have come to feel the situation is impossible, and I just would rather be out of it. I'd rather not even see her, not even talk to her. And yet I'm very uncomfortable about having these feelings, too.

So that's where I've created these little lies to avoid saying what I really feel—that I don't want to be around her. So when she calls and says: "Do you want to do something?" I've been busy. Or one time when we did get together for lunch, I seemed distant and distracted.

So gradually we have just drifted apart, and I think she has gotten the gist, and hasn't called me for a long time. So it's been easier that way. It just seems like we've grown out of the relationship, without there being a sudden break and it has felt easier that way.

LYING TO RELATIVES

When relatives turn into friends, because they have things in common and do things together, the usual patterns for lying to friends apply. Otherwise, relationships with relatives are quite different because of blood or marriage connections. But at the same time, these relationships can range from the very distant to the very close, so the possibilities for lying go through all sorts of permutations.

Lies of Avoidance

In many cases, people just aren't close to some of their relatives, so there is relatively little reason to lie, unless something pops up, such as an inheritance dispute. However, once there are less acceptable reasons to avoid or reduce contact with the relatives, the lies may begin. For example, Sandy's real reason for not wanting to see some of her nearby relatives was that she did not like them. She didn't like the way they had tried to impose their own values on her when she was a child, by expressing disapproving noises to her mother, so when she grew up she wanted them out of her life. But her mother, who was still in touch with these relatives, didn't want to let the relatives know the real reasons, so she found excuses to cover up, such as "Sandy is too busy" with this or that. A few times she persuaded a reluctant Sandy to send greeting cards. But even after Sandy stopped doing this "as a favor to me," as her mother put it, her mother still tried to maintain a face that said all was well.

Similarly, Raphael, the healer, encountered denial when he spoke to his cousin soon after his father and his cousin's father had a business fight.

Jack, my cousin, assured me that he didn't have any animosity toward my parents after what happened, although then he said something like: "Well, what your mom said didn't help matters." Then he said again that he didn't have any animosity and wished them the best of luck. But I didn't really believe him, and I said that: "I really don't believe that, I'm not sure I believe you."

However, he didn't really comment on or acknowledge what I said. I felt good that I said that, because it was truthful. But I feel he was just trying to hide his true feelings.

Finally, the lies themselves sometimes provoke avoidance. For example, Sandy reported that her parents effectively isolated one of her aunts who repeatedly exaggerated and lied about little things:

My mother used to tell me all the time about how my aunt lied about everything. She would say that things cost much more than they did. She would talk about her wealthy relatives and her connections with royalty in Europe, when none of that was true. She would claim that she had ins in the publishing and film business, when in fact, she just had a relative in a lower-level position who had very little power. She was constantly bragging about this and that, and my parents didn't like it.

So they avoided her as much as they could, though of course they didn't tell her why directly. They just found reasons why they would be busy so they could decline dinner invitations and they stopped inviting her to most things, too, other than general family gatherings, where it was hard not to invite her and her family.

Similarly, Storm, the writer, reported disconnecting from his own relatives who lied, though in his case, there seemed to be a whole parade of people who lied. As he described it:

I have a family of cousins, uncles, and aunts that is just full of liars. So I don't have anything to do with any of them. There are very few people in my family I'm close to as a result.

Some of my relatives are just crazy. I have one aunt, for example, who just doesn't know what she's saying. She's so insecure. She builds all kinds of fantasies. And then the other relatives—it's unbelievable the lies, deceptions, cheating, backstabbing, trying to steal property—it's like a whole "Dallas" scene though on a much smaller scale back in the Midwest, because they don't have that much money. But that kind of stuff has been pervasive in our family—it's a kind of small-town–type politics atmosphere.

So from the time I was a child, I never got close or connected with any of my relatives, because it was so obvious they were a bunch of hypocrites, and I'd hear stories from my parents or other people in town, or I'd see what they were doing. Or then other people would report what they said about something, which wasn't true. So the lies would get back to us.

Lies to Impress

Relatives may lie, too, to impress other relatives. Such lies are often born of a struggle between relatives to show how well they or their children are doing compared to the others.

Sandy, the marketing consultant, had parents who did this constantly, particularly her mother, who was a real social striver. As Sandy told me:

My mother always wanted to seem very successful, more successful than her three brothers, so she was always exaggerating what I or my father did, or concealing things she thought were not so good, so we would fit the image she wanted to present.

For example, when I was first starting my business and my mother sent me some money to help finance things, she continued to tell everyone about how well I was doing, even though I was still not making it financially, and she never let on she was helping to support me. Then, later on, when I managed to send her back a few hundred dollars on a loan for about $50,000 she had given me over the years, my mother announced that I had sent her this money as a birthday present and said nothing about the loan.

Lies about Money, Jealousy, and Revenge

Finally, there are the more intense lies that arise among relatives over money or when bitterness develops over things such as jealousy or a desire for revenge.

Dick, the sales executive, described how one of his customers manipulated his relatives to get them to sign an agreement about a property that had been in the family for more than a hundred years.

It's amazing. This client has bragged to me about how honest he is in business with his customers, and he says that's why he has been able to build up his business so he had become the largest distributor in the state. He doesn't lie, he says, so people trust him.

But as we were driving to the airport, he described how he had just sold his ranch, which had been in the family for about 120 years. And he had to get his relatives to agree to sell it in order to get the money and distribute the shares. Well, the way he went about it, he said, is he told each of the relatives that all of the other relatives had signed, though they hadn't.

"But isn't that dishonest?" I asked him. "Here you've been telling me how you built your business on honesty," and he replied: "Well, the way I look at it, there are shades of honesty, and I don't lie to my customers. But in this case, I don't think my relatives are very bright. They're idiots and I can't wait to get rid of them. So I felt I needed to shade the truth a little to get them to sign. And I don't see this as a real lie because everyone will sign eventually. The lie will become the reality, so it's okay to say something if it's going to happen." And he didn't really understand that this was a lie.

Yet, while Dick described this customer's actions as a lie, he earlier justified another customer's actions in getting relatives to sign a will everyone would eventually sign anyway, which reflects the fine line between justifying or disparaging a lie. In some cases, it seems that expedience may be used to justify a lie that is ultimately beneficial to those manipulated by the lie; in other cases it may be not, particularly when done by someone else. It is as if the decision to justify the lie or not is on a balance scale that could go either way, and the slightest change in the circumstances could change the balance, such as one's feelings about the individual telling the lie or the situation leading the individual to tell it,

For sheer drama, perhaps nothing compares to the story told by Susannah, the financial analyst and planner, of family betrayal, revenge, jealousy, money, and suicide—a painful illustration of the tragedy that can occur when a family's lies explode with emotional intensity. But let Susannah tell it:

My sister lived in a fantasy world half the time and was mentally ill. She would tell the most outrageous lies, though she would tell them in the most sincere fashion. I think that she honestly believed they were true.

The biggest one that led to the rift between us was when she tried to back out of a contract she had signed by claiming that she had not signed it; that I had forged her signature. It was a contract that when my mother died my brother, sister, and I would distribute the estate equally, which was drawn up by my father, because he felt that my mother would not leave me anything, since we had always been alienated. So instead of compensating for this in his own will, by leaving me more, my brother and I persuaded him to do this, because we thought this would contribute to more harmony in the family.

But when it came time to honor this contract, after my mother died some years after my father's death, my sister reneged, claiming she had not signed the contract, which would have meant paying me about $20,000. Well, eventually I sued, and when the handwriting experts we both hired agreed that it was a legitimate signature, I won the case and I ultimately collected, including damages. But after paying all of my legal fees, I came out about even.

By the time of the contract incident, Susannah and her sister had not spoken for about seven years, so all the communication about the contract agreement occurred through her sister's husband, who answered Susannah's letters since her sister wouldn't answer them herself. Meanwhile her husband contributed to the tapestry of lies as well. As Susannah described it:

After my mother died, I wrote to my sister to see if she would honor the contract, and when she didn't answer, I spoke to her husband several times. He claimed she was very shaky, very upset over the death of her mother, "So we mustn't press her"—the same kind of solicitous nonsense I had been hearing all my life.

So I backed off for a while, though after about a year or so, my lawyer told me that if I was going to sue, I better go ahead and do so. So I tried writing one more time and this time my sister made a suicide attempt—something she had been doing for years as a way to get her way. Usually, she would slash her wrist or take pills, though this time she shot herself. Well, my brother-in-law claimed she had done it because of the pressure I had put on her over the contract, and then he called me about once a week for the next two months to tell me that if I didn't back off, my sister intended to kill me.

Well, I believed him and backed off completely for the next three months, because after all, I thought, my sister could do this, since she had a loaded gun. However, when the case finally came to trial, I discovered that my brother-in-law had really lied about this to get me to back off. What had happened, as came out in testimony, is that my sister had only made the threat to kill me one time right after she had made the suicide attempt and was in the hospital. "I'll kill her," she said. But then, when her husband called me, he kept repeating this threat as if she was making it week after week. So he was trying to intimidate me so I would back off.

Finally, several months later, she really did commit suicide, although it would seem that the real reason is because her husband decided to leave her and had moved in with another woman. Though she dated a number of other men after that, his leaving left her really depressed. But in her suicide note to the police, she blamed me. Her very last act, and it was a lie. My lawsuit had occurred about six months before, while her husband moved out about ten weeks earlier. And when I met one of the men whom she had dated afterward, he told me she had been quite disturbed by the break. So I'm sure it was that. But she couldn't acknowledge that, and we had been warring for so long, since childhood, that it was easier to blame her suicide on me. She had been blaming things on me all her life, so why not her final act?

Thus, lies with relatives can sometimes become extremely intense when they are fueled by long histories of blame, competition for family love, and jealousy, as illustrated by Susannah's story. But more commonly, they tend to revolve around money, impressing one another, or finding ways to gracefully get out of having contact when the relatives don't like each other but don't want to admit it.

CHAPTER 10

When Men and Women Lie—The Dating Game

Another common area for lying is the dating and mating game. Perhaps that's one of the reasons it provokes so much lying—because it's a kind of game. People negotiate and bargain over whether there will be a relationship and what kind it will be.

People lie to themselves about what they want and whether the person they are seeing really fits this image. They lie to get to see someone—or to get out of a meeting. There are lies about making and breaking dates. Once people are dating, there can be lies to avoid intimacy. People who are dating or trying to date may lie to exaggerate their prestige, power, or personality.

And then there are the lies—more commonly committed by the male—to get sex or more sex or better sex.

Men use strategies such as the normalcy argument (i.e., "Sure, everyone is doing it"); hiding their marital status; concealing some type of deviant sexual interest or illness; or pretending to use birth control devices. Women may counter with their own form of sexual lying—telling the man how great he is when he isn't.

Both may lie about not seeing others to preserve an illusion of true loyalty. Finally, there are the most bitter lies of all, which can destroy a relationship, or often occur as the relationship is falling apart. These are the lies about money, the lies during fights, and the lies about endings—often committed because people hate confronting each other or the truth when things are breaking up.

Dating is also the arena where you are especially likely to see the differences in different types of liars emerge. On the one hand, the models of absolute integrity and the straight shooters will be much more likely to keep it honest and real; they are more likely to be who they say they are, and they like their dates to be similarly honest with them. If not, they are more likely to feel betrayed and hurt when a lie is exposed and more likely to end the relationship.

By contrast, the pragmatic fibbers, Pinocchios, and frequent liars are more likely to use deception from the get-go when it suits their goals in the relationship and they feel they won't get caught. Often such lies involve males exaggerating about their job status and income or women lying about their age, as well as about other markers of success, like job titles and who they know. Ironically, though, some may have a double standard, expecting others to be more straightforward with them, while others will be more forgiving if they catch their partner in a lie in the early stages of dating, since they consider this more of a game themselves.

You can keep these distinctions in mind as you think about the different types of lies that are common in a dating relationship.

LIES TO YOURSELF

Several of the counselors and therapists I spoke to pointed out that lying in the dating relationship frequently begins with lies to oneself. What commonly happens is a kind of exaggeration in which the suitor creates an ideal person and then measures the people he or she meets against that ideal. The result is usually frustration, because the real person fails to measure up.

A common fantasy for men is the young, beautiful, sexy woman. But for some men such a woman is unattainable, because they lack the trading cards in the dating relationship that are generally needed to attract such a woman. The men may be old, unattractive, or not have very much money themselves. So they dream. Conversely, some women dream of that attractive, successful man with money. But with many of these attractive, rich, successful men being drawn to the young, beautiful, sexy women, many ordinarily attractive and successful women are just not going to land these men, either. Thus, they feel frustrated, too.

People may have more specific fantasies and illusions. Susan Scott, a relationship counselor, pointed out:

Many people have fantasies. They'll meet somebody, and they'll make it into something that it's not and build an illusion and fantasy around it, rather than really look at it, tell the truth about it, and recognize that this really isn't what they want.

For example, say a person who wants to remain where he is meets a person in another state. He or she really wants to have a relationship with someone who lives within a hundred-mile radius. But then he or she spins a romantic fantasy about the new relationship that is doomed to failure. After all, how are they really going to create a relationship they want under the circumstances? It's an impossible relationship to begin with because he's not going to move and she's not going to move. But they each may create an illusion that the other will. So they kid themselves about where the relationship is going, when it isn't going to go anywhere.

Others may build up the relationship into more than it is because of their insecurities and fears of taking a chance on getting what they really want. This is what happened to Raphael, who described how his lying kept him in an unsatisfying relationship for more than two years.

Sometimes I have fooled myself to get into or stay in a relationship that I know isn't long term, but I would like to believe it is or will be. So I have concealed the real nature of the relationship from myself. For example, I stayed in a relationship once for two-and-a-half years that I knew wasn't right and I knew I had to get out of it. But I couldn't muster the strength to say: "Look, this is something we need to talk about. We need to end the relationship." I was afraid of hurting and rejecting the other person, and also feeling alone myself by making the break. So I just kept it going. But the real heart and love had gone out of the relationship for me. And I think she knew it. But I think she was fooling herself, too, because she was also afraid to make the break.

LIES TO AVOID GETTING INVOLVED OR MORE INVOLVED IN THE RELATIONSHIP

Men and women seem to differ over the roles they play in initiating the dating process or moving it on to a more committed relationship, because women tend to make up excuses for not getting involved in the first place (usually to avoid hurting the male's feelings), while men tend to find reasons or excuses to avoid getting more involved (usually because it's the woman who's pressing for commitment or intimacy).

Getting Out of Dates

Generally, it's the women who make excuses to get out of a date, because they don't want to hurt the man's feelings by saying no outright or giving the real reason for the rejection. But whoever the person saying no is, the goal is to be diplomatic and gentle.

Reba, a speaker and seminar leader, well expressed this spare-the-feelings approach when she commented:

Well, if someone called me to go on a date but I wasn't really interested, I might say something like: "I'm really flattered," but then I would probably make up something, such as "but I have a boyfriend," or "I'm busy this weekend," rather than say: "No, I'm not interested." I would do this rather than be direct, because I'm afraid I'd hurt their feelings otherwise.

It was easy for Reba to do this because the man would normally accept the rebuff and not try to press for the real reason.

Susannah, the financial planner, gave a good example of a typical lie she might tell, in this case an excuse about the things she had to do to avoid getting involved with a married man.

I lied to him just this morning. He's a nice man who's been a friend for about a year, and he comes over from time to time to help out around the house for me. He does things like repairing the electrical switches and wiring. I'm really grateful to him for doing that. But he's a married man, and I have no interest in a romantic relationship with a married man, so I've always kept things at arm's length. And in the past he hasn't pushed things.

However, recently he has been having a really hard time, because he just lost his job and I think his marriage has been under stress. It's just a sense I have, because he doesn't talk about this.

Anyway, he called up this morning and wanted to know if we could get together this weekend. I have been at some group social gatherings with him in the past. But this weekend he wanted to get together just with me by going out to a movie or dinner. But I felt that was too much like a dating situation, which I want to avoid with a married man. So I just made an excuse about the things I had to do. I felt like I wanted to let him down easy, because he's emotionally vulnerable right now, and I feel like I'm in a sticky situation. I want to give him some support while he's unemployed, as a friend. But I don't want to get trapped into something that's going to be emotionally sticky. I thought the excuse was a good way to keep things on the even keel they've been on.

While the women I spoke to may have seen this kind of gentle turndown as a way of saving the man's feelings, some of the men felt bothered by what they saw as women being devious or wanting to avoid a confrontation about the truth. For example, Roger, the philosophy teacher, felt this kind of upset over such lies most strongly.

It sometimes feels like the woman is giving me the runaround, and it bothers me. I just think it would save everyone a lot of trouble if she'd tell me how she feels up front.

For instance, I experienced a very painful example of this recently. I saw this woman in the hallway at the college where I teach, and I was very impressed with her. She was very attractive and I felt she had this strong sexual, passionate energy; she was just incredibly striking, and I wanted to get to know her.

So I followed her to her office and found out where it was. And then a few days later, I walked into her office and said: "You don't know me, but I'd like to introduce myself." It was a real bold move on my part, something I don't normally do, but she seemed receptive to getting to know me, although now looking back, maybe she was just flattered that I would go to such an extreme length to get to know her.

Anyway, after I introduced myself, she mentioned briefly that she was single, never married, and had one boyfriend, but nothing exclusive. So we made plans to get together. But then, she called to cancel, saying that something had come up that she had to do. And then I said, "Fine, well, let's set another time," and she asked me to call her to do so.

But when I did, I felt like she was trying to evade me. One time she said: "Oh, my boss is calling me so I can't talk now." Another time, she was just busy with work. And the third time she gave me her home number to call her there, but when I did, she said: "I can't talk to you right now, I've got company over." And the next time, it was: "Oh, I'm waiting for my cousin to call; I can't talk to you right now."

So after a while, with all these reasons, I began to think she was just putting me off. So I wrote her a card, hoping to find out what was really going on, and I said: "I get the impression that you're not interested in going out with me. And if that's true, fine, but I'd just like to know. Please let me know whether you really are interested or not."

And she did call back. But she seemed very defensive when I told her I was feeling very frustrated that it had been so difficult to talk to her. I had the feeling that she really didn't want to see me after all, from what she said. However, she was also very upset that I had seen through her and tried to confront her about this. So I thought that she just basically wanted to call to smooth things over and make peace, though she also didn't want to see me.

Another time, Roger was upset by a woman who took off without explanation after they had agreed to a date after getting connected through an ad. He described his frustration.

I had joined this date-by-mail service, and every so often I'd get a response from a potential date in the mail. I got this one from a woman who looked pretty good, and I called her and we talked on the phone for two or three times at the office where she worked. She was a professional in the biology field, and we both had Ph.D.s, so there seemed to be a good match.

We arranged a date, and she agreed to come over with the wine, while I was going to get the bread. Then we were going to go out. It sounded like a kind of romantic evening—maybe too much for somebody one doesn't know.

But when I got there, a little late, I'll never forget the expression on her face. It's like when she saw me, her face just fell. She had this look of total disappointment, and perhaps this was because I hadn't had a haircut in a while, because the man who cuts my hair had been hit by a car, so my hair was a little shaggier than usual. Anyway, whatever it was, I got the impression that she didn't like the way I looked, though she didn't say anything.

We went inside, and we had this real tense conversation, though we had had great rapport on the phone, and then we talked about where we would go to have the bread and wine. We finally agreed on a nearby lake that has a public park, after she turned down the first place I suggested as being too isolated. And then, when I asked, "Whose car shall we go in?" she suggested that we take separate cars.

I thought this was a little unusual but agreed, and then she agreed to pull her car around, and while she waited in front of the house, I went to get mine. But when I got back after a few minutes, she was gone.

I felt really devastated by this. What had I done to offend her? I wondered.

When I called her and asked if I did anything to offend her, she just said no. So she wouldn't tell me what bothered her. Was it because I was a few minutes late getting my car and meeting her? Was it because she didn't like my appearance? Whatever it was, it really bothered me that she wouldn't say. Maybe this was a case where she was withholding the truth to save my feelings. But I felt it made it worse. Not only did her driving away bother me, but her not telling me why bothered me even more.

Similarly, men finding themselves in an undesired dating situation might attempt various tactics of diplomacy to avoid being direct—as several women reported. Some common ploys:

- One man in an introductory phone call with a woman suddenly claimed to hear the doorbell ring and said he would call her back, but never did. "God knows what I might have said to dissuade him," said Sandra, the marketing consultant who told me about this. "I was just answering some question of his when suddenly I had the sense that he turned off, and I think his excuse of the doorbell was his diplomatic way of saying good-bye."

- Another man, on a first date after responding to an ad in a local single's paper, suddenly remembered he had to check to see whether he had left the lights on in his car. When he returned, he said he had to take the car to a garage. The woman who had just met him didn't, of course, believe him, but what could she do?

- In another case, Sandra and several of her women friends had a dinner party for some of the men who replied to a single's ad. They thought they had screened the group carefully, based on the letters and in some cases photos the men had sent. But it turned out that one man, who had sent a picture that didn't really look like him and had used a false name, knew two of the women already and seemed not especially interested in talking to the others. So during dinner he made a point of talking about how he not only worked in the cellular phone business, but carried one with him, and he said he sometimes got calls for emergencies where he had to call his office. Then, a few minutes after dinner, lo and behold, he claimed he heard his phone beeping, though no one else did, and he quickly ran to a phone in the kitchen. Then, according to one of the women who was helping to clean up the dishes, he went through the motions of pretending to make a call to his office. After a few minutes of this, he emerged triumphant, saying how sorry he was, but he had to leave early to take care of some unexpected important business at his office. Then he left, saying how much he enjoyed the evening, though everyone else clearly knew the truth, and for several minutes talked about his elaborate attempted ruse. Why couldn't he have just told the truth?

As these stories illustrate, in early dating situations, people will sometimes go to great lengths to avoid admitting the truth—that they don't like the other person and don't want to get involved. So why not just call to cancel? Or let the other person know gently that they aren't interested? Generally, the passive resistance is viewed as easier and more comfortable. The person really wants out but doesn't have the courage to say what he or she really feels, commonly because he or she wants to spare the other person's feelings or just doesn't want to risk an unpleasant confrontation.

Lies to Avoid Intimacy

In the later stages of a relationship, other lies may be used to avoid intimacy. Here it is generally the men who come up with such lies, since it is usually the women who want a more committed intimate relationship.

Susannah reported this sort of problem. She had been dating Allan on and off for several years, and at one time broke up with him because she felt he wasn't as serious as she would like. Now they were back together again, but though he talked vaguely about how he would like to get married—sometime—she felt the same lack of commitment from him, an unwillingness to talk about it, and the use of various ploys and lies. It was Allan's way of avoiding a messy confrontation about the nature and future of their relationship while keeping it going at a more casual level. As Susannah commented:

Allan often used these little white lies to get away from me or avoid facing the truth about things. For instance, he would spend Saturday night here, and then he'd get up on Sunday morning and would suddenly say, "Well, I've got to leave. I've got to go to work." Then, I might ask him: "Allan, what kind of work are you going to do on Sunday?" and he'd say, "Well, I've got a whole bunch of things I need to take care of."

I found out one time when he did this, he really went home and turned on the football game and spent the whole day in front of the TV with beer watching football.

I think the reason he did this was he was avoiding intimacy, which is what I sometimes accused him of. Paradoxically, he couldn't stand being around me on a protracted basis, even though he kept talking about wanting a relationship. So at the least bit of pressure, he would slip away. I feel he did this because he doesn't know himself. He's very confused and mixed up.

LIES TO EXAGGERATE, SHOW OFF, AND INCREASE SELF-ESTEEM

Many people in dating relationships lie to exaggerate, show off, or impress others with how terrific they are. It is a way both to build their own self-esteem and to get the other person to respond and give them what they want. As the common equation goes, men use these strategies to get sex; women use them to get a more serious, committed relationship.

Sandra, the marketing consultant, described how one man she knew regaled his new women acquaintances with tales of all the property, jets, and yachts he owned—when he owned none.

Others may lie to seem more exciting and daring. For instance, a man Dee dated described how he went through a fire and was burned all over, along with other stories of great adventures. Dee was quickly able to see through the guise.

I could tell he was lying about the fire because I was a nurse then, though he didn't know it. So I asked him to show me his scars, but he didn't have any. And I knew he would have to have them if he was burned as he said. So I knew he was lying. And I guess he was doing this to impress, but didn't know I had the background to see right through him.

While such exaggerations of self may be blatant, other exaggerations may be more subtle, puffing, or slanting to appear in a favorable light, so that the line between what is true and false can become very fine indeed.

Raphael, the healer, described wrestling with this issue in his effort to lead what he considered a life of integrity.

I'd like to be more honest, but sometimes I wonder if it's completely possible. For example, with this current woman I've gotten involved with, the day I met her, I had led a dance workshop involving dancing and moving. I told her about doing this and I said I like to consider myself a dancer.

But then, thinking about it, I wondered: Can I really consider myself a dancer? Is that really accurate? Is it a fabrication? Is that more of a fantasy? Am I really a dancer, or a therapist doing workshops on dance or movement?

These things can sometimes be hard to define, and generally, I try not to fabricate with friends. If anything, I try to be really open about who I am, and I feel I admit more of my weaknesses than most. So I think I'm more honest at that level than most people.

When I spoke with clinical sexologist Louanne Cole, she noted that men tend to exaggerate about money and family connections. And men often exaggerate their sexual conquests, a point that Dick, the sales executive, made:

You know, men sometimes make things up about women, such as that they've been to bed with someone. It's a way of showing off. I experienced this just last night when a gentleman I introduced to this lady told me some things I knew aren't true. They've only known each other for a month and have only gone out twice, but he told me that they've already been in bed together. But knowing the woman, I find that incredible. I know her well enough to know that's not her style. She needs a more long-term, committed relationship first.

By contrast, women tend to use exaggeration and manipulative tricks to show off their popularity and desirability to others, as relationships-counselor Susan Scott described. For example, a woman who has a man visiting her might have someone call her on the phone every hour or so, so it appeared as if she were popular. Or a woman might pretend to be busy when a man called. In fact, I remember learning such tricks from my mother and girlfriends as part of the dating game. It was part of playing hard to get to exaggerate my self-worth and thus make the male think me more worth getting. Indeed, a woman I once worked with pretended to have another love interest and threatened to break up with her long-standing boyfriend because he didn't want to get married. In this case, her exaggeration worked and he married her because he decided he didn't want to lose her.

PERSUADING BY USE OF LIES
ABOUT WHAT OTHERS DO

Doctor Cole calls these lies of persuasion "normalizing lies." The idea is to persuade someone to change his or her behavior to what others do or to embarrass him or her for doing something by claiming it is not normal to do or be or think that.

Cole gave me examples, many used by men to get sex or a particular kind of sex from a woman who was hesitant. For instance, the man might argue that "others are doing it" to persuade an unwilling woman. Or if the woman said she didn't want oral sex, he might say: "If you don't enjoy oral sex, there's something wrong with you. You're not normal." Conversely, a man or woman—though more commonly the woman—might use such a normalcy lie to discourage some sexual behavior, such as claiming: "People who look at pornography aren't normal," or "Using some kind of sexual accessory isn't normal."

While such statements may definitely be false, they may or may not actually be lies, because in some cases the person using this technique may actually believe the statement. Rather, he or she is calling some common behavior normal as leverage to win the other person over, a little like a lawyer using a particular spin or emphasis on evidence to win a case. Whether a real lie or just leverage, this technique can be effective, because, as Cole pointed out, "most people want to be normal. So when someone else convinces them that a certain way to act, think, or believe is normal, they want to conform."

Still, some people may challenge the normalcy claim. When they do, there's a risk of jeopardizing the relationship. But they are willing to do so for the sake of standing up for themselves. Otherwise, according to Cole, if they are afraid of losing the relationship, they will go along with their partner's normalcy claim, whether they truly believe it or not.

And then what? What is the challenged person making the claim likely to do? Sometimes the person making the claim is only bluffing, pushing the partner as far as he can to get what he wants until he hits resistance. When this resistance occurs, he is willing to back off, because he wants to maintain the relationship. On the other hand, the person may want this goal so much that if his or her bluff is called, the relationship will end. As Cole commented:

The response is extremely varied. In some cases, the relationship will end; in other cases, it will not. For example, say the man argues for oral sex, using the normalcy claim, and argues that "If you don't give me oral sex, I'll leave this relationship, because I just can't imagine being in this relationship without it." Then she doesn't give it to him. Sometimes he may stick around, but find another alternative, such as getting oral sex on the side from another woman or a prostitute. Other times he may forgo his sexual desires. And then still other times he may leave.

So there can be a lot of claims of leverage that are not followed through on, though there has been an ultimatum. But at other times, the claim is true. And then the relationship will end.

LIES TO CONCEAL AN IMPORTANT TRUTH ABOUT ONESELF

Still another common lie in dating is the concealment of an important truth about oneself to initiate, maintain, or deepen the relationship or to get sex. One of the most common ones is claiming one isn't married when one is or that one is getting a divorce when one isn't—usually this kind of lie is told by the man. Or one may state that one hasn't had a sexual relationship when one has—usually this is a lie told by women. Another reason for lying is to conceal some deviant or undesirable trait or behavior—such as one's age (usually done by women) or one's interest in some unusual sexual activity (most commonly told by a man). Still other examples might be concealing or denying problems or weaknesses such as alcoholism, using drugs, a lack of earnings, sexual difficulties, and the like. Then, too, other common concealments or denials might revolve around past relationships—how many, how often, or even how lonely or how desperate one is—in order to be with someone.

Dee described several instances in which her girlfriends were courted by a man who turned out to be married. These men usually were concealing their affair from their wives as well.

A lot of my friends have been taken in by married men who have been cheating on their wives. And then they say they aren't married. So they're lying to their wives and the women, too.

For example, one girl told me the married man she was going with was going to leave his wife. But in the beginning, she didn't even know he was married; she thought he was already divorced. So when she did find out, he told her this "I'm-going-to-leave" story. However, though she wanted to believe him, it seemed pretty clear he would never leave his wife, and I told her that. Why? Because he had secretly seen other women on the side. And he already had three children. So why should he leave? Even if he didn't really love his wife anymore, he would probably have to give up 50 percent of his income to her in child support and maybe in alimony. So any divorce was unlikely.

Finally, after several months of his stalling, she realized this was true. He was just lying to her because he was interested in her for sex, so he pretended to her he was the available guy she wanted. But the reality was that he was really married and intended to stay that way. And finally she found this out. She broke up the relationship when she realized this was true.

In Reba's case, she concealed prior affairs from a man whom she was afraid would be jealous and maybe break up the relationship. As she described it:

In my last relationship, I didn't want to tell him I had a couple of affairs. So when he asked me if I had done this, I just said no. I thought he might be angry and it might hurt the relationship or he might leave.

Eventually, he did find out, though I didn't tell him. He heard it from some person I used to be friends with who got mad at me because I had mistakenly revealed something about him, and when he found out, this was like his way to pay me back. As it turned out, the man I had been seeing was quite upset about this knowledge about me, so I feel I was right not to tell him early in the relationship when he asked me, though I don't like to lie. However, by the time he found out, the relationship was really ending anyway, and this helped to end it. Though eventually we made our peace about this and now we're just friends.

So should I have been honest in the first place? It bothered me to lie at the time, and I talked to a couple of my women friends about this. But they said: "No, what's done is done." So I never told him myself. But I still think what I did is a lie.

As for the lies used to conceal deviant or undesirable traits or activities, Susannah, the financial analyst and planner, described how one man had concealed his interest in being a transvestite (a liking to dress up in women's clothes) from her. She thought this was a significant concealment because she doesn't consider this normal. In fact, it was one of the factors that contributed to her eventually breaking off the relationship. As she explained:

Jerry didn't exactly lie; but he didn't tell me he was a transvestite. At one point, perhaps, he hinted at this, when I asked him if he had any idiosyncrasies that I should know about before he moved in with me. Well, at the time he mentioned that his dead wife Joyce had a skirt that he liked to wear around the house. When I asked him why, he told me it was because it was more comfortable, since pants can be very hot, and air circulates under a skirt. So, because he and his wife were about the same size, he sometimes wore her skirt.

Then, because the skirt belonged to his wife, I asked him: "Please don't bring any of her clothes with you when you move in." So he didn't. But the first time I did his wash, I found all these women's underpants. And when I asked him about it, saying: "I thought you promised you wouldn't bring any of Joyce's clothes with you," he told me: "Oh, those aren't Joyce's. I bought them through a catalog."

So that's when I realized that he was a transvestite. But he hadn't told me that. And I didn't like his not revealing this. I felt cheated. On the one hand, in an intellectual sense, I felt he had a right to do this, a right to have his own lifestyle. But at the same time, I don't get sexually turned on by transvestites. I don't like men who dress up. So this materially affected my relationship with him after I discovered this. And I probably would not have invited him to move in with me had I known in the first place. So I'm sure that's why he didn't tell me. He thought if he told me I might change my mind. But when I found out, I eventually decided to break up the relationship anyway.

While Susannah may have been sufficiently turned off by this behavior that it contributed to her ending the relationship, in other cases, the initial concealment might provide time for a relationship to develop, so that later this deviation might be accepted.

For example, Harvey, a doctor I met when I was doing research on a community of people experimenting with erotic dominance and submission as a lifestyle, did this quite successfully.[1] As Harvey described it, he enjoyed being submissive to a woman and engaging in various forms of S&M and bondage-and-discipline play. But when he first met a woman, he didn't tell her this, because he felt she would think he was weird or sick. However, as he got to know the woman, he would drop hints, and then if she seemed responsive, or at least receptive, he would let out a little more. If not, he would back off.

For instance, he might mention that he had seen a movie recently or heard someone relate a fantasy about something, and what did she think about it? Gradually, if the woman seemed open, he would lead up to sharing and acknowledging his own fantasies, and eventually he would get her, if willing, to participate with him in acting these out. In turn, he found this strategy worked because the woman got to know him and came to see him as an otherwise ordinary, normal, respectable person, so that as he gradually revealed his real interests, she was willing to accept them, because she had come to accept him.

Similarly, Don, the engineer, concealed his herpes condition when he first met a woman, to permit the relationship to flower, although eventually if the relationship turned intimate he would reveal this. He explained his approach and justification:

I've met some women through personal ads I've placed in a local paper, and I've been mostly honest in describing myself. But I did decide to leave one item out—the fact I have herpes. Because I felt if I put this in, women might not answer this.

However, I felt it was okay to do this. Why? Because my rationale was that if this information turned out to be important, because a committed relationship develops, then I will reveal it. But if it doesn't turn out to be important, because the relationship isn't going anywhere, then I won't. There's no need to reveal such personal information in that case.

OTHER LIES TO GET SEX OR AVOID UNCOMFORTABLE DISCUSSIONS ABOUT IT

Still other lies are used to get sex or to avoid talking about it in a way that might be uncomfortable. A good example of this is the way men—and usually it's the men who tell these kinds of lies—lie about their interest in the woman to get sex. They pretend they are more interested than they really are and claim they want more of a relationship than they really do. Women, on the other hand, are more apt to use sex to seek a relationship or more intimacy.

In a sense, the man may be honest initially because, excited by the power of sex, he really does anticipate the beginnings of an enduring relationship. But after the sexual experience, he may feel satisfied, so the desire for the relationship recedes. So what was the truth may turn into what seems like a lie, when it's actually the paradox of differing male and female cultural training or biology.

In any case, these male reassurances about the future to get sex now are common in the early stages of many male–female relationships, since men tend to have a more recreational attitude toward sex—"Let's have fun now"—while women tend to have a more long-term view of it—"Will we see each other again?" or "Do you love me?"

In turn, these kinds of male lies or promises can add to the uncertainty that women tend to feel in the early stages of a relationship, as sexologist Louanne Cole pointed out.

For example, a woman hears him say: "That was wonderful," or "I'll call tomorrow." At this early stage of the relationship, she may be unsure whether it will continue and whether she will hear from him again. So she may wonder if she became sexual too quickly. Should she have waited? And if she doesn't hear from him, she may worry about whether things might have been different if she had put him off.

Meanwhile, the man promises to call, but he doesn't. In some cases, he may have the intention of calling, but other things come up. Or he may just say he will call to help protect the woman's feelings. Or his promise to call may be a strategy just to gain sex, since he thinks the woman needs that promise to be willing.

And what if he told the truth? In Cole's view, it might be nice theoretically if he could express his desire for short-term recreational sex, so the woman could agree on this basis. But many men don't do this because they don't want to take the chance that the woman will say no. As Cole put it:

Say the man lies about his future interest in a woman to get sex now. He's taking the risk he might sully his reputation if she tells others what he did. So he's weighing out the benefit of sex now versus the risk of the bad reputation and being thought ill of by the woman when he doesn't call.

It's a weighing that happens very quickly. For example, if he decides to lie, he may think to himself: "Oh, she'll never tell anybody; she'll be too embarrassed." Or maybe he'll think: "I don't care what she says; I don't know any of her friends anyway." Or perhaps he might decide: "So what if the woman hates my guts. Who cares?" And then, seeing no risks to telling the lie, he goes ahead.

The women hearing the lie may respond in various ways. Some may acknowledge that the man is seeking just recreational sex, even if he hasn't stated this directly, and agree that this is fine, even as she is going along with his game that they will see each other again.

Other women may think that although he really is seeking just recreational sex now, even though claiming otherwise, once he has sex with her, he will want to form a relationship with her. In Cole's view, this thinking is often a delusion, because the woman doesn't know the man's inner desires and intentions. Also, such an attitude is often a kind of "magical thinking," based on believing that the man will change his interest to something more permanent or committed just because of having the sexual experience with her, when in fact, many men tend to have the opposite reaction, feeling that if something comes too easy for them it's not worth much.

Thus, caught between the uncertainty about lies and truth in the beginning of a dating relationship, women walk this delicate line in trying to figure out what's too soon or too impetuous and what's just the right amount of waiting and assessing, if their purpose in the encounter is to build a relationship. For some men, this uncertainty contributes to the conquest mystique or excitement of the chase that stimulates their libido.

Complicating this whole equation are the women who would rather hear the man go through the pretense of "I'll call you," when he has no intention of doing it, because, according to Cole, they don't want to face that reality so soon after having sex with a man, because they would experience that as demeaning. Others would rather hear the truth right away and not sit waiting and wondering whether he's going to call.

Another common male lie might be the claim to be safe, by either using contraception or being sterile, so the woman can't get pregnant, although the men

I spoke with about this didn't think such a lie was either common or justified, because of the potential dangers that a pregnancy might bring. Still, one
of the men, Roger, the philosophy teacher, had used this, hoping there would
be no bad consequences, and not feeling good about telling such a lie later.
As he described it, sounding very much like a model of absolute integrity or
straight shooter who had fallen off the usual path:

I don't normally lie to get what I want in a relationship. That's not my style. I try to be
very open and frank. But I do remember one lie I told and I didn't feel good about it.
What happened was I was seeing this woman and we usually had intercourse with con-
doms. But one time, I got carried away and didn't have anything on. Well, she thought
I'd used a condom, though I had not. But I didn't tell her that I had not used it, because
I knew she'd worry about being pregnant, and I didn't want her to worry about it.

Well, fortunately she didn't get pregnant, which would have really been a disaster
for us. So we were lucky, and I just took my chances in telling her that I was protected
when I wasn't, so she wouldn't worry.

Both males and females might also lie to avoid talking frankly about some
area of sex that bothers them. For instance, Dick, the sales executive, described
how one woman told him she had told one of her sexual partners that she used
no birth control when she really did, in order to get him to use a condom. As
Dick commented:

She told him what she did because it was more embarrassing for her to sound like she
was accusing him of maybe having something. So her lie was a more diplomatic, gen-
tler way of asking him to use something.

Also, her lie was a way to avoid the AIDS issue, which no one wants to address or
talk about. So it's much simpler for her to tell him that she doesn't have birth control
and it's up to him, rather than get into the whole AIDS issue. Besides, if she did get
into this subject, maybe she might get answers she doesn't want to know. Plus, many
women tell me that most men are not truthful in discussing venereal disease or AIDS
anyway. No one wants to know or admit it if he has it.

Other lies might be used to reassure the other person—usually the woman
lying to the man—about his sexual performance. For instance, Dee reported
that she and some of her friends had sometimes told men they were fantastic
in bed when they were not—a common sexual lie, according to Dr. Cole, who
told me:

One partner may try to show the other she is enjoying herself, because there is fear
of hurting someone else's feelings by exposing the truth. That's why a woman may lie
about whether she was having an orgasm—because she doesn't want to discourage the
man into thinking that he's inept or that she is sexually unresponsive. So she might just
pretend or create a scenario to make him think he's doing the right thing, when in fact,
he's not exactly doing so, though he may be on the right track.

A good lie? Cole didn't seem to think such lies were usually a good idea
because she tries to encourage people to be honest while learning how to tell

a partner the bad news about his or her performance in a gentle, constructive way that encouraged improvement. As Cole explained:

Sometimes it may be better to hold back or alter the truth a little, if a person is afraid he can't communicate in a way that is going to be taken well. But when possible, it's better to be honest and tell the bad news in a gentle way. For example, if a woman doesn't feel the man is doing something she likes, she might say something like: "I really appreciate the effort you put into our sexual relationship, and there are just a few things that I need to have changed for it to be really fulfilling for me."

In other words, the person who wants some change can acknowledge the other person's effort and care, and then explain that there are some future refinements that are needed to make it good or satisfying or ideal. I think that's better than setting up a deception that the person is doing everything right, so he thinks he's right on track when he isn't. That's why I encourage people to be honest about what they feel and need. Then they can inform their partner, so he or she can try to correct what's wrong, and they are more likely to get what they want that way.

LIES IN THE HEAT OF PASSION

There are also what might be called "the heat of passion" lies—lies uttered during sex, when people may say all sorts of things. The person may actually mean them, at least for the moment, but often they are just a kind of romantic wish fulfillment or enticement for the other person, not really meant sincerely, but part of the sexual play.

All this can be fine when such talk is part of a shared fantasy and both partners know the boundaries and don't take it too seriously. For instance, partners in the throes of passion fantasize about going off to live together on some wonderful island. Such talk can be used for fun, and as part of the play, according to Susan Scott, a relationships expert and author of the book *Create the Love of Your Life*. Yet there can be a danger in this for some people if they take this play for love, when it is really just sex, which can happen because sex is very powerful and is often mistaken for love by very vulnerable people. Also, this shared fantasy can become a problem if one person believes what the other person is fantasizing about and acts upon that lie. Misunderstandings and disappointments can result.

A good example of this is the story that Judy, a teacher and seminar leader, told me about a woman she knew who had been having an affair with a married man for four years. During the affair, in the heat of passion, the man had spoken of things they would do together and about the gifts he would give her. He emphasized his intention again and again in what for him was really a fantasy sparked by the heat of the moment.

She was lucky to come to this realization, so she could face the truth, disengage from the relationship, and get on with her life. But not all people do this or escape the great pain of coming to terms with reality, for as Scott commented: "People can sometimes get so caught up in the fantasy that it hurts so much when they have to face the truth. And there are some who may never face that reality."

LIES ABOUT SEEING OTHERS

Some dating couples may agree that it's okay to see others, but many pledge mutual loyalty. Just as in a marriage, deceptions may be used to maintain a monogamous ideal while one partner (or both) sees others.

For example, before he decided to change to a monogamous lifestyle, Dick, the sales executive, reported frequently seeing two or more women at one time, while denying it to them. As he told me: "There were several times where I was intimate with a couple of women at the same time, and they would ask me if I was sleeping with anybody else, and I would say no."

At times such denials can lead to uncomfortable confrontations. This happened when Alison, a counselor, decided she didn't believe her boyfriend John, who claimed he was going on a ski trip with male friends. She suspected that wasn't true and that he was really seeing another woman. She decided to check his story by waiting near his house and watching him leave. Soon, just as she suspected, the other woman showed up, and Alison decided to confront John.

Needless to say, a raging, embarrassing argument ensued, with lots of yelling and tears. When John finally departed with his date, Alison felt devastated. Her relationship with John cooled quickly, and they soon broke up. She felt both vindicated and relieved at having exposed the lie, telling herself that it was better to be free of the "lying, deceiving bastard," however painful it was initially. Yet at the same time, she regretted the loss and felt upset and lonely for many months until she was able to find someone new. In the long run, she felt the exposure worth it, because she ended up with a very deep, committed relationship with someone she trusted fully and eventually married.

In the other cases, some dating situations turn into long-term stalemates in which there is a series of lies, confrontations, exposures, explanations, and still more lies. Why? Because the person to whom the lie is told hesitates to let go of the relationship and comes to accept, tolerate, or avert her eyes to the cheating at least for a time—and usually it is the woman who tries to overlook this. Meanwhile the person who is lying eventually lies again, since his partner doesn't want the truth, and he wants to continue seeing others on the side. Susannah, the financial planner, had such an ongoing relationship with her on-again, off-again boyfriend Jerry. As she told me:

I got involved with Jerry because he swore to me he was interested in a serious relationship and really wanted to make it work. Well, we had gone together before, and we had broken up, because he kept seeing other women while telling me he wasn't going to do this. But now, he promised again he would be faithful.

And I thought he was. But then I happened to get a copy of this magazine that he publishes, and when I glanced through the personal ads, I saw an ad that I knew he had put in. He described himself just perfectly, and he even mentioned his new apartment with a view, which I had been helping him fix up.

Now I thought that was really outrageous. He was advertising for women on the one hand, and telling me that he's interested in a serious relationship with me on the other. So I confronted him about the ad and he admitted it was his. But then he insisted it was only for business reasons. Supposedly, he said, he wanted this ad to measure the response. Well, I told him, he could measure the response by counting the number of envelopes that come in for other people's ads. And he didn't really have an answer for that.

So afterward, we didn't see each other for a few weeks. We were supposed to go out that weekend, but I said no, and then I didn't hear from him for a while. But then he sent me a valentine, and I wrote him a note thanking him for it. And then he called me up and asked me out, and I said no. But after a while, he kept calling and I said yes again. So once again we've started seeing each other.

But the problem is still there, because he sees himself as an eternally available bachelor, while a part of him wants a permanent girlfriend. So he wants to have his cake and eat it, too, and he'll lie if necessary to do it. So do I call him on that or not? If I do, he just tries to deny it and maybe we'll fight. But if not, things just drift along as they are with Jerry's seeming commitment, though I know that's not really true. And I haven't decided which is better—what I have, which isn't really what I want, because I don't feel I can really trust Jerry, or no relationship at all.

MIXING LIES, LOVE, AND MONEY

As in other sorts of relationships, lies about money in dating and intimate relationships sometimes come up. It is often those feelings of love, friendship, or trust that are used to nourish the lie, as happened three times to Frances, the computer-systems specialist.

In one case, a lawyer friend she dated told her he was going to file papers to incorporate a business, and she paid him to do this. But he took the money and never created the business. In another case, a man she had been seeing claimed that money was being wired to him in New York and said that if he could just get the money, about $1,000, for the plane trip to New York, he would pick up the money and come back. Though Frances explained that she was lending him her rent money and she desperately needed it back within a few days, he never repaid it. In fact, Frances lied herself in claiming this was rent money, because she did have a financial cushion and was using this claim as leverage to suggest how much she was sacrificing and risking to help. Even so, her occasional boyfriend didn't pay her back. And later, a third boyfriend took her for about $6,000 as a result of a series of loans that he promised to repay, as Frances complained:

But he never repaid me either. In fact, his last lie was to ask me for another loan of $2,000, claiming that if I didn't loan it to him, he wouldn't have enough money to make it through the month to be able to have the money to pay me back what he owed me from before. And I thought that was a bit much, so finally I said no.

Frances hurt even more because with him it hadn't just been a business venture; she had been in love. This hurt and betrayal led Frances to hesitate to trust any male. Frances explained:

I've just been afraid of getting involved again—with him, with anybody. For example, he's called me recently about trying to repay me. It was the middle of the night, and he announced that he was here and had about half the money. He told me: "If you'll see me tonight, I'll bring the $3,000. I've got $3,000 cash right here in my hand right now. And there don't have to be any strings attached. If I come to your door and I give you this $3,000 and if you decide that you don't want me in your place, that's all you have to tell me. And then I'll leave."

But I didn't believe him. I just thought, with the door open, he could force his way in. Or maybe he didn't really have the money. Or maybe he'd just tease me with it, promising to give it to me, but then he wouldn't. He'd find some excuse to hold it off.

So, what it came down to is that I didn't really trust him. So I said no. I said, "It doesn't feel right to see you right now," and I suggested that he call me for an appointment sometime during the day. He didn't call, so I think I was right not to trust him. I can't.

Now I find I can't trust anyone else either. All of these situations have been so hard. I just feel like in the past I have had no control. I was like a wet rag. And so now I can't trust at all. I just say to myself "No, no, no." I feel I was hurt too much to trust again.

LIES IN FIGHTS

Arguments can be another time when lies come out and are used as weapons. Don, the engineer, described how he had experienced lies used as insults during fights with lovers. As he commented:

Say you have a rift, a little misunderstanding with your primary person. I've sometimes had the experience of them saying things that aren't quite true just to throw a little barb at you. It's like they want to dig in their nails.

For example, a couple of times I have been trying to heal the rift and have been talking about meeting again, when all of a sudden the other person will say something like: "Well, are you really sure you want to meet again? I thought you didn't ever want to see me again." Well, it's like putting thoughts and feelings in your mouth, maybe because they're really worried that might be true, and they want you to deny it and reassure them. Or maybe they want you to imagine the possibility of never seeing them again so you are concerned it doesn't happen.

Anyway, for me, when this happens just before we say good-bye, it leaves me wondering and a little unnerved. I've been trying to patch up the quarrel, and then I start wondering "What's going on?" It's like having a rock thrown in some water that's just becoming calm, which starts stirring things up all over again.

Insulting digs, like direct hits, can hurt even more. Sarah, the educator, and one of her former boyfriends had been having an ongoing argument over their differing interests. While the fight had been patched over for a while, the raw feelings and resentments still simmered under the surface. As Sarah described it:

One of our problems was our differences. I'm normally a social person and I also like to dress up and go places at times, though I can wear jeans and do things informally, too. So being in the city is comfortable for me. But my boyfriend was often very uncomfortable in the city or with my social settings. And sometimes things got very tense because of this.

This one night we went to a restaurant after going to the opera. And we had this incredible fight. I had really enjoyed the opera and I liked this restaurant, so I was in heaven. But my boyfriend, though I wasn't aware of this, was very uncomfortable. So all of a sudden, while I was really having a good time and feeling very, very good, my boyfriend suddenly lashed out at me and said that I was being just horrible. He claimed I was ignoring him, that I was making eyes at someone else, when I wasn't doing any of that at all. I think he was just making that up to start a fight, because he was feeling tense and irritable.

Then a few days later, he sent me a letter filled with lies and he told the counselor we were seeing that I didn't want to see the counselor anymore, when that wasn't true. Maybe he wanted to stop, but I didn't want to cancel the appointment. In fact, he even told the counselor I wanted to do this because I needed the extra hours though this was not true. But I was relieved that he canceled it for me. Additionally, he sent a letter to the counselor, describing how I had been very angry that night and how he had tried to calm me down, when in fact I was the one who tried to calm him and stop the fight.

So he really misinterpreted everything. He tried to get me angry that night by what he said. And then he tried to get me angry again by sending me this untrue letter. I felt like he was like a child, trying to get me riled, maybe to get his own way or upset me because he felt he couldn't have what he wanted.

THE RESPONSE TO LIES

How do men and women respond to lies that sometimes pepper a relationship? At what point do the lies break up the relationship?

It would seem as if the occasional lie can be forgiven, particularly if the rest of the relationship is good and the lie is not serious. It also depends on the individual who has been lied to. Some people are more willing to forgive or see the lie as a reflection of the other person's insecurity. So they decide it's not such a big deal—this is more common for the pragmatic fibbers, Pinocchios, and frequent liars, because they are more concerned with what's pragmatic to do. Others may become incensed by lies about anything, especially the models of absolute integrity and the straight shooters.

Though she didn't use these categories, sexologist Louanne Cole made these suggestions in describing that the willingness to forgive has to do with differing personality dynamics. As she noted:

Some people have a real sense of righteousness and justice, and they feel that being lied to is a major offense; while others are more tolerant. They take into consideration how big a lie it is. So if it's a big lie, then they would react against it more strongly. But if it's a minor lie, they wouldn't take it so seriously.

And then there are those people for whom any lie undermines trust generally. They may feel if the person has lied about one thing then he may lie about others. They think: "If you could lie about that, then I don't know if I can trust you any more." Then, if they don't have an understanding of or an empathy for why the person lied in the first place, they may be closed to further understanding, and so it can be very hard for that trust to be rebuilt.

The response of the person lied to may depend on how the liar responds. Commonly, lies come out not because the person recognizes the lie at the time but because little things happen later to reveal it, sometimes by illuminating discrepancies. Cole gave examples that come up in man–woman and dating situations:

Other people or creditors call, and the other person picks up the phone and gets the gist of what is really going on. Checks bounce if there's a lie involving money. Or maybe families have disputes or family problems come to light, so the relationship turns out to be not what it seems. Or perhaps the weakness in the relationship is revealed when one person is in trouble, asks for help, and the other person doesn't respond. So various events can happen to bring the lie to light.

Once the lie comes out, people can respond in different ways that make the lie easier or more difficult to accept. Sometimes the response is denial, which, according to Cole, is especially common when there has been a liaison with someone else—"No, I wasn't really seeing someone else." Other liars accuse the victim of lying to get out of seeming to lie themselves. And then others, relieved to be caught lying, may actually confess. A person may explain the lies as something he or she did because "I didn't want to hurt you, and I thought if you knew, it would hurt. And so the better choice seemed to be to lie."

In any case, if the response to being caught in a lie works and the victim accepts or forgives, the relationship can continue. But this kind of repair work commonly works only so often—perhaps once or a few times, depending on how forgiving the other person is and whether the lie doesn't seem all that serious. However, if a pattern of lies builds up, that can lead to the end, as occurred for Dick, the sales executive, in one of his relationships. It happened with a woman he "really loved and could have been very happy with." As Dick described the breakup:

There were just too many things to accept so after a while I had to end it. For instance, when we first started dating, Judy called up and canceled a date with me at the last minute. She was supposed to come over to my place, but she said she couldn't be there, because she was with a sick friend. I knew she was breaking off a relationship with another guy to see me, and so I immediately suspected that she might have been with this guy.

I wanted to know the truth, so I asked her not to be offended, but could I speak to the sick friend? But she said, no, because the sick friend was in bed. So then I asked if she would mind if I came over and talked to her in front of her sick friend's house because I needed to talk to her about something. But she said, no, you can't do that. And I asked why? But she had no reason. She just said you can't do that. So I felt that here she was probably lying.

I let that one pass, because I really did feel I loved her. But another time, when we were supposed to go out of town together, I suddenly found out I had to go on a business trip the next Monday, so I said I couldn't go. She claimed she could go with me, and I wondered how she could do this, because I knew she had all these customers. And she said she would just call them tomorrow to make other arrangements. But she told me this on a Saturday morning, and I knew she couldn't really do this, because people don't work on Sunday and you can't reach them to reschedule appointments. That's not how business is done.

Then another time she said she was supposed to be speaking at an engagement, and when I said I would like to go hear her, she said she didn't want me to go because it would make her nervous. But I wondered about that because she is a professional speaker and she was going to be speaking to two hundred people. So how could I affect her that way? So finally she agreed that, yes, I could go. And I drove her to the engagement. But when we got there, she announced that she had gotten the wrong day, and she really wasn't speaking that day after all. Then she wouldn't let me speak to the woman who had supposedly booked her.

So I think she probably was never really ever scheduled to speak there. I think she just made the engagement up to impress me, because there was a big fair going on and there were going to be other speakers. And she just wanted to make it seem like she was going to be speaking too.

Anyway, though I loved her and thought she was a fantastic person in other ways, these little incidents began to build up and bother me. So finally I told her that. I told her how I loved her and thought she was great, and that I wasn't sure about what happened with the speaking or her sick friend and all that. But I wanted to ask her from this point forward to be sure to tell me the truth and that this is what I needed to continue the relationship. And she said fine.

But, as Dick related, she didn't do this, and finally one incident led to the end of their relationship. By itself, the incident might have been minor. But as a part of a pattern of lies, it was just too much. Dick described what happened:

The last straw occurred when we took a trip together. We drove to the country and we stopped in a restaurant. Suddenly, during dinner, she began to choke on some food, and the emergency medical people arrived and took her to the hospital for a little check-up.

While she was in the emergency room, I went through her purse to get her license so I could check her in, and I found that her license had a different age than what she had told me.

So later, after she left the hospital and we were driving home, I asked her how could that age discrepancy be. She replied that the DMV had made a mistake. So I said that I never heard of the DMV making a mistake on a person's birthday, or if they did, I thought it was pretty unusual for a woman to go along with letting her age be listed to show her as older than she really was—in this case four years older. But she insisted, no, this really was a mistake.

So I asked her to do me a favor and get a new corrected license. But she said she couldn't, so I was sure this was just another lie. Had she told me she was four years older in the first place, it wouldn't have made any difference to me. And maybe if this was the only lie she had told me, it wouldn't have mattered. Just a little lie about her age.

But there were just so many lies before that for me this was the last straw. I loved her, but I just didn't want to deal with any more lies. So for me, that was enough, and when we got home, I told her I wouldn't be seeing her anymore. The relationship was just over for me, and so that's how we broke up.

THE DESIRE FOR AND THE DANGERS OF HONESTY

As these stories show, while people may sometimes express the ideal of honesty in the dating relationship, leading to a greater intimacy based on honesty and trust, if the relationship becomes more serious and committed, in fact, lying is commonly part of dating relationships. So while someone may feel acceptance to anger when one is the victim of a lie by a dating partner, one may often engage in different types of dating lies oneself, based on what's expedient or practical in that situation. In other words, though the model of absolute integrity or the straight shooter may represent some kind of ideal, in practice, people are more like pragmatic fibbers, Pinocchios, or frequent liars when it comes to dating.

Perhaps a reason for this is that part of the intrigue and excitement of the dating relationship comes from the mystery of the not fully revealed self. Raphael, the healer, made the distinction between being seductive in a relationship, which is okay, and being deceptive, which is not. The difference is in intent. In being seductive, one combines being warm, inviting, welcoming, open, and receptive with a kind of gentle and aware drawing in. But with deception, one holds something essential back.

The paradox is that while this open honesty and giving of the self may sometimes cement the relationship through trust, at other times this openness may reveal too much that destroys the relationship. The reason is that the person who receives this truth is not always as tolerant as he or she may like to be. And that breeds a need to conceal.

Dick, the sales executive, described how he confronted this essential paradox:

I realize that if you can say anything you want to, and the other person will still love you, then it is okay to be honest. That takes away a lot of the reason for lying because the fear of losing your relationship is gone.

But can you really do that? I've had the experience of telling a woman that I want to be really honest, and then I asked if she's only seeing me now, hoping she will say yes and knowing that if she says no, it will turn me off. So I'm asking her to tell the truth. But if she tells me the truth I don't want to hear, I know that will end the relationship for me. I find it difficult to be receptive, forgiving, and accepting.

So there's always that danger in being honest. It can destroy that very intimacy that it's designed to promote.

This is what happened to Sandy, the marketing consultant, when she told a man she had just met through an ad that she didn't feel any chemistry between them:

This man had put an ad in a local singles paper, and as soon as I met him, I thought he was a basically nice, sweet person, but not right for me. I just thought we had very little in common, and I thought to save us the time and energy of trying to struggle through a conversation together over coffee, I would just tell him what I felt. So I told him that the chemistry was not right for me, though I thought him a nice person. And he seemed very insulted. So I've wondered since then about whether it's good to be so direct. It seems like some people just don't like to deal with the truth when it's so blunt.

Similarly, Roger, the philosophy teacher, seemed to feel as if he might have gone too far in trying to share his deepest, darkest secrets with a woman who encouraged him to open up and be more emotionally intimate. As he explained:

I usually like to get everything out on the table, and if there's something standing in the way of me being connected with someone, I want to know what it is. Well, as it happened, I was seeing one woman, and we had a great deal of sexual activity in our relationship. She complained that our relationship was just sexual and she wanted to share more emotional intimacy. So when she mentioned she had this diary she had been keeping for about seven years, I said I would like to read it, and she agreed as long as she could read mine.

So I gave it to her. But afterward, I wondered if this was such a good idea, because it contained my deep subjective feelings about what I do, and some of it is in X-rated language. Also, it included all the dates I had with this woman. So there were things there I didn't really want her to know about me. But I gave it to her, and I read hers.

And there were things in hers that I'm sure she really didn't want me to know about her, such as the fact she had had an abortion, and other things she had done. Afterward, I felt like we had maybe told each other too much. So this mutual revelation didn't really help the relationship. I think in our search for emotional intimacy we might have gone too far, because we both felt a little awkward about what we read.

Then she decided to go back to dating her former boyfriend, so our relationship ended anyway. But I think sharing too much helped to put a bit of a strain in it. So I guess I'm all for seeking that deeper intimacy. But at a certain point, you have to draw the line.

What complicates this ideal of honesty is the fact that women and men often have different ideas about how much should be shared and how much should be concealed for the relationship to be an honest one. Again and again, the individuals I interviewed and the therapists and business consultants I spoke to observed that women tend to reveal and want to have much more revealed. They reveal it to the men in their lives, and they reveal it to their friends and associates in talking about their men.

As speaker and author Judith Briles, who did several studies of male and female differences in the workplace,[2] commented to me:

Women are far more likely to divulge personal information to anybody. We women talk too much. We really share too much too soon. For example, at one group I spoke to, I remember saying:

"You know, I could sit down with any one of you, not knowing you, over a cup of coffee and within a very short period of time I would know about your love life, your married life, what kind of problems your kids have had, and what kind of female problems you have—information I'm not entitled to know."

Well, with that kind of orientation, the man may feel under pressure to talk about what he doesn't want to share. And the woman may perceive a lie (of concealment or denial) when the man does not. Perhaps as a counterbalance to this, women may also be more apt to suffer in silence at what they feel is a lack in the relationship, whereas men are more likely to act. As sexologist Louanne Cole observed: "Women sometimes tend to suffer a little bit more in the state of deprivation, whatever they're feeling deprived of, while the men will more often take matters into their own hands to do something and get what they want."

CHAPTER 11

Lies with Husbands, Wives, and Intimate Others

When it comes to spouses and intimate others, the ideal of honesty becomes even stronger, so that lies become even more frowned upon. Yet here, too, there are all sorts of lies, ranging from the common and usually harmless "You look great today, dear" lies to make the spouse feel good, to the lies that threaten the heart of the marriage because they are about affairs. Then, too, in a marriage or more intimate relationship, the lies bring up even more intensely that central puzzle of when it is best and most appropriate to lie to benefit the relationship—and when the truth should be told.

As in the case of other personal relationships, the model of absolute integrity or straight shooter is more likely to be open and honest, or at least to feel guilty in those rare instances when he or she slips, while the pragmatic fibber, Pinocchio, and frequent liar are more prone to using a lie to evade or wriggle out of a difficult situation. By the same token, the first group is more likely to uphold vows in a marriage or to be faithful with a partner, while the latter is more apt to respond to an opportunity to cheat and then cover up after the fact and not feel any guilt, only remorse over being caught.

As an example of the first two types, Stan, the high school teacher, described a few of the lies he told his wife to promote her well-being, while pointing out that he considered their marriage to be based on a high degree of openness and mutual integrity. So why did he lie? In one case, to hide a doctor's verdict about her health problems from her so she would feel better; in other cases, to hold back a contrary opinion about things she had bought, to keep peace.

Such lies in a close relationship may be quite common and accepted, because their purpose is aligned with strengthening the relationship. Yet, despite the good intention, such lies may at times actually harm the relationship because they leave real thoughts and feelings unexpressed, and that can lead to misunderstandings and a build-up of resentment and anger.

Sexologist Dr. Louanne Cole pointed this out when she observed:

Sometimes lies can paper over unexpressed anger, such as when somebody asks what's wrong and the other person says: "Nothing," when in fact something is. I think it's important that people should get out their real feelings, because otherwise anger can build up and just fester, and then it will come out in some other way eventually.

So it's really important that people talk about what's bothering them or making them angry in a relationship, and they can do so in a way that is healing and releases the anger. They can do this by using "I" statements, in which they express the idea that "I think that . . ." or "I'm feeling that . . ." or "When you do this, it makes me feel this way . . ." or "When you do this, there's a consequence which is this and I don't like it." Such statements are designed to express the way the person feels and reacts to what the other person does, not blame the other person for those actions and reactions. So then the other person can be more receptive to listening and making a desired change.

However, if such concerns don't get expressed, this just messes up the relationship, because the anger will come out in one way or another—maybe in sex, maybe in money disputes, or in fights about how to raise the children.

In any case, the ideal is to be as honest and open as possible, since honesty is seen as the basis for true intimacy and commitment.

Alison, the relationships counselor, expressed this ideal quite intensely:

When I decided to get married again, I was real clear that I wanted somebody I could really trust. I knew I didn't want the uncertainty about trust to be an issue in my relationship, because I find that very draining, and I needed all my energy to put it into my work. So that was really important on my list, and I feel my present husband has lived up to that completely. I feel I can trust him in every way, and that's critical to me now.

Yet along with this ideal comes the problem of defining just how honest partners should be—what should be revealed and what should be concealed. It is not always an easy decision because with openness comes vulnerability.

For example, Raphael, the healer, had gone through just such a period of uncertainty and ambivalence during a very close relationship with a woman he had considered a "significant other" for about a year. As he told me:

In our relationship, I think we were real honest with each other, although there were certain concealments. But were they really? Were they something that we should reveal? For example, suppose something has happened in the past, such as a previous extramarital affair or extrarelational affair? When do you share that? In the beginning? After the relationship has reached a certain depth of intimacy and bonding? Or never?

It can be a drag if you always have to say everything that's going on. I mean, there's a certain acceptance that's needed, a certain respect for privacy, secrecy, and autonomy of the other person. So how much should you share? What's honest and what's not? When does that line get crossed, indicating that you should share? How is that defined? And then, if you should share, when is the right time? It all can get very complicated. There's so much that's uncertain and undefined, and you have to develop your own definitions as you go.

LIES AND SEX

The sexual relationship itself can be a big source of lies because it involves such emotional intensity, and when people don't feel comfortable about saying what they are really thinking and feeling, they may prefer to lie. But again the paradox is that lying sometimes can help the relationship by avoiding unpleasant truths one partner doesn't want to hear. Yet at other times, lying can interfere with the relationship by keeping one partner from getting what he or she really wants because he or she doesn't ask for it or says he or she wants something else (such as the classic case of the woman feigning the orgasm).

Sexologist Dr. Louanne Cole pointed out such an example—a woman had fantasies about the things she wanted her husband to do with her sexually, but she feared sharing these ideas with him. So she denied them, leaving her tense and in conflict. Finally, with therapy, she was able to open up and reveal them, resulting in an improved relationship. As Cole told me:

This one woman was really upset about her sexual relationship with her husband, because she had some fantasies that involved him dominating and infantilizing her to make her feel like a little girl by embarrassing her and humiliating her. Somehow that turned her on. But she was very conflicted about the fact this turned her on, and she didn't want to reveal this to her husband. So she didn't talk about this.

But finally, after a lot of therapy, she was able to reveal some of this to her husband, and he had no trouble, it turned out, playing into this fantasy once he got the hang of what her script needed to look like. Also, he had no objections to doing this on ethical or moral grounds, just because her fantasy went outside the bounds of what might usually be considered normal. So in this case, it helped the relationship for her to be open and honest about what she really wanted.

Still, as Cole advised, it is important that people approach such revelations in a tentative way, much as the doctor I described in the previous chapter did in revealing his S&M desires to his girlfriends. As Cole commented:

It's best when people do some what-if scenarios to see how their partner responds. Then they can watch how that person responds to other similar kinds of things in the news or on TV or in the movies or books. For example, when the movie *9 1/2 Weeks* came out, some women dragged their husbands off to see it because they had submissive desires, and they used the film as a testing ground to see if their husbands might want to put them in that role. Other people I know took their husbands to see that very erotic movie based on Milan Kundera's novel, *The Unbearable Lightness of Being*.

So people use movies frequently as testing grounds for some of their own desire. And some bring home porn films and books occasionally that reflect their own desires, and then they check on how the other person reacts to see if they can bring their own desires out in the open.

However, there are times such openness would not be helpful and could actually harm the relationship, so it might be better to lie. Some people need to keep certain areas of their life private and they need that space from their partner. In such cases, the denial or lie for concealment might be better than feeling a sense of personal invasion, which might undermine the relationship, too.

Cole described how some people have a need for pornography but must keep it secret from a spouse who might not approve. She felt in many cases it was quite justified for one spouse to have this separate part of his life to preserve his own sense of independence and privacy. As she commented:

Say a man wants to go to see pornography or explicit movies. Or maybe he might want to subscribe to *Playboy* magazine or see sexy films on the Playboy channel. But his wife or significant other might think this is just disgusting. Well, what sometimes causes problems in relationships is when people think that because they are married or in a very close relationship that they have a license to run the other person's life. They have this idea that they have a right to possess this other person, and they think they know how that person should best live up to their own potential based on their own ideals.

But if the person didn't demand that, then a lot of lying wouldn't happen or be perceived as necessary, because what it can lead to is someone lying to avoid confronting the other person with the fact that a part of their life doesn't live up to the other person's idea of what their life should look like.

Ideally, of course, it would be preferable if the person insisting on this behavior could give up this insistence, so the lie would not be necessary.

I have found that some men choose to live double lives to hide their occasional participation in dominance-and-submission activities because their wives couldn't accept their taking a role that didn't fit their image of how he should be. If the man wanted to play a submissive scene or dress like a woman, he might conceal it from his partner but express it by going to some activity put on by some group in the D&S community. The men did not consider this to be the same as going to a prostitute or having an affair, since they experienced no sexual intercourse, just erotic arousal and release, and it seemed to work well for them.

Dr. Cole seemed to think this kind of double life might be appropriate for some. As she told me:

I think if people can tolerate that kind of double life and everything else is good about the relationship and this approach works for them and they don't absolutely need their own partner to be involved in the S&M or D&S scene with them, then that may be a choice that they should make rather than other choices, such as disrupting the family, breaking up the relationship, or revealing the variation that might bring about unnecessary embarrassments.

But then other people may want to come clean about their sexuality so badly that they can't tolerate any of that kind of subterfuge. So in that case, perhaps they should tell. They should be aware that the price may be high if they want to come clean, but if they need to do that, perhaps they should.

Likewise, there may be times when it is better to keep secrets or tell lies in the sexual relationship to make the other person feel better or maintain the sexual mystique. Cole pointed out that it might be best to keep it a secret when one's partner doesn't measure up to a physical ideal. As she put it:

I think there are better kept secrets, such as a woman's preference for penis size or a man's preference for breast size and that sort of thing. This is the case because a partner may have a preference for a particular size body part that seems important. But if he or she looks at the relationship as a whole and everything else about that relationship works very well, should he or she throw it all away because the partner doesn't have the ideal penis size or breast size that he or she is looking for?

Likewise, it may help to tell a little lie about what he or she thinks if the partner asks for an opinion about that part in the heat of passion. For example, suppose he says in the midst of passion: "How do you like my penis?" or something of that sort in more romantic terms. I don't think it's a terrible thing for her to say: "I think it's great, sweetheart." Or if she should ask him the same sort of question about her buttocks or her breasts, I think he should be similarly supportive, whether he thinks they're the greatest or not.

And the reason I think the lie is useful in such cases is because the person's body is not going to change. For the most part, there's nothing the person can do about his or her body, maybe just a few minor alterations here and there. So I don't think it serves the person to know that his or her partner has a critical feeling about such physical things or that they aren't really his or her ideal. Rather, I think it's better for the partner to be gentle and kind in saying what he or she thinks, so the partner feels better and that helps the person's self-esteem.

But if the partner was just being kind rather than saying what was true, would the other person really believe him or her? Cole didn't think this mattered, feeling that both would feel better through this shared romantic fantasy.

Other common fantasies are also better left unspoken. As Cole observed:

Sometimes people may think that if their partner fantasizes about other people, the partner doesn't love them, so that can encourage the lies such as: "I never fantasize during sex with you," or "I never look at other men." Or maybe he or she asks the partner: "What are you thinking about?" and he or she says "You," when in fact he or she is thinking about someone else.

Sometimes that can be a good response, because many people think that if one fantasizes about somebody, one really must feel that way or one will go and do it. But that is just not true. There are many, many fantasies that many people have that they have no intention of following through on.

Such fantasies may be about having sex with someone else, having a group-sex orgy, or a woman being forced to have sex. In the fantasy, this activity may seem like fun. But in real life these people would never go and do it or want such a thing to happen to them. The same goes for having fantasies about being dominated or embarrassed or humiliated in some way. There are some people who have such fantasies, but that's all they are. These things will never happen, and they don't want them to happen for real.

So sometimes if the other partner asks what you are thinking, it may be better to say "about you," or else not reveal the fantasy if it's not something the other person can understand or accept. Sometimes the other person has an idea of what he or she thinks the partner ought to be and won't budge from that position. So if he or she hears a fantasy that is different from that idea, they may think it bad or awful, which may hurt the relationship, and for no good reason, because the truth is just a fantasy. So for them I say, don't tell. It's better in such cases to keep the secret or deny.

And that's what many people do—lie about or deny their fantasies and feelings. Stephen, the writer, described what happened when his wife Nancy asked him to express feelings for her that he wasn't feeling at the time. As he told me:

Sometimes when Nancy asks me: "Do you love me?" and at that moment I'm not feeling love for her, I still say: "Of course, I do." That could be considered a lie, since I'm not feeling it at that moment. And there have been other times when I might say: "Yes, I love you," but I don't have any real conviction or passion about it right then.

And Nancy's reaction?

Sometimes she'll just accept what I've said whether she really believes me or not. It's not that big a deal to make an issue about it, and I've said what she's wanted to hear. But sometimes she'll call me on it by saying something like: "You're full of shit" or "You don't mean that."

But generally that's as far as it will go. I'll just say something like: "Oh, sure I do," to keep the peace, or maybe I won't say anything at all. And then usually she'll let it drop and that will be the end of it, because neither of us really wants to pursue this, neither of us wants a fight.

LYING AND AFFAIRS

The lies with the most potential to do damage involve affairs or outside sexual liaisons, because these go to the heart of the marital or intimate relationship, which is usually based on mutual monogamy. When such outside sexual relationships occur—and reportedly they do in about 30 to 50 percent or more of all marriages[1]—they usually are accompanied by lies designed to deny or cover up. The cheated-on spouse may know or suspect but may keep secret or deny his or her awareness to avoid bringing the affair out into the open, which might threaten the apparent calm of the marriage or relationship.

Such affairs occur for many reasons, ranging from a passing attraction to a way of coping with a marriage breakdown without breaking up the marriage. The affair can be beneficial by providing an outside release, although it also can create distance between the partners. Meanwhile, the lies about the affair become another layer in the mix.

Don, the engineer, described his own ambivalent feelings about having the relationship and lying about it:

Lying in a monogamous relationship is not an acceptable lie to me, although I admit that sometimes in the past I have done this. And then I have felt guilty about doing it. I just feel it's an essential dishonesty to the relationship.

Why, if so many couples have extramarital or extra-significant-other relationships, do they not admit it and work out ground rules? According to Susan

Scott, the expert on relationships and author of *Create the Love of Your Life*, the reason many do not do this is because of the power of the monogamy-fidelity ideal. As she observed:

Sometimes people have open relationships. But most of the time the spouse is never told, because the person having the affairs knows it will never be okay with that spouse, and they fear the loss of the spouse, even though they may be unfulfilled at home. So even though they are still unhappy, they want to hold onto the relationship, and fear disrupting it by telling and admitting they have violated this monogamous ideal.

Also, a person may conceal a past affair to maintain his own image of purity or integrity and to prevent the other person from feeling hurt, again because of this monogamy ideal. Joyce, a personnel counselor, described how she kept secret a past affair with an accountant because she didn't want to worry her husband. As she told me:

My husband and I have an extremely open and intimate relationship with each other. It's completely monogamous and based on an ideal of sharing everything with each other.

But there is one thing I never told my husband about and that's that I had a sexual affair with one man who is still our accountant. He was my accountant as well as my lover before our marriage, before I divorced my previous husband. And after our affair was over, I still wanted to use him as an accountant because he is very good.

So I never told my husband about the affair. It feels like a lie to me not to tell him, because we are so honest and open about everything else. But I can't see any reason to tell him. If I did, I think he would just feel uncomfortable with this man and wonder about the relationship in the past or worry about it happening again where there's nothing there and won't be again.

Although this lying and secrecy associated with current or past affairs can produce feelings of guilt for many people, for many others this lying and secrecy are part of the excitement of the affair. Doing something forbidden heightens the sense of romance and physical passion. And for some people feelings of excitement and guilt along with fears of being found out are interwoven, alternately drawing the person more intensely into the affair or making him or her reconsider it.

In some cases, of course, guilt can lead a person to stop the deceptions by finding an alternate outlet, such as becoming busy. Some common ways of doing this might be by volunteering for something, becoming more active in one's business, or even cleaning up the house, according to Scott. For example, Judy, the teacher and seminar leader, told me about a friend who couldn't stand the deception after he cheated on his wife with a one-night stand, so he threw himself into community work to escape a marriage that was going downhill. He couldn't handle the guilt and secrecy of an affair—which is much like the way a model of absolute integrity or a straight shooter might respond.

Other people who feel guilt usually work through it by rationalizing or saying that the benefits of the affair are well worth it.

And many people find ways to compensate for their guilt, such as the man who buys an extra nice present for his wife because he is cheating on her. Still others channel their guilt into being supersensitive about discovery, and they become extra cautious to keep their secret.

TYPES OF CONCEALMENTS AND JUSTIFICATIONS

How do people who have affairs conceal them? Some—most typically the pragmatic fibbers, Pinocchios, and frequent liars—use fake excuses and explanations such as "I have to work," "I have to go out of town," and the like. But as the outside relationship goes on, the person may have to come up with more believable reasons, particularly if there is a change in the person's situation that makes the outside relationship more difficult to carry on.

Scott pointed out that concealment strategies can lead to difficulties because the cheating partner may lead what becomes a double life. For instance, Annie, a communications consultant, described a friend whose husband was fairly successful in keeping an outside jogging-sexual relationship carefully hidden.

This one man I know has a woman friend he jogs with two or three times a week. They also take time out to have sex together. And sometimes they go off on runs together, which take them away for a weekend or so. And they have been enjoying this relationship with each other for a couple of years.

But at the same time, he has had to maintain the lies with his wife and lead a double life.

And ironically, what's fascinating is that the two people who are affairing are often more honest with each other than they are with their spouses, because they aren't responsible for each other's overall well-being.

For example, the man doesn't have to worry about being Mr. Macho and taking care of the woman, because she is being taken care of someplace else. So he can be more himself and allow himself to be more vulnerable and therefore more honest. It's not likely that this kind of outside relationship will lead to marriage, since most people in affairs stay with their mate. And they use the lies and the cover-ups with their primary partner to help maintain this dual state of affairs.

Some couples may also use their friends to help them maintain their cover-up. A classic example of this is when a person having an affair gets a friend to open up his or her home, so the couple can have a supposedly safe place to go. But more generally, in the interest of secrecy, friends will be kept out of this. One reason is that many people having affairs don't want even their friends to know, because their friends may disapprove or that knowledge provides one more loose end that could lead to exposure. Then, too, it may not be a very good idea to involve friends in actively protecting the affair, because if the affair comes out, they might be targeted by an angry mate.

Such lies can work for a long time, because the other partner wants to believe and trust, and even may try to screen out any potential suspicions.

Then, too, the people lying can often be quite convincing, especially when they can push away feelings of guilt and compartmentalize their lives, so that leading the double life causes no qualms.

While there is much uncertainty about male and female differences in their success in managing the affair, the popular view appears to be that men have an easier time of doing this, since they are better able to compartmentalize their lives—say by having a wife at home and a lover at work or putting lust in one category and love in another. This may be because some men tend to be more in control of their emotions, or at least don't express their emotions so openly, because from early childhood males are taught to show control and not express emotions. Thus, when having the affair, such men may feel or express their feelings less openly, because their emotions are more underground. As a result, they are better able to conceal their feelings for the other women or any effect of this on their relationship with their married or primary partner.

By contrast, because many women may be more apt to experience or express their emotions openly, women may be more apt to act in a way that triggers their partner's suspicion. But then, whether there are these male or female differences or not, those married people who have successful affairs are those who have learned how to be more in charge of their emotions to maintain concealment. As Scott commented: "Those that are able to compartmentalize have a strong survival motivation to keep the affair going by keeping it secret, and they do this for that reason."

Of course, some lies unravel, and the secret comes out. In some cases this happens because the partner has just gone too far in trying to invent and create, so the lie sinks of its own weight.

Blanche, the public relations executive, described a situation with her first husband, who had gotten his mistress pregnant and then let the cat out of the bag, so to speak, when he tried to figure out what to do about it. As Blanche described it:

I was in my early thirties, married to my first husband, and one day he asked me for the name of a girlfriend of mine who is a nurse, and then he called her and asked her for the name of a doctor who would do an abortion for a co-worker of his.

Well, my friend came to me and said that this was a funny thing for my husband to ask her, and she suggested: "I bet he's knocked up someone in his office." At first, I said: "Oh, that's impossible," and I just thought her idea was funny.

But then, her suggestion acted as a kind of a trigger, and I soon put two and two together when one of his partners at a social engagement said how much time my husband was spending with one of his co-workers at a luncheon counter. It was the same woman he had asked about the abortion for, and so I became suspicious, and when I confronted him about it, he admitted it was so, and that helped me realize that our marriage had been going along, not being very good. And so, though the incident and the lie weren't the cause, they really served as the beginning of the end of our marriage, and we soon got our divorce after that.

While the revelation of a lie may lead to the end of the relationship in some cases, it may lead to further concealments and lies in others, building a foundation of lies.

A good example of this is the wife one interviewee told me about who uncovered her husband's affair and made him call his mistress and tell her the affair was over while she listened. But, in fact, he called the mistress back later and the affair went on, though now the partners worked even harder at keeping it secret. They changed their meeting places and times; they set up signals to use in calling each other, so each would know when it was safe to take the call. Also, they paid more attention to small details, and generally became even closer to each other.

This greater intensity in an affair may in turn result from this greater fear of exposure, according to Scott, because this fear and the added concealment efforts can strengthen the power of the affair. Why? "Because," Scott commented, "different things turn people on. For some people, the taboo of the forbidden is more exciting. It acts like an aphrodisiac to make the affair more intense and stronger, though for other people that same fear can kill the relationship."

REVEALING AND REACTION TO THE LIE

Sometimes, even with all these efforts to conceal, the lie is revealed. Often a mistake, some sort of chance happening, brings the secret out, although according to Scott, there may be other clues, which the other person may be able to pick up, if he or she is ready to see them, even though these clues can be quite subtle. As Scott commented:

When someone is really close and tuned into someone else, he or she will always be able to see the truth. Although if someone isn't ready, he or she will miss it, because he doesn't want to see what's there. This is so, because if you use your intuition, you will always see the truth.

For example, some of the clues a person might see might be clues given off by the sense of touch, taste, or smell. There could be visual clues in the way the person acts; sound clues in the way the person says something. Some examples of this might be one partner acting nervous or not looking into the other person's eyes. Also, perhaps out of guilt or as a way of making up for having the affair, the person may become unusually nice or thoughtful, such as bringing flowers or an extra present, that seems unexpected or inappropriate.

However, whether the spouse experiencing this recognizes these differences is another issue. The spouse may not always do so, because he or she may not want to see what is happening, so it is easier to lie to oneself. But these differences, these clues to the truth are there.

One reason for not wanting to acknowledge is, of course, the underlying betrayal and shock to the self-esteem such involvement with another may bring. But another reason is that in facing the situation, the person will have to do something about it, and may not want to face the pain of taking this action. A wife, Scott observed, might have to confront her husband, which frightens her, because it would shake up the marriage. Also, she might be called on to make decisions about the marriage that she doesn't want to make, and she might lose everything. Thus, by maintaining a state of denial, she can keep what she thinks she has in the relationship.

In other cases, the spouse really may not be aware, because he or she hasn't been paying attention or the clues have been too subtle. But then, all of a sudden, their spouse does something that gives the affair away, and all of the clues become apparent.

Because of traditional roles and upbringing, the wife may be slower to suspect and the husband quicker to become aware earlier, because he is more likely to be jealous or possessive and so be on the alert for such clues. But, regardless of gender, Scott feels that the person who wants to hold onto the illusion the most is the last to suspect, and one cannot generalize about whether men or women are more likely to do this, because roles and situations today vary so greatly.

Another traditional pattern that still seems to be common is that when men do find out, they tend to be more angry, hurt, and violent than women, and they are less ready to adjust, accept, and forgive, perhaps because of this tendency to be more jealous, possessive, and ego-involved. At least the high level of statistics on wife abuse and male violence against ex-wives or wives who have tried to leave seems to bear this out. Then, too, men may be more apt to express their hurt outwardly through action, rather than release the pain by talking about it, as is more common for women, who may find more support from others in sharing their grief. Yet, again, such patterns may be changing, as men increasingly learn to get in touch with their feelings today, and in Scott's view, those who are better able to express emotion will be less apt to express it in angry, violent ways and will be better able to adjust, accept, or forgive.

So what happens when the spouse finally finds out or admits that he or she knows? The spouse might continue to deny it openly, hoping the affair will go away without a confrontation. So in this case there can be a collusion in which the spouse, usually the wife, decides not to make an issue of it, to keep the relationship as it is. Such a person might be feeling a great deal of emotional pain, according to Scott. But he or she just doesn't want to risk the possibly greater pain of losing the relationship he or she has. But then, when the person does finally find out or acknowledges what is really going on, Scott feels it will help the person to break free and move on.

A woman in this situation, according to Scott, might be able to rationalize that as long as her husband pays the bills, takes her on nice vacations, and otherwise treats her well, she doesn't want to rock the boat. She might overlook the situation. But, according to Scott, when a person is settling for less than what he or she really wants, that person won't be really happy, because he or she won't truly respect him or herself.

On the other hand, some people who do bring everything out in the open can be quite devastated on the surface, leading to all sorts of reactions—from tearful discussions to angry confrontations to wives or husbands hiring private detectives to confirm their worst fears and finally to divorce.

When Dee, the real estate investor, suspected her husband was cheating on her, she started playing detective.

I hated lying to my husband. But I felt I had to because I thought he was lying to me. So I tried calling his office or calling him when he was home, and then when he answered, I would hang up, because I just wanted to know if he was there. When he asked me sometimes about this the next day, asking me, "Did you try to call?" I would just say no. Though I'm not sure if he believed me either. So things started to get quite uncomfortable.

Eventually, as their relationship deteriorated, the affairs started to come out into the open. Her husband didn't seem to care whether she knew, so there was no more need to lie. She even saw some of his women come to the house, and finally he moved out entirely. The marriage was over, and so were the lies.

In other cases, marriages have been healed after a period of upset and turmoil following the revelation of the lie. Louanne Cole pointed out how this had occurred with one of her clients.

He had been having an affair because he needed variety in his sexual partners after 20 years of being married to one woman, who started to devalue the importance of sex in their relationship. However, he didn't want to disturb the marriage. But eventually, the affair was revealed when the husband of the other woman he was seeing became suspicious, taped a phone conversation between the lovers, and then played it to the wife.

One result of this was that the woman herself went through a period of renewed sexual activity with him to show him that she could do it. Then, proving herself and arousing his interest again, she pulled away. So it was her way of making him feel bad about what he had done. But then, gradually, with extended therapy, they have been repatching their 20-year marriage, in part because she was motivated to stay married to him for financial reasons.

In other cases, the revelation of the affair might in the long term actually be very healing for the original relationship. The result might seem paradoxical, but, as Scott observed, sometimes this can renew the partner's sexual interest in each other. As she observed:

The revelation of the affair can act like a wake-up call on not taking each other for granted any more. Also the feelings of jealousy can show the partners that they really care about each other.

So the revelation can be used in a positive way if people really have a good intention to make the relationship work again, although this kind of result is rare. Generally, people don't have the skills to deal with this situation. But if they can, then the discovery of the affair can act as a turning point to shake up the marriage, since trauma can lead to positive change. So possibly it could lead them to correct the problems in their relationship and move on to a better relationship and companionship, much deeper and much stronger than before. Though it will take work in dealing with the issues in the relationship to get to this point.

LIES TO THE OTHER MAN OR THE OTHER WOMAN

While such lies to the spouse are an inherent part of the secrecy and intrigue involved in any affair, very often there are lies to the other man or woman as well. Although the partners in an affair may be more honest with each other, because they have no formal responsibilities to each other or public images of a marital relationship to maintain, in many other cases their relationship is shrouded in lies.

One big lie, of course, is that the other person isn't married or is planning to get a divorce. When the partner in the affair finds out the truth, it can be devastating.

Blanche, the public relations executive, described having this experience several times when she had an affair. As she told me:

The first time I discovered this man I was seeing was lying to me, it was terrible. I had just graduated from high school, and I was dating this very tall, handsome medical student who was a basketball player, and I was very much in love. I thought everything was dandy. We had spoken about marriage.

And then one day I got a call from this woman who told me she was married to him and was having his baby. I was shocked. I couldn't believe it. Here is this man who was two-timing the woman he was married to while she was about to have his baby, and he was two-timing me, too.

I felt so hurt, and I cried and cried. It was so hard to break up with him, but of course, I did. I couldn't go on with the situation after that.

In a situation involving another man, she discovered the truth when she went to his apartment after several broken dates.

I wanted to see him to find out what was going on, so one night, I went to his apartment and sat outside until two in the morning. I just waited. And when he didn't come, I realized he was out all night. So I went home and about ten in the morning I called him on it. Well, he tried to cover his tracks and give some excuse why he was so late.

But I knew. I knew he had been cheating on his wife to be with me, but he had explained that was because he didn't love her and they just had this marriage of convenience. But now he was cheating on me, though I had come to expect him to be faithful. So it hurt me a lot, and after that I tried to work on finding him unattractive. If I couldn't have him completely outside of his relationship with his wife, I decided it was time to get him out of my life.

LIES WHEN THE MARRIAGE ENDS

Lies often come up in the marital relationship at the bitter end. Two types of lies are common—those used to get back at the ex- or soon-to-be-ex-spouse and those used to get more money.

Revenge lies express anger. Dick, the sales executive, described how one of his divorced friends told lies about his ex-wife to smear her reputation out of bitterness. As Dick commented:

He just wanted to hurt her. For instance, one time I went to a class reunion, and he and his ex-wife were both there, because they had gone to that school together. Well, he was going around telling everybody there that they should go get into her pants, because she was so easy. And that was a lie. He was really libeling and disparaging her, because he had lost her, so he wanted to put her down.

After her own divorce, Sarah, the educator, discovered that her former husband was lying about her to their children, now living with him and his new wife. As she explained:

He was just saying awful things about me, telling them I didn't really care about them, that I was being promiscuous with other people, things like that. He was really blowing things about me totally out of proportion.

So finally I called his wife and told her about this, and then I spoke to him. I told him: "I don't say things about you, and if the kids say anything disparaging about you, I try to help them see things from your point of view. So why are you doing this? Why do you feel you have a need to say bad things about me?"

Well after that, he didn't have much to say, and I thought I had made peace with him about this. But later, as the kids were growing up, I found out he was still doing this. I thought I had smoothed things over and we were friends again. But apparently we weren't. He was still feeling very angry about what happened, and I think his lies about me were his way to get this out.

As for the lies to get more money, some partners may simply do this out of greed, others because they feel their partner is not being fair to them, and the lie is their way of fighting back. This is what happened when Alison was going through what she described as "a really nasty" divorce. Her husband was "hateful and vengeful," and he was trying to give her as little as possible from the business they shared. So she used her own bluff to get him to give her a loan to buy a house she wanted. As Alison told me:

When my husband and I were married, we owned a small manufacturing company. And since I was the bookkeeper, as well as one of the co-owners, I knew what the business was worth—almost a million dollars. In fact, we had started with most of my money.

Then, when we got divorced, he was very unhappy and spiteful about this, and he tried to give me as little as he could. So he lied, claiming the business was only worth $200,000, and he had phony books, though I knew it was worth closer to $800,000.

However, I had the kid. He was just about four at the time, and my ex was worried that I was going to move out of the area and take the kid with me. So when I found out he was worried, I decided to use this information against him. This happened when I decided to buy a house, and I found I needed $25,000 for the down payment. I had ended up with a much smaller settlement than I should have gotten, only about $100,000, instead of $400,000, because of the way he lied. So I didn't have enough for the house, and I asked him for this extra amount. But he wasn't going to give it to me.

Well, that's when I decided to lie myself. So I told him that I wanted this money, and that all he had to do was to take a loan from the bank against the business, which would be easy for him to do. And I told him that if I didn't get this money to buy this house, I was moving. Well, I was bluffing.

But he bought my bluff, and so I got the money to put down to buy the house. And now it's worth three times what I paid for it, so that way I almost got back what he cheated me out of.

Then the business he cheated me out of got demolished in the recent San Francisco earthquake, so I feel that's a kind of karma or justification for what he did to me, too.

Usually, I don't like to lie. It's always been very important to me to be totally honest with people. But in this case, I feel proud of getting away with that lie to get the house. It felt so justified to do that because that was my only trump card. That lie was the only thing that I had to get a piece of what was mine.

Then, too, the lie was also for my son, because I wanted him to grow up in a nice neighborhood. So, yes, I'm quite proud of that lie and getting away with it.

CHAPTER 12

The Lies of Parents and Children

Parent–child relationships are peppered with lies. Likewise, children lie to each other, and the lies become more complex as they grow up. Commonly, children are taught very early not to tell a lie, and it's part of the tradition of religion and morality passed down from parent to child. Yet very young children begin to lie as well, sometimes because they experience lies from their parents and other adults or older children. Then, too, children soon discover the benefits of lying for much the same reason that adults do—to impress others, to avoid punishment or disapproval, or to get out of something they don't want to do.

So, early on, children begin to develop the patterns of lying they will continue to express in later life along the continuum from the model of absolute integrity to the frequent liar.

WHAT PARENTS TELL CHILDREN ABOUT LYING

The ideal of honesty has a long history, wrapped in notions of traditional morality and religion, with admonitions against lying derived from the Judeo-Christian tradition and from other religions. And there are all sorts of outside supports for this idea as well. For example, traditional stories such as Pinocchio, about the little boy whose nose grows long when he tells a lie, support the notion that the lie will be discovered and punished. Religious leaders convey this message, too—it's wrong to lie.

The people I spoke with pointed out how they had been given this message early: Don't lie; it's wrong to lie; the lie will be revealed. For example, Alison, the relationship counselor, said:

My parents made me afraid to lie. I don't remember specifically, but they led me to believe that something bad would come back and get me or something bad would happen. Somehow the lie would haunt me.

Don, the engineer, stated:

I recall my parents telling me I wasn't supposed to lie and my mother could tell by looking in my eyes if I was doing this. She really couldn't, but she claimed she could.

For Storm, the writer, there was always the threat of hell if the lie was serious enough.

They told me that lying was a sin, but if it was just a simple lie, I wouldn't go to hell. Instead, there would be purgatory, though it would have fire and damnation, but one could get out of it someday. But then, for a really serious lie, there might be no possibility. So I had that drilled into me when I was a child—lying was a sin, with the appropriate punishments for the lie.

While this message of "don't lie" may come through loud and clear, children very often may get a double message when they discover that their own parents lie.

Susannah, the financial planner, described this confusion:

I remember my parents telling me how it was wrong to lie, and they used stories to illustrate their point, such as the story of George Washington and the cherry tree.

But then, even though they expressed this ideal, they behaved differently. For instance, my mother lied all the time, and my older sister did, too. So perhaps that's why I tried to become exactly the opposite as I grew up. I thought what they were doing was so hypocritical and wrong.

WHEN PARENTS LIE

When do parents lie? Very often it's to guard their children by concealing information or opinions to protect their feelings or to keep inappropriate information from them. Then, too, parents may want to keep back painful information, such as a family secret, or conceal their disapproval. Or they may lie simply to get their kids to do something. Parents commonly justify their lies to children as being in the best interests of their kids, although again and again, the people I spoke to told me that, however painful, they really would prefer to know the truth.

Lies to Protect Feelings

Parents may lie to protect their kids' feelings by telling them they are doing something better than they really are or by not sharing a negative opinion. The goal is to help their kids feel better about themselves and build self-esteem, and the parents I spoke to felt quite justified in doing this. After all, these were helpful, benevolent lies.

Stan, the high school teacher, described how he did this with his daughter:

I'm not always absolutely truthful with my kids, particularly my daughter. She is really very competent, and I get angry sometimes that she doesn't do more academically than she can. But I try to keep that back.

For instance, one time she said: "You know, I only made a C," and I said: "Well, that's all right. You did the best you can." But I know that was a kind of a lie, because I really think she should be getting a B, because I know she could do it if she tried.

Stan continued:

I told her the lie because she's easily discouraged. She has two academic parents and a super-bright genius brother, and that's really hard on her.

Thus, though she is perfectly competent and could do better, she has decided that there's nothing wrong with a C, which is average. She feels more comfortable thinking of herself as average, so she doesn't have to feel she is competing with others in the family. She really is above average because she tests above average, and she could be above average if she wanted to. But much of the time she doesn't, and so her mother and I try not to press that because it just makes it worse. We just let her think we think what she is doing is okay, though really we think it's not.

Lies to Conceal Opinions or Disapproval to Avoid Undue Influence

Sometimes parents lie, particularly as children get older, to conceal their opinions or disapproval of certain behaviors to avoid a conflict or to influence their kids in a choice they feel the kids should make themselves. While some children might appreciate the freedom from parental opinions, others felt a sense of distance at not knowing what their parents thought.

Stephen, the writer, commented:

My parents often wouldn't tell me the truth or share their ideas about how they felt about what I was doing or what I had done or who I was living with or that sort of thing. They just seemed to find it difficult to tell me what they thought or share their feelings. I think it's because they wanted to keep the peace. They didn't want to rock the boat or get me upset if we had different ideas about something. But I really would have liked to know.

Lies to Conceal Inappropriate Information

Parents also may lie to keep their child from knowing something they think he or she shouldn't. This can be something that puts the parents or the family in a bad light; at other times they just feel the children are too young or that this is inappropriate information for them.

With very young children, the Santa Claus or Easter Bunny tales fall into this category. Parents want their children to believe in this kind of childhood fantasy, and they don't want to be the ones to break the bubble of childhood innocence.

On a more serious note, parents may conceal the reality of death from their children. Alison, the counselor, recalled that her first experience of being lied to occurred when she was four years old and her grandmother died.

But nobody told me she died. My parents just kept me in the dark. They just gave me excuses about why I couldn't see my grandmother, why she couldn't come to visit. And I didn't find out until years later about what really occurred.

Did Alison believe the lie to be a good one? "I felt like they were keeping something from me, and I felt helpless, like I didn't have any control."

Another such example occurred for Raphael, the healer, when his parents tried to conceal their experience of the Holocaust. His father had gone through the horrors of a concentration camp, and Raphael seemed to think that his parents should have told him about this so he could better understand his own background and heritage. But they held it back to protect him, as well as themselves, from the memories of such suffering.

Still other concealment lies concern the parents' sexuality, particularly when the children are young. Parents just don't want the children to know about this, and may feel uncomfortable talking about sex generally as well. So the lie or denial becomes a handy way of covering up.

Frances described how her own parents used these gentle lies.

When I was a kid I remember that my parents always lied about this. For example, they would say they were so tired that they had to go to bed at 8 o'clock when I was a little kid. But later in life, you learn that there's more in bed than that you're dead-tired at 8 o'clock.

Joyce, a therapist and mother I spoke with, felt it appropriate to disguise or evade to avoid giving young children inappropriate sexual information, using her own experience with her three- and five-year-old daughters as an example. As she commented:

I basically regard myself as an honest person, but I've used disguise or evasion with my young daughters to keep information I think is inappropriate from them.

For instance, say I am in a public lavatory with my daughter, and she says: "Oh, is this where they put the diapers?" I'll say: "Yes, it's for babies' diapers," even though it's used for something else, for used tampons, because I don't think it's timely for her to know this. There will be a time when I will tell her all about the subject, but at age three or five, I don't think it's appropriate.

Another example might be explaining other inappropriate or taboo subjects, such as where babies come from. I'm not going to get involved in some long and complicated explanation of sex at this point. It's not something a child of that age needs to know. So I might say something quite honest, such as the baby is pushed out from "down there." But I wouldn't go into any big explanation about the mechanism of what happens. So instead, rather than do this, I might evade or disguise or tell white lies. I try to give out the appropriate information and be honest about that. But beyond that I think it's appropriate to lie and evade.

Lies to Get a Child to Do Something
or Not Do Something

Finally, another big category of parent lies is made up of those little lies they tell to get their child to do or not do something. For parents, such lies may seem like clever tricks to help shape desired behavior, but they can seem quite hurtful for the child, as well as providing a model of deceit for the child.

Sandra, the marketing consultant, ended up going to the college her parents wanted her to attend because of the way her parents used deception to guide her choice. Later this recognition contributed to her growing distance from them. As she explained:

When I was young, I always had this fascination with the West. There was something about its old mystique, the myth of the frontier, the romance of the cowboy, the image of the old farmstead, that helped to intrigue me, even though all this was long past in the modern day. Also, I had long listened to country-and-western hits on the radio; so in many ways I felt this connection with the West.

Thus, when it was time to go to college, I wanted to go to a western college, though we lived on the East Coast. And my parents actually did take me visiting to many colleges in the Midwest, as well as to schools in New England and New York.

In the end, there was a school I decided I wanted to go to in Minnesota, because when we were there I had really liked hearing stories about the early frontier days there. It had many stories about the escapades of the old outlaws, and I loved the countryside, too.

But I also won a scholarship to a school in the East, and my parents really wanted me to go there, because they would save some money. So they worked on convincing me. And one of the arguments they used was that this was really a western college, because it was so close to Ohio. So they played upon my old fantasies and my lack of real knowledge of U.S. geography to finally convince me.

And I did go there, though I always felt like it was the wrong choice, like I didn't belong. And for a long time after that, I resented my parents for tricking me into making this choice, because they really wanted me near to them and wanted to save the money. Eventually, I hated it so much that I finally ended up leaving and breaking away to go to California. And that helped me break away from my parents, too.

WHEN CHILDREN LIE

Whether children learn it from their parents or do it for other reasons, they learn to lie very early. According to psychologist Paul Ekman, author of *Why Kids Lie*[1] and numerous articles about children and lying, by the age of four, or even earlier, "children can and will lie—not simply making excuses or confusing fantasy with reality, but deliberately attempt to mislead."[2] According to Ekman, the usual reason is to avoid punishment, commonly by claiming "I didn't do it."

Initially, parents may have this notion of childhood innocence. They may think of their young children as "sweet innocents, uncorrupted speakers of pure truth," and they like to think their own children wouldn't lie or try to deceive them, according to Ekman.[3] But the truth is that children discover sooner than parents think that they can get away with their lies at least some of the time, and as they get older they get better and better at it at the same time that they become better at detecting lies. They learn to control the sound of their voices and the looks on their faces and avoid the obvious inconsistencies or obviously untrue alibis. They also tend to feel less guilt about lying, particularly by the time they reach adolescence. One reason that guilt may subside, despite the early admonitions against lying, is that children simply get used to lying more; they become desensitized to it and increasingly discover that others around them, regardless of any moral principles against lying, are lying, too. Then, too, the decline in guilt may be related to the rejection of parental values that comes in adolescence. As Ekman suggests:

One reason adolescents are more successful liars is that they feel less guilt about lying to their parents or teachers. Rejecting parental values—noticing the clay feet that authority stands upon—is a common form of rebellion. For some teenagers, lying may be one way of establishing their own identity, of achieving independence—a necessary task of adolescence.[4]

Lies to Escape Punishment

The people I spoke to recalled plenty of examples of the lies they told when young to try to avoid making their parents angry or escape being punished when they knew they had done wrong. Usually they were caught, because they weren't very good at lying, or they felt bad, because they still were impressed with the traditional childhood admonition that lying is wrong.

Stephen, the writer, recalled taking a music box from his mother when he was about four or five and then denying that he took it.

I didn't really steal the music box. I just really liked it and I took it. Then I was caught and punished. I tried to deny that I took it, but my mother didn't believe me, and punished me. I'm not sure if that was for lying or for taking the box.

In Sarah the educator's case, the crime was taking candy from a store, though eventually she felt so guilty that she finally admitted what she did.

I was about six or seven, and at first I acted like nothing had happened. But then I started to feel so guilty that I told my mom. Then she had her boyfriend take me and her back to the store so I could confess what I did. I felt relieved when I did it, but it was also a horrible feeling, too, because I felt like such a criminal for what I did.

Many times these lies were caught, but in many other cases they were not, often because the parents did not want to think their child had lied. For example, Dick, the sales executive, described how he got away with many lies because his parents thought of him as a "good" boy.

They didn't catch me when I lied about all kinds of things. For example, they would tell me to stay home, and I would go away, and then I would tell them I stayed home.

Or they would ask me who broke a window, and I would tell them somebody else broke it, though I did, and other things like that to escape punishment.

But they tended to believe me, because they had instilled in me the idea that it's wrong to lie, that lying is a sin, and you had to confess it. Well, I would confess it, and I did feel better after that. Also, when I went to confession, I would promise not to do it again. But then again, sometimes I did. I would be better for a while, but then something would happen and I would lie again.

Some kids evade discovery of both their lies and their transgressions by becoming better at lying. Don, the engineer, and a friend played a prank on a third boy and ably denied it. As he described this early adventure:

I was about five or six, playing a game with another boy, and we saw another boy who we didn't care for very much who was playing by myself in a hole in the ground. He had taken his shoes off and left them outside the hole, so we decided to play a trick on him and we grabbed his shoes and we hid them.

Soon he came out of the hole and he couldn't find his shoes, and so he went and told his mother. Then his mother told my mother that we had been playing nearby, and my mother asked me: "Did you take his shoes?" So I said: "No, of course not, in no way would we do this."

Then we offered to help and we wandered around looking for his shoes, and finally we found them as if we had come across them by accident. And that was one of the times when my mother believed me. In fact, I remember her looking closely at me when I told her, as if she was looking for a sign that I wasn't telling the truth. But I could tell she couldn't tell whether I was or not. It felt a little scary at first, when I wasn't sure whether she would believe me or not. But when she did, I felt a little more confident that I could do this, that I was able to trick my mother in this way.

Thus, while a lie might be caught, overall the people I spoke to seemed to find they or others who lied were able to get away with it or at least avoid any punishment if they were found out, thus perhaps setting the stage for more lies. In fact, in some cases, their parents might even overlook the lie or respond to its revelation by being willing to help.

Lies to Conceal Unapproved Activities

Kids also learn to use lies to cover up unapproved activities. For younger kids, common lies involve homework or other responsibilities. As kids get older, all sorts of lies sprout up around, as one person I interviewed put it, "drugs, sex, and rock 'n' roll."

Stan, the high school teacher, described some of the dubious excuses he had become used to hearing from his kids.

They were supposed to be home by a certain time, but then they would be late, and they would say something like: "The teacher kept us after school." One time my daughter told me: "I had to go downtown with my friend. She wasn't feeling well." Another time my son said he stayed at school to watch the game. But there was no sick friend, there was no game. They just wanted to do something else.

These lies often worked, because even if exposed, Stan, like other parents, might let them go or give a simple admonishment because confronting the lie would be too much trouble, create too much conflict. Dealing with such lies became a little like dealing with brushfires—stamping them out if they became too serious, looking the other way if they didn't, and knowing they would probably start up again.

Teenagers start testing their independence and experiment with all sorts of things that, for parents, are forbidden or taboo. Alison, the counselor, had many such occasions to lie when she was 16 and wild about a boy. As she described it:

I had a boyfriend in another state when I lived in New York, and we had a very erotic, intimate relationship. I knew my parents wouldn't have understood, since I was only sixteen, so when I went to see him, I would say that I was going to stay with a girlfriend, but I made up this friend. Then, I would go to stay in his apartment for the weekend, and my parents never found out.

I did it because I have a very strong will, and when I really want something to happen, I'll make it happen no matter what.

In fact, I managed to see him one time when I was punished for something else. I was locked in my room, and my father said: "You cannot go out. You have to stay in your room." But I found a way to get out. Maybe I described some emergency that happened to my friend or something like that. I don't remember exactly. But I did get out and I got to see my friend.

Similarly, one of Stan's teenage daughters lied to conceal her drinking.

She was in high school, and one day she came home with her two front teeth chipped. When I asked what happened, she told me: "I slipped on the kitchen floor at my friend's house," and I knew that she had been there and there had been a party.

But the reason she slipped was because she had been drunk, although I didn't realize that at the time. Instead, she just said she had slipped while talking to someone in the kitchen, and all of her friends were backing her up. So I just believed her at the time.

I similarly believed her when she said she was working on her studies, although I later realized she was doing a lot of fooling around with guys at school and cutting classes to do this. I just wanted to believe her, though later I realized there were many signs that this just wasn't true, such as her lack of success academically. But I just looked the other way for a long time, and eventually, as she got older, she did straighten up.

Other lies might be used to conceal illegal, immoral, deviant, forbidden, or socially unacceptable activities in one's own community, such as using marijuana or other drugs, having sex, being gay, or dating someone from a different racial, ethnic, or religious group when one's parents object to this. Also, lies may be told because a child has a different value system than his or her parents.

For example, Nancy, a business consultant, had this kind of experience when she was drawn toward going to church, although her family wasn't religious. As she told me:

When I was growing up, I lied about a lot of the standard things kids do just for survival.

Then there were other things I ended up lying about because there were things my parents didn't believe in, such as going to church. My parents weren't religious at all, and they had no idea that I decided I wanted to do this. But I felt I needed this in my life from the time I was a little kid, and so I would lie and tell them I was going somewhere else, when I was really going to church.

In fact, I had myself baptized when I was eight years old, but they never knew it.

Also, they had no idea that I spent a great deal of time with another family which really became like my real family to me. I just felt very alienated from my own family. So I retreated into a kind of fantasy world, and then I was drawn to this other family. But of course I felt I couldn't tell my parents I was drawn to this other kind of world, this other kind of life, so I just didn't. I kept it hidden and didn't tell them, so they never knew.

Because fear and uncertainty can lead to lies, some therapists encourage families to be more open and yielding in sharing their concerns.

Sexologist Dr. Louanne Cole commented:

I think that if families can talk more openly and candidly about anything, and not have taboo subjects that we don't talk about or taboo emotions that we don't dare to express, such as it's not okay to be angry, it's not okay to be sad, it's not okay to do this or that, then there can be less censorship and lying.

For example, parents or other adults may make the assumption that a young child shouldn't hear about sexual things.

So when kids have questions about sex or these other things, they don't dare to ask mom and dad. Instead they try to ask a friend or find a magazine or they get some misinformation rather than ask their parents. Or if they try to bring up the subject, their parents may ask where they learned about that, and tell them, "Don't you dare talk about that subject again."

So that tells the kid never to bring up that subject again, and that shuts off communication or it leads to cover-ups and lies. If parents have a more candid attitude, that can lead to candor on the part of the child.

Lies to Impress

Children also may use lies to impress and build themselves up, or conceal their weaknesses—just like adults. For example, instead of talking about having large amounts of money or property to inflate their worth, kids talk about things like having a better toy, being more popular with playmates than they are, or having some special magical powers. But the basic impulse to show off and increase one's self-esteem seems the same.

Raphael, the healer, used lies to cover up his loneliness, anger, and feelings of abandonment when he was a child. But as he got older, he learned to bring such feelings out, and he felt better about being able to acknowledge the truth with others. It helped him feel closer to the people who were important in his life.

Lies may also be a way to cover up the little childhood thefts that children may resort to in order to impress or they may be a way to get even or get revenge when they think someone has done something to hurt them.

Lies to Help and Protect Others

Children learn early on to use lies to help and protect others, often with their parents showing them how and when to use such lies to conceal their feelings instead of coming out with the real but hurtful or discomfiting truth.

Sandy learned the virtues of being less than forthright about things after she managed to thoroughly mortify her parents. As she described it:

I was about three or four at the time, and my parents had some of their friends and relatives over for a dinner. Well, while they were having dinner, I happened to wander up to the bathroom, and saw this little boy in there. Well, when I got back, I made this announcement that my daddy's penis was much bigger than little Jimmy's.

Well, needless to say, my parents and everybody else were really shocked, and afterward my parents talked to me to tell me there were things I shouldn't say even if they were true. It just wasn't polite to say such things, and then later I learned there were many other things I shouldn't say.

Parents may advise children on what they should say to cover up their real feelings or hide the truth to smooth over social relations, such as telling someone he or she looks good when the child doesn't think so or acting as if he likes the person when he does not. For example, I remember how my mother used to tell me things such as: "Now be nice to your cousin," or "Tell your aunt you liked her cake." It was part of what she called learning the social graces. Similarly, Blanche, the public relations executive, covered up her real feelings about her sister, who was very much overweight. As she explained:

I just learned early that it's good to protect people's feelings. For example, even though my sister was very fat, if she asked me: "Do I look pretty?" I would say: "Yes, you look beautiful to me," because I didn't want to tell her what I really thought. I wanted to make her feel better.

So it's no wonder that people continue to lie in social situations and to protect and help others when they become adults. It's something they learned very early when they were children.

Teenage Dating Lies

As kids become older, there are the familiar going-out and dating lies—focused around gaining more independence from parental and establishment rules.

The ID lies, for example, are probably quite familiar. To be able to drink or get into places when they are too young, kids try to pass for being older, and some even get a fake ID. Bartenders or doormen may be willing to go along with the pretense, as long as the person has the paperwork or appears old enough, because that means one more paying customer.

Typical dating lies are probably also quite familiar. They revolve around manipulating the dating game to get desired dates and get out of unwanted ones. For example, while males come up with come-ons to get dates or sex (e.g., "Of course, I love you" or "Everyone else is doing it"), females find ways to come up with believable excuses to gracefully turn someone down.

Stan, the high school teacher, recalled a number of these:

I remember a couple of times using a lie to get out of a date. For example, there were times when I decided to cancel a date for some reason but I didn't want to say it, so it was easier to lie. Some examples might be that I just decided afterward that I didn't want to go out with the girl or something came up that I wanted to do more. But I didn't know how to say that nicely, so I would just make up an excuse.

On the other hand, I knew there were many times that girls lied to me. For instance, some girl might say she couldn't go out with me because of some reason, but I would know it was a lie. It just didn't sound right or there would be something in her tone. But I figured, that was the way it was, and I didn't make a big deal about getting what I thought might be a phony excuse.

Sandy, the marketing consultant, recalled strategies she learned from her mother and friends:

I always felt uncomfortable saying no when some boy asked me out whom I didn't like. But of course you don't tell someone "No, I don't want to see you because I don't like you." So I learned very early to give excuses and even be creative.

For example, I would say I was busy, already had previous plans, had to baby-sit, or something like that. And then if he became persistent, I would find other reasons why I couldn't, such as I promised someone else to do this or that.

But sometimes this kind of approach really did backfire, because I remember once liking this boy who called me to ask me out several times, when I really did have to baby-sit. We had just had a fight and had broken up and he wanted to get back together. Well, he asked me about going out again on two different nights, and when I told him about the baby-sitting, he just got mad. I tried to explain it was really true and I did want to see him. But he didn't believe me. And even though I called him back saying I could cancel one of the evenings by telling the people I was sick, it was too late. He was too hurt and didn't want to go out with me anymore.

CHAPTER 13

Lying to Oneself

While most lies are designed to deceive others, people also lie to themselves—and for much the same reasons: to avoid some unpleasant truth or achieve some desired gain (or at least imagine one has achieved it).

For example, a man with a drinking problem may lie to himself that he doesn't have the problem. A woman with a personality flaw may pretend that she doesn't have this and find other more acceptable reasons for explaining why others don't have much contact with her. Someone with great dreams but little ability to realize them may fantasize that he can turn them into reality or imagine he already has. Such lies may turn into what appear to be lies to others, as the person acts on his own false beliefs and draws others into his reality, such as the travel promoter described in the introduction who came to believe in the fantasy of his travel programs. At the extreme end, such self-lies can turn into delusions, schizophrenias, and paranoias, which can lead to the mental hospital.

To some extent all of us lie to ourselves, if only to dream about possibilities. We enjoy the fantasy of getting away from everyday reality. Sometimes, if we act on these lies, we may be able to turn them into reality—such as in the Horatio Alger myth of a great desire that becomes true. However, between these extremes are the bulk of the self-lies that are used for self-protection and gain as a kind of personal barrier against truth that might disrupt one's view of oneself or the world.

Here the differences in patterns of lying for different types of liars may be hard to determine, since self-lies are often not revealed. After all, if one lies successfully to oneself, who will know? However, it may be that the models of absolute integrity and the straight shooters are more likely to lie to themselves in the event they do tell lies to others, because they don't want to admit to themselves that they have lied. Or they may try to explain away the lie, based on claiming they didn't say anything and that the other person just got the wrong impression—but that's a lie of omission. Or they may redefine the little social lies as something other than lies, because they are designed to make someone feel better.

I got into a number of discussions during radio interviews about these finer points of when something was a lie with some listeners who claimed they never lied to anyone—which I think is impossible based on defining a lie as anything which isn't the truth, including misrepresentations or omissions about something that should be revealed or that give a wrong impression. Repeatedly they sought to claim that small lies or omissions weren't lies, and they were fervent and determined to hold onto the image of themselves as completely honest people.

Thus, such models of integrity and straight shooters may also have more of a reason to lie to themselves to preserve their self-image of integrity and avoid feelings of guilt for lying. By contrast, the pragmatic fibbers. Pinocchios, and frequent liars may be more likely to level with themselves, because they see themselves in more pragmatic terms—so if they have to lie, that's just the way things are. It's perfectly fine to misrepresent, exaggerate, and otherwise modify or cover up the truth as long as it's practical to do so—so why lie about doing this?

WHY THE SELF-LIE?

Self-lies are self-protection, and they are, according to psychologist Daniel Goleman, who wrote a book about this subject, *Vital Lies, Simple Truths: The Psychology of Self-Deception*, a basic strategy used by the individual to protect against anxiety.[1] His main thesis is that the mind can protect itself against anxiety by dimming awareness; this mechanism creates a blind spot: a zone of blocked attention and self-deception. Such blind spots occur at each major level of behavior from the psychological to the social.[2] In other words, we hide things from ourselves to keep ourselves from getting upset about something, which parallels some of our reasons for lying to others—to keep from upsetting our social relationships by smoothing them over with a lie.

According to Goleman, this use of self-deception through dimmer awareness has deep biological and psychological roots, and it operates much in the same way that the brain acts to relieve pain, by inducing numbness. As Goleman puts it:

Whether physical or mental in origin, pain registers in the brain via a system that can dampen its signals. In the brain's design the relief of pain is built into its perception.[3]

In particular, the brain uses a pain-numbing response in an emergency, which helps to induce calm. It's a life-saving strategy, Goleman points out, because once the individual is numbed and calm, he can better assess the situation.[4] While this kind of response developed early in evolution to help the individual survive physical dangers and pain, Goleman suggests this same kind of response occurs in reaction to psychological pain—such as an "affront to one's self-esteem, apprehension, or loss."[5]

The Forms Self-Denial and Lying Take

In turn, this denial and lying can take various forms. According to Goleman, citing a list of denial mechanisms described by psychiatrist Mardi Horowitz, we can deny in these various ways:

- Avoiding associations, so we short-circuit the usual connections with something said or experienced because we don't want to experience them;
- Becoming numb, so we turn off our emotions and don't feel the appropriate emotions;
- Showing a flattened emotional response, so we constrict the usual expectable emotions we might feel;
- Dimming attention, so we avoid focusing clearly on information, including thoughts, feelings, and physical sensations that might bring pain;
- Going into a daze, so we cloud our alertness and avoid recognizing the significance of events we don't want to acknowledge;
- Constricting our thoughts, so we don't explore the likely avenues of meaning beyond the obvious one;
- Experiencing memory failure, so we are unable to recall events or their details, or we just selectively recall what happened again to blot out painful information;
- Disavowing what is so, which involves saying or thinking that obvious meanings are not so, because we want to avoid them;
- Blocking through fantasy, so we avoid reality or its implications by having fanciful thoughts of what might have been or could be.[6]

When we do deny, we aren't aware of it. Instead, the mind scans, filters, and selects information, and it does all this outside our conscious awareness.[7]

What information do we deny or deceive ourselves about? One big source is any information that threatens the self by not supporting how one feels about oneself, and therefore threatens self-esteem, according to Goleman, because such a threat is a major source of anxiety. The process is equivalent to the numbing reaction in animals. But whereas animals usually experience stress when their life is threatened, for humans, a challenge to self-esteem is enough to trigger anxiety. And then that anxiety triggers the denial self-deception response.[8] For example, the mind starts selectively remembering events, or reinterpreting and slanting them.[9]

Lying about One's Own Abilities or One's Business

One big source of self-lying concerns abilities, skills, and success in business, because ideas about accomplishment and achievement go to the heart of our self-esteem. If we do well, we feel good about ourselves. But if not, we feel bad, so there can be a great incentive to lie to oneself about personal failures.

Business consultant Robert Middleton described how he noticed many of his clients had this problem. They at first didn't want to face the facts that their business wasn't doing well or that they were making key mistakes. But as things continued to spiral downward, they finally had to admit they needed help. As Middleton observed:

A lot of people in business sometimes hold onto the belief that something has to be such and such a way. But it's not really true, and that can limit or destroy their business.

For example, someone might think, I can only charge this amount. But who says so? Maybe he can really charge more. Or again, maybe someone thinks he should sell this, but the market isn't really there for it. So he just thinks he should try harder, when in fact, he should give that up and not try at all.

Then, too, people can have self-limiting beliefs or beliefs that they can do more than they can. And either can hurt the business. On the one side, I think the self-limiting beliefs come out of fear. A person doesn't think that he can do all he can. But on the other hand, a person can build himself up so much that he ultimately falls. So there can be these two kinds of lies—lying about how great we really are or lying about how small we really are, and either can be damaging.

Besides leading to failure, other kinds of self-lies can make one miserable because one is doing more or something different than one wants. And this can lead to conflicts with others when one doesn't face up to what's really going on or what others need and want.

THE EFFECTS OF SELF-LYING IN RELATIONSHIPS

Self-lying can also lead to problems in relationships because the reality of the relationship is out of step with what is wanted.

A good example of this is what happens in the codependency relationship, according to therapist Rose White, who specializes in codependency and addiction issues. In the codependency relationship, which is especially common in cases where one person is an alcoholic or addict, the partner—the codependent—modifies his or (usually) her life to adjust to the afflicted partner. But very often, this adjustment is based on living a lie or self-delusion, because the codependent is not seeing the truth about the partner or is denying his or her own needs or truths. As White commented:

Codependency is a relationship in which we are not telling the truth about what our needs are. Usually, in the codependent relationship, there's a form of denial about what is going on presently, what has gone on in one's past, what has gone on in one's family life.

Typically, the codependent is denying his needs and feelings. Emotional responses become flattened out, or reactions are projected onto something else, because the person is trying to deny or avoid recognizing what the actual situation is. He or she is trying to elude the truth. The person is lying to him or herself, though there's no awareness of this lying. It's not conscious and is used as a form of self-defense.

White gave examples of how such self-lying or denial could alter the course of the relationship.

I have some clients that talk about how they have this wonderful, happy family, when that's not true at all. Or they say they have a terrific marriage when that's not true. They're just kidding themselves.

But such lying is a form of protection, so they don't have to deal with what the true issues are, because many times, dealing with the true issues means you have to do something about them.

For instance, sometimes, if you face the facts, this might mean you have to leave your partner. Sometimes looking at the true issues may mean recognizing that you have denied yourself for your whole life for other people, and then you're left with this vacant, empty feeling, because you realize you have left yourself out.

Also, looking at the true issues might mean recognizing that you didn't have a happy childhood, that you had a miserable one, and you were never able to trust your parents because they never really protected you the way they were supposed to do.

Such recognitions can be very painful, and may mean the person has to do something about them to change them. And for many people that's hard, so they don't want to look.

Also, as White pointed out, people in codependency relationships might be deluding themselves about control issues and find it especially difficult to deal with them. She explained:

Codependency can range from being a good, helpful human being to being totally compelled to helping other people and controlling their life. And often, people lose sight of who's really in control.

For example, someone in a codependent relationship with an alcoholic may feel like she is keeping control, because she is the sober one. But in reality, what is happening is that she is being controlled by the other person's behavior.

So in dealing with codependents, a key aspect of therapy is helping the other person not only become aware of how he or she is deluding herself but in how to gain or regain control.

Other types of relationships may harbor self-delusion and denial, leading to anger and conflict. White described another couple she was seeing:

For eighteen years, everything has been seemingly wonderful. They've had what has seemed like a great marriage. But what has happened is that for eighteen years, she has gone along with everything that he has asked, according to her, and all of a sudden, she started realizing and admitting to herself that over all this time she has been denying herself things she's wanted.

What sorts of things? White continued:

Friends, relationships with other women, for example. The family unit was so important to her and her husband that she would do everything for the family.

For instance, her husband and son were involved in some male-dominated sport, and she went along with her husband and son in supporting them in this. But in reality she wasn't that interested in this activity and felt left out, and her involvement in all their interests cut out her own.

So her husband, too, is upset and surprised, because he never knew what she really wanted, because she concealed it from him, since she was concealing it from herself. So now the healing involves bringing her real feelings out, discovering who she really is and wants, because she's concealed that part of herself from herself for so long.

LYING TO ONESELF ABOUT PERSONAL PROBLEMS AND LIMITATIONS

Self-delusion can be especially common when one has a personal problem or limitation one wants to avoid, especially a habit or addiction. Self-lies, such as "I don't have a habit," "I don't have an addiction," or "I can stop whenever I want" can help protect the individual from accepting an uncomfortable truth.

Storm, the writer, experienced this with his own drinking problem. Eventually things got so bad and he got so much input from his friends that he had to face the problem. As he described it:

My liquor problem got so far along that I couldn't deny it anymore. It was so obvious. I was turning yellow. I had trouble walking straight. I wasn't even drunk when this was happening. There was a continuous effect. Then, too, I was always sneaking a drink, and the pattern started to show to my friends.

It can be easy to be able to deceive one person. You can just slough off their complaints with some explanations or excuses. But when you try to do this with a lot of people, and they get together and talk about this, and they all tell you they know, then you know you've been nailed.

So eventually, I came to realize this and decided to go into a clinic to get over it. So that was for the best. But I felt bad that I had to get to that point, because I could have corrected the problem long before, if only I had the guts to face it when it first started happening. And then I also felt bad that I had been deceiving my friends into thinking everything was okay with me when it wasn't. At first, I guess I was successful, because I was lying to myself, too. And that makes it easier to lie to other people, when you actually end up believing it yourself, that you don't have a problem. But I did.

However, I finally came to recognize this, and I also came to realize that at a certain point you can't lie to yourself any more, because you're only fooling yourself. And eventually, if you do that long enough, you can destroy yourself, too. So at that point, I had to face what was true, and that's when I knew I had to change.

OVERCOMING THE SELF-LIE

One of the big problems with these self-lies is they can turn out to be even more devastating to the individual than the conscious lies to others, because they have the power to hurt the individual in two ways. First, he may hurt himself because he is not aware of his own lies and he may act on this false notion of what is true, with harmful results. Second, the individual who is acting or telling untruths that he is not aware of may end up having conflicts with others because of these lies. Plus, others may imagine he is untruthful as well.

How does a person overcome the lies to the self? Some of the therapists I spoke with emphasized the importance of making the individual aware of them. They pointed out that when a person was lying to himself or his therapist in treatment, the therapist could not help him in that area; it was necessary to first get to the truth and uncover and overcome the lie. But it could take a lot of personal work to do this because the person might be afraid of facing the truth.

Michael Gelbart, a therapist specializing in a combined mental and body approach to healing, observed:

Often, what a person says is just the tip of the iceberg to what is really going on in him or her, and he may not be aware of what this is. Thus, the person may not be consciously lying when I work with him and he hasn't told me some important thing about his life. In some cases, the person may just not think it's important and so doesn't say it. But in other cases, the person may be scared of saying what this is. Or the fear may be so deep that the person isn't even aware of how and what he really feels.

The only way I can help my clients is for them to tell me what is really going on for them. Often, even though a person may be sharing a lot, there's still a lot that is held back, because of all of the protections and fears, some of which are conscious, some of which are not. There are some things that clients may not be ready to reveal to me or themselves.

What sorts of things? Gelbart had a few suggestions:

Sometimes what is blocked are things the person is ashamed of, things that show him in a bad light, or maybe something he thinks is terrifying, hateful, or wrong about himself. Perhaps a person may be afraid of his or her own feelings in dealing with something if it comes to the surface, such as might be the case for someone who has been abused as a child. He or she might be afraid to say something for fear of not being believed, since many people aren't when they first reveal this. Or the person might fear that he'll be humiliated, shamed, or laughed at. For whatever reason he or she may hold this back.

At first this holding back may be conscious. But then it might also become repressed, so the person even denies this happened and the repression of something he doesn't want to face turns into the lie.

Rose White worked with clients with a codependency problem who were lying to themselves about their relationship. One of the first steps to help them was to get them to be aware of what they were doing, including the double messages they were sending themselves, so they could overcome them. As she commented:

All of us have been trained to give double messages to some extent. We were trained to not tell the truth in certain circumstances, to tell little white lies, to be nice even when we didn't feel nice, to smile when we didn't feel like smiling.

Well, when you are consciously doing that and in control of the process, that's one story. That can be healthy because then the person is coming from a place of choice. He or she knows what he or she is doing. But when a person continually denies his real feelings and thoughts, there's a problem.

Thus, one key to a successful therapy is to help make the person conscious of what's real for him so he can be responsible for his own life. He can make the choices he wants, because he is aware of what those choices are.

To get to this point might be quite difficult because of the individual's resistance to looking at the problem. Much of therapy might involve helping to support the person in looking at this painful past so he or she can face it and move on. For example, say the person has created self-delusions to cover up fears and inadequacies dating from childhood. A therapist might work with the person this way, according to White:

Say the person is lying to himself as a form of protection to keep his sanity, say because he was neglected or abused in his childhood or because his parents simply weren't there for him.

In the therapeutic process, what may happen is some of these truths may start emerging. Now, as things start opening up and revealing themselves, it may feel like a horror story. Because the process is like opening Pandora's box in some way. Well, that's when people truly need to have a support system around them, and that's when it's very helpful working with a therapist or perhaps a support group.

Then, too, it can be useful to have this outside support, because as a person goes through recovery in a codependent situation, the other partner may do everything he or she can to subvert this change, even though they may not be aware of what they are doing. It's like the wife who decides to go on a diet, and the husband brings her a box of chocolates to subvert her efforts, to keep her the way she has always been. So the person gets a double message.

Thus, in any therapy, it's important to look at the whole family system any person is involved in as well as the way they may have been deluding themselves, because the family is a system, and any system maintains itself by seeking a form of homeostasis or balancing itself out.

As a result, if one person changes in a family, the family will do what it can to pull that person back, to keep them the way they have been before. Thus, it's necessary to let the client know that people may not like them changing, may not like them giving up their past self-lies, because this change is going to make the other people uncomfortable. So they have to work on working out these adjustments with others as they let go of their lies. And all this can be a difficult process—not only facing the truth, but also maneuvering through this process of change that the truth brings in its wake.

CHAPTER 14

The Strategy of Deceiving and Perceiving

Why is lying so common? Are people who lie simply good at deceiving? Or are people who are lied to poor at perceiving? And what can be done to deal with lying? How can people recognize when someone is lying? How do people learn how and when to use a lie when it might seem justified, such as to keep someone from knowing information that may be harmful to him?

And how can you better tell when someone is lying to you? As you read the following discussion, you might keep in mind the basic difference in telling when those least likely to lie (the models of absolute integrity and the straight shooters) and those more likely to lie (the pragmatic fibbers, Pinocchios, and frequent liars). Generally, the former will be more likely to give away signs of lying, because they lie less and feel more anxious or guilty about telling a lie. By contrast, the latter will be less likely to give away the lie, because they are more practiced in telling lies more frequently and they feel relatively little or no guilt or anxiety in telling the lie itself—they are more concerned about the potential for being caught. In short, the former are more likely to be revealers, the latter concealers when it comes to finding clues and cues to detect the lie.

THE SUCCESS OF DECEPTION

Lying is common because, in general, the ability to deceive is better than the ability to perceive. In other words, lying works because people more often will be able to get away with it than people will be able to recognize the lie.

This development is linked to the evolution of lying as a survival and defense mechanism discussed earlier. To briefly recap here, researchers have found that the ability to deceive can help an organism survive, so the genetic capability for deception has evolved through natural selection. As psychologist Charles

Bond and others point out, for hundreds of generations, those who are the most cunning have left more offspring, while those who are less cunning have left fewer, so the ability to deceive has increased in the gene pool.[1]

When Bond and his colleagues set up a research study in which undergraduates told lies and truths about their own job, the liars were able to conceal their lies from most observers, with only about a quarter of the lies being detected.[2] Other psychological experiments on lying and detection have had similar results. For instance, when R. E. Kraut reviewed the results of nine studies judging whether people told the truth, he found that, on the average, the participants were able to make accurate judgments only about half of the time.[3] In turn, applying a correction for chance guessing, Bond and his colleagues estimated that only about 14 percent of the would-be detectors were able to expose the typical liar in a psychological experiment.[4]

The greater success of deceivers is also shown by the problems of people who are trained in lie detection. For example, when Kraut and D. Poe studied a group of U.S. customs inspectors—lie detectors by profession—they found the inspectors couldn't reliably expose deceit,[5] a finding that may be expected, considering the obvious failure of inspectors to stop more than a small percentage of the people who smuggle various goods and drugs through customs.

According to researchers, this better ability to deceive than perceive lies makes survival sense. Bond says:

Though both deception and lie-detection capabilities have been naturally selected, they may not have evolved to comparable levels. Deception skills may have evolved further. If so, one may infer that—over generations—an organism's survival has depended more on its ability to deceive than its ability to detect deceit.

For example, the rabbit runs faster than the fox, because the rabbit is running for his life, while the fox is only running for his dinner. This "life-dinner" principle of unequal selection pressure could explain the imbalance in the deceptive struggle.[6]

There are a number of reasons why perceiving lies may be so difficult. Not only may perceivers be unable to tell when skillful liars are lying, they may think that truth-tellers who seem deceptive are lying, too. This is what researchers call the Othello effect. In Shakespeare's classic *Othello*, the title character falsely accuses Desdemona of infidelity, believing her emotional outburst at this accusation to be further proof of her lies. In fact, he is mistakenly interpreting her fear of being disbelieved. When Charles Bond and associate William Fahey investigated this difficulty of sorting truth from lies, they found this quite true. Subjects seeing videotapes of people lying or not lying about their feelings could not distinguish the lies from the truth.[7]

Research on sales pitches has shown that experienced sellers may be so good in their ability to deceive that they fool subjects who are cued to look for the body movements and speech patterns associated with deception. The problem is that although the judges might pick up nonverbal cues associated with lying, these cues don't correlate with the seller's lie. Thus the researchers in these studies have concluded that experienced sellers, confident in their ability to deceive and having no qualms about doing so, are not likely to inadvertently give away their lies with nonverbal cues.[8]

Why can't people perceive lies? Generally, the people I spoke to talked about being unaware or gullible. They didn't pay attention or didn't know the cues of lying, or they just tended to believe—or wanted to believe—that someone was telling the truth. As a result, the usual discovery of a lie tended to occur when something the liar said just didn't seem to make sense or fit something the listener knew from before or later on, when the inconsistencies contained in the lie began to unravel.

For Don, the engineer, the big cue to a lie came through external information that showed up the lie, but otherwise it was hard to tell. As he commented:

It's hard to know if someone is lying, unless you have some sort of validity check that comes up. Otherwise you don't know. For example, suppose somebody says X, and the result is Y, then that's an indicator that there was something wrong. Otherwise there may be no way to tell if someone's lying.

Or another possibility might be if something doesn't fit someone's usual pattern— such as say someone says he just likes to go to thrilling movies, but then he wants to see a calm, thoughtful one, you might wonder about the discrepancy. There's a lack of congruity that might suggest a lie. But otherwise, who knows? It's usually hard to pick up anything in someone's voice or tone.

THE STRATEGIES FOR TELLING A LIE

What makes a successful liar so good? What strategies do liars use? Good liars—who are more likely to be the Pinocchios and frequent liars—are aware of the attitudes and preferences of the targets of their lies, according to psychologists Bella DePaulo, Julie Stone, and Daniel Lassiter.[9] These practiced liars may even construct their lies with such information in mind, much like the salesman who figures out what to say to push the prospect's button, or the so-called psychic or spiritual reader who senses what her customer wants to hear and then says it.

Second, good liars learn to control so-called channels to present themselves in a convincing way. Generally, the verbal channel is most easily managed, and it's also the channel that's especially important for listeners as they hear words, react to them, and hold the speaker accountable for what he says. They also may be able to control the nonverbal channels of communication, such as their face, body, and tone of voice, although researchers such as DePaulo, Paul Ekman, and others have found that these channels are much more difficult to control, because emotional reactions are registered automatically.[10]

On the other hand, as liars become more motivated to lie successfully, they may actually lose some of their advantage because they may pay too much attention to what they are saying and not enough to the nonverbal cues they are giving off. This is what DePaulo and her associates found in an experiment with male and female college students who sent and received truthful and deceptive messages. The more the subjects were motivated to lie, because they found their targets more attractive, the more their lies were detected. This led the researchers to conclude that the senders paid more attention to the more salient verbal channel they felt they could control more (i.e., what they were saying) and less to the nonverbal cues, which were what eventually gave them away.[11]

THE STRATEGIES FOR PERCEIVING A LIE

Although it may be difficult to distinguish the truth from a lie, there are techniques that help even up the odds, though they may not be correct all the time. These techniques don't always work because it is easy to err in either direction—misinterpreting seemingly suspicious behavior for a lie when the person is telling the truth, or not noticing little behavior cues or verbal inconsistencies that point to a lie.

Researchers have found certain patterns of behavior that may point to a lie. Many have been discovered by a San Francisco psychologist, Paul Ekman, who has studied techniques used by liars. According to Ekman, there are two types of clues to deceit. These clues essentially are mistakes that reveal the truth or may suggest that what was said or shown is untrue without revealing the truth. One clue is "leakage," which occurs when the liar's behavior suggests he or she is lying without revealing the truth.[12] Then, too, there may be something in the overall social context in which the lie occurs that gives off clues that things aren't quite right.

Discovering Leakages

Leakages may be the most difficult to discover, because these usually come from verbal slips, and the liar usually has control over the verbal channel. But the liar may not always remember what he says or to whom. So there may be inconsistencies and contradictions that build up. Later on, the liar may give the wrong name or information to someone, so he must backtrack to conceal the holes. Such discrepancies can be a clue to lying, but not always, because people really do forget and make mistakes.

Still another reason, pointed out by Ekman, is that liars can't always anticipate when they will need to lie. So they don't always have the time to prepare the line to be taken, to rehearse and memorize it.[13] Even if the liar has had plenty of advance notice and has prepared what he is going to say, he may not be able to anticipate all the questions or think through his answers, so he may slip up, be unconvincing, or even blurt out the truth.[14] Or the liar may forget what he has said previously and have trouble answering new questions quickly and confidently. In short, as Ekman sums up, any of these three common types of failures can produce easily spotted clues to deceit.[15]

Discovering Deception Clues

Assuming the liar maintains control over the verbal channel or his little inconsistencies or slips are unnoticed or overlooked, the other big key to perceiving lies comes through the behavioral or "deception" clues the liar gives away.

In this case, there are a number of major types of clues, again suggested by Ekman's research. These include the way a line is spoken, the difficulties a person may have in lying about his feelings (including his feelings about lying, his fear of being caught, his guilt at deceiving another, and his delight at making someone else a dupe). As Ekman points out, these signs of guilt, fear, or delight can show up in the person's facial expression, voice, or body movement, even when the liar is trying to conceal them. Even if there is no nonverbal leakage, the struggle to prevent these leaks may produce a deception clue.[16]

Here are key clues that can be a sign of lying (though sometimes not—remember the Othello effect).

- *Carefully considering each word before it is spoken.* This can occur because the liar hasn't thought through what to say next to keep the pretense going or has trouble remembering what was said. So he may need to be more careful in thinking about what to say. Thus, pauses during speech or other gestures associated with thinking might be a clue.
- *The difficulty in concealing or falsely portraying emotions.* Real emotions may leak out, or, if the person is trying to feign an emotion, it may be hard to do this, too. According to Ekman, there are several big problems in concealing emotions.
    - The first is that when an emotion begins gradually or is only slightly felt, the changes in behavior are small and could be readily concealed if the person was aware of them. But many people may not be aware of such changes, and so don't control them.
    - Second, if the emotion is a strong one, then the problem is in controlling it, and it can be difficult to conceal the changes in the person's face, body, or tone of voice. Even if the person can conceal these changes so his real feelings don't leak out, the struggle itself can be noticeable and so provide a clue.
    - Falsifying emotions can be problematic, too, because the deceiver must put together the right movements and changes of the voice that reflect a particular emotion, and many people may find it quite difficult to perform these movements voluntarily.[17]
- *The way the person feels about lying.* The emotions associated with the fear of being caught, one's guilt about lying, or one's delight in duping another person might be the giveaway. Signs of nervousness and anxiety could be a clue that one is fearful of being trapped in a lie, although the danger here is the Othello effect, since, as Ekman notes, "it is always a problem to distinguish between the innocent's fear of being disbelieved and the guilty person's detection apprehension."[18]

- This problem is even worse when the perceiver is known to be suspicious or has caught the liar in a lie before. Conversely, as the liar becomes more practiced and has more success, this fear of being caught will go down, although the risk to the liar of making careless errors grows. So, according to Ekman, some degree of detection apprehension helps the liar by keeping him more alert. But too much apprehension can give him away, because of the difficulty in controlling these emotional clues.[19]
- Moreover, as the stakes get higher this apprehension can increase because, initially, the person tells a lie to gain a reward or advantage. After a while, the rewards may no longer be available, but the person has to maintain the deceit to avoid getting caught and being punished for the lie.[20]

Also, a person may experience guilt just because of lying and that can be a clue as well. This guilt may turn out to be more than the person anticipated, or it can increase over time if the liar finds that his original lie was not enough, and now he has to repeat it or must even elaborate and expand upon it to protect the original lie.[21] Ekman also points out circumstances when such guilt can be most severe and hence most likely to give away the liar, such as when the person's lies are not authorized by some higher or legitimate authority or when the person lied to is trusting and doesn't gain or suffers from the lie as much or more as the liar.[22]

Finally, there may be some people who let their delight at duping the victim give them away.[23] They brag about their lie to others, who reveal them or show signs of excitement or enjoyment at lying, which betrays the lie.

- *The behavioral cues from the liar's words, voice, or body.* According to Ekman, liars usually give off behavioral cues, because they are not able to monitor, control, and disguise all of their behavior. As a result, liars usually concentrate on concealing or falsifying what they expect others to watch most, which is usually their choice of words and then their facial expression. Liars control their words because they know they will be held more accountable for what they say. And they are likely to try to control their face, because it receives the most attention from others.[24] Even then there can be leaks and clues from the voice or face.

These facial and vocal cues can be especially important giveaways because the individual's face and voice are directly connected to those areas of the brain involved with emotion, whereas the person's words are not, according to Ekman. When a person's emotions are aroused, the muscles on his face begin to fire involuntarily, and there will be changes in his voice. Although a person can learn to interfere with and override these involuntary reactions, there can still be leaks, such as when a person forgets to exercise this conscious control or when he initially experiences the emotional arousal, before applying the conscious brakes.[25]

The body is more subject to conscious control, because most body movements are not directly tied to the areas of the brain involved in emotion, as

Ekman notes. But most people don't bother to control their body cues, because they have grown up thinking such controls are not necessary, since people are usually not held accountable for what they reveal through the actions of their body. Rather, the emphasis is on watching the face or evaluating the words to detect lies, so people just ignore the body.[26]

Then, too, there might be a discrepancy between what the person says and what his voice, body, or face reveals, which can point to a lie.[27]

Major Clues in the Words, Voice, or Body

In his book, *Telling Lies*, Ekman describes a number of the major clues in the words, voice, or body that suggest lies. Some of the key clues:

- *Words.* Liars might be given away by such things as slips of the tongue, forgetting familiar names, and mistakes in reading or writing.[28] Sometimes the build-up of emotion, concealed by the lie, might escape through an emotional outburst or tirade, which can lead to specific slips of information, too.[29] Also, evasions or circumlocutions may be giveaways, although some liars are too smart to be evasive and indirect. Sometimes a person is normally evasive and indirect in the way he speaks, so this isn't always a signal of lying.[30]
- *The voice.* A big clue to deceit is overly long or overly frequent pauses. This is a sign the person is trying to think about or craft a response. Another may be speech errors, including nonwords such as "ohs" and "uhhs," and repetitions or partial words. The sound of the voice, particularly pitch, can signal an emotion underlying the lie, such as the person's fear, anger, or other feelings of upset. Ekman notes that pitch becomes higher when someone is upset or excited, while the pitch may drop when the person feels sadness or sorrow. Making it even worse for the liar is the fact that changes in the voice due to emotion are not easy to conceal, especially if the lie is designed to cover up emotions felt at the moment or if the lie itself has led the person to feel a strong emotion.[31] On the other hand, the voice isn't always a giveaway, because some people may not show emotion in their voice, or a person may not be emotional about a particular lie. So someone's voice can be calm even though he is lying.[32]
- *The body.* Some of the key clues to lying come through what Ekman calls "emblems" and "illustrators." Emblems are specific gestures with a particular meaning to a particular cultural group, such as a wave that means hello or good-bye or a head nod for yes. However, when there is a slip in the way an emblem is normally performed or only a small part of the emblem is performed, this could be an indication that the person has something to conceal.[33] An example of this might be the person who starts to raise his middle finger in a traditional gesture of anger, but then thinks the better of it and instead responds with a smile suggesting friendliness.

Likewise, an unconsciously performed gesture outside of the normal position in which it is used could be a clue.

Illustrators are the open movements that illustrate speech, such as a big, open gesture to describe a large house. In this case, according to Ekman, the clue to deceit is not in the particular illustrator used, since these can vary with personality style or culture, but in the decrease in the number of illustrators normally used by a person. The reason for this is that people tend to use more illustrators when they are very involved in what is being said, because then they are more excited or aroused in some way, whether positively or negatively. But when people use fewer illustrators than usual, it could be because they are being cautious about what they are saying, which sometimes may be due to deceit. If people are trying to feign an emotion, they may be given away by their failure to illustrate as much as they would usually do if their heightened emotional arousal were true.[34] However, to interpret these clues correctly it is necessary to know what the person usually does. If you meet someone for the first time, you generally can't use an illustrator as an indication of dishonesty, though sometimes an emblematic slip might give a person away.

The other major type of body movement is what Ekman refers to as "manipulation." Essentially this occurs when one part of the body (often the hand or a finger) manipulates another body part (such as by massaging, rubbing, scratching, pinching, and the like). Many people think an increase in such movements is a sign of deceit because when people are uncomfortable or nervous they fidget or make restless movements. But Ekman considers such movements quite unreliable. One reason is that many people show an increase in these movements when they are relaxed and feel they can let their hair down, so they let go of their formal controls. Then, too, people vary a great deal in the types of manipulators they use and how often, so a prior knowledge of the person is generally necessary to evaluate him. Also, people may use more manipulators when they are uncomfortable about anything, not just lying. Finally, it's relatively easy to inhibit these manipulators, so a person who is lying can often succeed in controlling them.[35]

- *The autonomic nervous system.* Ekman also suggests that changes produced by the autonomic nervous system due to emotional arousal could be another source of clues to deception. These are the sorts of changes measured by the lie detector. Many of these changes are visible, such as changes in the pattern of breathing, frequency of swallowing, amount of sweating, and the changes reflected in the face, such as blushing, blanching, and the dilation of the pupils.[36] According to Ekman, the autonomic-nervous-system changes appear to be specific for each emotion, so that an aware person might be able to tell just by observing not only whether a person is emotionally aroused, but what emotion he really feels. Moreover, such observations might be especially telling because these reactions are relatively difficult to censor, whereas other body and facial reactions may be more readily controllable.[37]

- *The face.* Still other signals of lying can come from the face, again because real emotions trigger facial responses involuntarily, although a person can control and interfere with these actions, according to Ekman.[38] What is especially helpful in deciphering real feelings is the fact that some facial expressions, such as those indicating happiness, fear, anger, disgust, sadness, and distress, are universal, and many others may be, too.[39] As a result, while people can sometimes be taken in by false expressions (such as the friendly smile of an enemy), many times people can see the real feelings leak out through a person's facial features. According to Ekman, people may be fooled because when people lie, "their most evident, easy-to-see expressions, which people pay most attention to, are often the false ones." By contrast, people usually miss the more subtle signs and fleeting hints that reveal the true and concealed emotions.[40] Some of these are what Ekman refers to as "microexpressions," which flash on and off the face in less than a quarter of a second, and these are an indicator of the emotion that is really felt.[41] However, these don't occur very often. Instead, what is more common and telling, Ekman has found in his research, are the "squelched expressions," which are the emotional responses that are suppressed just as they are beginning and the liar becomes aware of them. Since the liar doesn't want this response to show, he shuts it off, sometimes covering it up with another expression, such as a smile, which is the most common cover or mask.[42]

While there is always the chance of being wrong—because some liars are experts at controlling their features, while others may just be showing emotion because they are upset, not because they are lying—there are clues to detect lying from these subtle sources of expression. Some of the major ones reported by Ekman are these:

- *Increased blinking or pupil dilation* are signs of increased emotional arousal and could indicate lying if this is the source of the arousal and not some other emotion such as the fear of being disbelieved.[43]
- *Blushing,* which is a signal of shame or guilt, could suggest the liar is embarrassed or ashamed about what he is concealing. Or the person could simply be embarrassed. Also, the face reddened with anger could be a sign of hidden anger underlying a lie.[44]
- *Blanching,* a response to controlled anger or fear, may be a sign of a concealed emotion, too, though so far not much is known about this response.[45]
- *Increased eyeblinks, pupil dilation, or facial sweating,* as signals of increased emotional arousal, may also be clues that something is going on, although these can be triggered by various emotions, too.[46]

In addition, the face may betray a person's attempt to feign an emotion, such as when a person tries to show he really cares for someone but doesn't or a salesperson tries to fake his enthusiasm. Some of the cues to look for include:

- *Any facial expression that lingers for five seconds or more*, such as a prolonged smile or look of amazement because most real facial expressions fade after four or five seconds.[47]
- *Crooked or asymmetrical facial expressions*, such as a crooked smile. Most people cannot control all movements of their facial muscles, so when they try to fake something, they can't get the expression exactly right.[48]
- *Smiles that show a muscular action around the lips*, such as a narrowing or tightening, can indicate a hidden negative emotion such as anger, disgust, fear, contempt, or sadness. By contrast, true smiles don't show this muscular movement, and instead show a movement of the outer muscle that circles the eye.[49]
- *Facial expressions that are out of synch with body movements or changes in the voice.* These suggest the person is trying to control and falsify an emotion. For example, anger is likely to be expressed before or at the beginning of a statement (i.e., "I don't like what you are doing"). But if the facial expression comes afterward, it is more likely that the person might be just trying to act as if he were angry.[50]

Ekman identifies dozens of smiles associated with different emotions, including fear, contempt, and misery. By knowing the differences, the perceiver may be able to pick up when a person is trying to manufacture an outward appearance and when he is expressing what he really thinks.

In short, there may be numerous clues to lying in what a person says, how he says it, and in the emotional reactions he expresses in his voice, face, and various parts of his body. If a perceiver pays close attention and is knowledgeable about these clues, he may be more able to pick up lies. At best, being aware of these clues can only increase the possibility of identifying the liar, since these clues can also arise because the person is feeling other emotions. Then, too, some people are good at controlling emotional expressions or masking them.

Discovering Clues in the Overall Social Context

There may also be clues in the social setting itself, notably in interactions that indicate something is being hidden or in special arrangements made to conceal or hold back the flow of information (such as a seemingly greater-than-usual effort to look something up). For example, author and management consultant Judith Briles described clues that might be found in a business setting:

Say people are talking about you or saying something they don't want you to hear. You can usually tell this when you walk into a room and silence falls.

Or suppose an employer walks into a room, and all of a sudden things get shuffled together or books get closed. That can indicate things that the employees don't want the employer to see.

Another sign that things may be hidden in the workplace are phone calls that are very hush-hush. Or maybe there's an unexpected abruptness. Also, a lot of things may get locked up all the time, or there may be many meetings behind locked doors.

Still another clue may be when an employee asks a question he feels is legitimate to understand something that he perceives going on in the office, but he doesn't get a straightforward answer. This may suggest that something unusual is up.

Clues to Look For

There may be clues that experts in lie detection such as Ekman look for, but I also wondered about the clues that common people usually look for.

In general, the people I spoke with indicated they could easily be duped and often were unaware of people lying to them. However, there were indicators that led them to be suspicious.

For example, inconsistencies or claims that didn't make sense were one sign. Also, there were certain types of statements that raised red flags that someone might be lying, such as someone bragging about social status symbols, suggesting they weren't all that they said they were and were compensating to make up for it.

People also may see nervousness as a sign of lying. Dick, the sales executive, looked for such clues in customers. As he commented:

I find it difficult for a customer to lie well because he knows he's lying and gives it away by the way he acts. What do I look for? I find customers have a hard time looking you in the eye. They also fidget. They're interrupted frequently and welcome interruptions. Also, they try to get the meeting over fast, because it's not comfortable for them. The situation is tense, they're tense. It's just not normal.

Other signs were the clash between body language and the message the person was saying. Raphael, the healer, tended to be quite conscious of this when he worked with clients.

I look for an incongruence in the way they are and what they're saying. If things are just not jibing, that leads me to suspect that someone might be lying. What kind of incongruence? Well, there may be a discrepancy between the tone of the voice and what they're telling me they really feel about something. So I listen for that, or sometimes, just get a gut feeling I can't really explain—something just doesn't feel right.

Alternatively, a person pushing something too hard might be a danger sign, too, especially in a sales or persuasion type of situation. As Reba, the speaker, observed:

When someone's coming on so strong, it just makes me wonder if they're sincere. Why are they pushing so hard? I think that if they were really being honest, would they have to sell that hard? So that kind of behavior leads me to distrust.

Much of the time, people felt they were at the mercy of practiced liars. Storm, the writer, described this frustration:

Sometimes you just can't know. Say someone is really lying. Well, usually, they'll be poker-faced. They won't give any clues away. And people are so different; there's a different read on everybody, and some are able to lie better than others, or people lie in different ways.

Usually there's no one tip-off cue, like suddenly the person starts looking out of the window or doesn't meet your eye. In my experience, the people who are good at lying do meet you in the eye because they are used to being bald-faced liars. So eye contact doesn't give me any clues.

For me, the best thing is to know what we're talking about, so I can call the person on something if it doesn't seem right. And then maybe they'll get nervous and fidgety because I seem to be onto them. But others may just plow ahead with some logical explanation as if nothing is wrong.

That seems to be the way it is for most people. They pick up on occasional clues such as inconsistent information, incongruent behavior, or signs of evasiveness and nervousness, but still very often are duped or just don't know.

Perhaps if people learned to pay more attention to the clues to lying they might be better at knowing when someone is lying. But, as the experts have pointed out, as the perceivers get better, so do the liars in this never-ending escalation of the ability to lie versus the ability to perceive.

Conclusion

As the preceding chapters have illustrated, we may say we don't like to lie, but often we do. It is a way to defend ourselves or gain rewards. Then we usually find justification for why we do it, while decrying the lies of others.

Lies strike us as hurtful, as betrayals, as indicators of uncertainty, because they make us unsure about relationships, about whether promised things will happen, about whom and what we can trust.

In turn, there is a biological basis for lying—for the ability to lie, to be good at it, and to get away with it. This has been programmed into us from our animal heritage. Deceit is a survival mechanism, and those with the greater ability to be deceitful survive. The paradox here is that those with the greater ability to detect deception have been more apt to survive as well. Overall, the probabilities favor the likelihood that people will lie. Perhaps using a kind of conscious or unconscious cost-benefits analysis, people weigh the risks of telling the lie against the importance and degree of the potential gains or defensive advantages in telling that lie. And maybe they factor in the guidelines of traditional morality and current social practice in deciding when and what lies to tell.

At the same time, there is a continuum of lying from those who fall on the morality end of the spectrum and lie less and feel guilt at times when they do to those who fall on the pragmatic end, lie more when practical to do so, and feel less or no guilt; their main concern is getting away with the lie and not being caught. On the one end are the models of absolute integrity and straight shooters; in the middle is the pragmatic fibber, who can lean either way, trying to do the moral thing yet willing to lie when practical; and on the other end are the Pinocchios and frequent liars.

Another paradox occurs because traditional morality forbids lies. The principle is encoded in the religious teachings and in the folk tales and stories that we hear as children, such as in the Pinocchio story that first appeared in 1883 in *The Adventures of Pinocchio* by Carlo Collodi and has since become a classic. Yet so often our social activities demand a lie, such as the white lie designed to help smooth over social relationships or keep someone unknowing about something harmful.

Thus, there is continuous tension between the immediate gains to the liar versus the potential damages to society if the lie is told or the truth is concealed. It's as if lying helps to illuminate what has always been a source of tension in human society—the desire to act out of the self-interest of the individual versus the need to conform to the demands of the social order. Most individuals usually use the lie for personal ends, while social groups discourage the lie because of its power to disrupt relations. Yet at times the truth can be more disruptive or damaging, such as when knowing that truth disrupts a personal relationship or makes a society vulnerable.

TO CONFRONT OR NOT TO CONFRONT THE LIE?

Suppose you suspect or know of a lie or a concealment. Do you confront it?

The answer is: It depends—it depends on your personal style, on the nature of the relationship, on the importance of the situation, on the potential gains versus the losses of exposure, and so on.

A common response for much of everyday, not very important social lying is to simply let the lie go to avoid hurting people's feelings, embarrassing them, or disrupting relationships with a confrontation over something relatively trivial. Letting it go may be a good strategy for many minor lies if we don't want to derail an otherwise good social or business relationship.

Is the Confrontation Worth It?

Deciding whether to confront the lie sometimes results in an analysis in which the victim will bring it up if he sees a payoff for doing it. But if there's no gain, he lets it go.

Others considered confrontation in terms of the importance or endurance of the relationship. If it is just a casual social encounter, they might let the lie go, feeling that the relationship is too fleeting to merit raising the issue. But if the relationship is an ongoing or long-term one, they might say something to deal with the lie, because it would interfere with closeness and trust.

Robert Young, the therapist I spoke with, had this advice:

My advice on what to do would depend on their relationship to that person who has lied to them in the first place. If it's a spouse or a family member or someone they are close to, I think people tend to confront it and should, because they're going to have to continue to be in a relationship with that person, whether they raise the issue or not.

I think with a boss or co-worker, it's the same sort of situation. It can be difficult to live or work together if one person suspects a lie.

However, if the lie is from someone one has met in passing, then I would suggest that the best strategy might be to simply avoid them because they aren't trustworthy. But there may be no reason to confront them, because there's no need for a continuing relationship. It's just as easy to avoid them and deal with the lie that way.

The Importance of Being Diplomatic or Tactful

Suppose someone does decide to confront a liar. How should he do it? A good approach is to be tactful and diplomatic so the person who has lied has a way out, can save face, or feels support for confessing. Then the liar is most likely to reveal the truth and not get angry and defensive about doing so.

On the other hand, if a person is too openly confronted, he might react as if he were being attacked or invaded, making him angry and increasing the possibility of conflict—and perhaps more lies to cover up.

Raphael, the healer, described the dangers of confronting someone too openly:

I once lost a client because I found I was too confrontational in trying to get him to face the truth. I thought our relationship could withstand it, and it didn't.

So I think it's very important to take into consideration the timing and be sensitive about how someone is going to receive something. That way he may be more ready to face the truth.

On the other hand, if the lie is important enough, if the relationship is important enough, and if confrontation fits with one's personal style, then it might be good to confront. In fact, some of the therapists I spoke to generally recommended this as beneficial both for the individual and the relationship.

Therapist Sylvia Mills emphasized the need to check out and confront inconsistencies, such as one might check out something in a house that didn't seem quite right. As she put it:

I think if people feel or suspect they are in a situation where someone is lying about something that matters, they should check it out, the same way they would check out the wood and the floorboards when buying a house.

How? You go and you stamp on the floor in a few places, put some pressure on it, and test it. Likewise, I think people should test out things in a relationship when they have suspicions. If you have an "instinct" something is not right, apply a little pressure to see if the person is feeling and thinking inside the way he is presenting himself on the outside. You need to do this for your own psychological health and the good of the relationship.

Then, too, confronting the lie might lead to a sense of release, leading to feelings of greater personal strength, a closer relationship, or the removal of barriers to a business or personal relationship.

For example, Sarah, the educator, felt renewed strength when she began confronting the man she was in a relationship with about things he had lied about or concealed. As she described it:

At one time, I thought it better to save face or not confront people. But I came to realize that this was because I wasn't willing to be in my own power and say what was really happening. And that was because I was insecure myself. I was afraid of rejection, afraid that I wasn't going to be accepted. I was afraid to make someone else angry or upset by bringing up something I knew to be the truth. But what I didn't realize at the time was that I was losing my own self-respect and their respect by not calling them on it when they weren't being honest with me or by saying what I really felt about something.

For example, a man I was in a relationship with was relating something that happened to us, which wasn't so, and at one time I would have just let this go. But this time I called him on it, and I reminded him about what really happened, and he finally admitted what really did. So I was willing to say that something was a lie, which was new for me. And I felt much better about myself when I did.

Giving hints that one might know something and giving the person a chance to retreat and change his story or explain might also be an effective strategy in some cases.

For example, Dick, the sales executive, described how he used this approach effectively with his clients:

When I sense someone is lying or fudging, I don't believe in calling them on it directly. I think that's cutting off your nose to spite your face, because that just makes people defensive or hostile. They feel challenged and that can put them on guard.

What I do is I let them know in a subtle way that I question what they are saying, and I would just like to see some support for this. And I also might allow that I could be wrong or not understand them exactly. So I give them a chance to back down.

For instance, say we're talking about price, and they give me a quote that seems out of line. I might say something like: "Well, we'll be glad to match that pricing as soon as you can show me in writing the competitor's quote," and then I'll move onto a different area to give the person a feeling of space. Then, if he does show me some supporting evidence to back up what he has said, I'll go along with his proposal. But if not, there's just a tacit understanding he'll accept my view of things and my proposed rate. So his attempt to state something that's wrong just isn't brought up again. That way I'm not directly challenging him on it; I'm not trying to suggest he's a liar. So he can back down quietly if my suspicions are correct, and at the same time the business relationship can go on.

Similarly, Blanche, the public relations executive, used much the same approach when she had suspicions about her employees. As she put it:

Say I suspect someone in the office of doing something, like taking things, but I don't have any proof. I think it's important to use tact. For instance, in a meeting I might let them know that I've noticed that things are missing, that things have been disappearing, and I might ask if they have noticed any of their things disappearing, too.

Likewise, if I've said something that's not true, say at a staff or client meeting, I would feel better if someone just gently said: "Well, Blanche, that's not exactly the way it is; it's this way," rather than trying to catch me in an exaggeration or lie. Then, I might simply say: "Oh, there I go again," and let it drop. I'll feel I've got a way out, a way to save face, because I may know they know I've tried to bend the truth a little, but they haven't made a big deal about it, either, so I can more easily back out.

Providing a supportive environment for helping the person reveal the truth can work well, as Judith Briles, the author and management consultant, described in working with her own employees:

I think when you know someone has lied, we need to give them the opportunity to open up and deal with it. And for that I think it's important to be understanding, to show them you want to listen and try to solve the problem. You want to help, not punish. So when you are trying to get them to open up in this confrontation, this is not the time to go in with a sledge hammer and hit someone over the head with what they have done. Rather, you want to create an atmosphere where you convey the impression that "whatever you have to say, it's really best to be direct with me." And that takes tactfulness. It takes loving. It takes caring, showing your support for the person.

Say a person has made a mistake. At first, he or she may not want to admit it. Well, I would encourage them to talk about it, giving them the assurance they would not be canned. I would let them know I believe in the possibility of change.

I had a person who worked for me who made some mistakes in doing some things that were a bit over her head. So I sat down with her, and I began by assuring her: "You don't need to make excuses. Let's look at where we are and what we need to do to make things work for you." That way I feel she felt more free to be open, so we could deal with the problem head-on.

WHEN TO CONFESS OR WHAT TO DO ABOUT GETTING CAUGHT

The other side of dealing with lies is, of course, deciding what to do about lying oneself—whether to tell one, whether to reveal one voluntarily, and what to do about getting caught. Again, there are no hard and fast answers, just considerations that may apply in different situations along with considerations based on personal style.

A key to dealing with personal lying is to be more conscious of these various considerations so one can determine when it might be best to use a lie, when to reveal, and how to respond when confronted over a lie, perhaps by weighing and assessing various strategic and personal-values considerations.

Although the ideal may be "don't lie," the overall reality is that at some point all of us do it. The problem is that many, if not most, of us are not really aware of how, when, or why we do it. Rather, the lie is more like an automatic defense or attack mechanism we use under various circumstances.

Thus, it may be useful to develop a management-of-lying approach so we're more conscious of when and how we do it and when it might be best to reveal lies. Ultimately, each person will have to develop his own way of approaching this, based on the situation and what he feels personally comfortable with. So this section is not designed to be a manual on how to lie! Rather, it is designed to raise final considerations and suggest the importance of being conscious about the process of lying and its results and ramifications.

You might also keep in mind where you fall on the lying continuum and consider if you want to change yourself. For instance, if you fall toward the moral end as a model of absolute integrity or straight shooter, consider if you are being taken advantage of or are getting into too many conflicts with people who are more pragmatic in their approach to lying. Maybe it's time to be less forthcoming and be more practical yourself. Conversely, if you fall toward the pragmatic end of the spectrum as a Pinocchio or frequent liar and this approach is creating dissension in relationships over trust issues or lost work because people don't trust you, maybe it's time to tell fewer lies yourself. And perhaps the compromise of the pragmatic fibber might be a middle ground to aim for, where you adhere to the principles of morality and avoid lying whenever possible, but when necessary you do lie—yet strive to keep lying to a minimum. It seems to be a compromise that many people have made today.

Some Considerations on Whether to Lie

Some possible considerations in deciding whether to lie might include:

- The importance of the situation lied about.
- The possible gain to oneself from the lie.
- The risk of getting caught and how one feels about this.
- The potential damage to one's reputation from being caught.
- One's own personal values and morality.
- The possible benefits to others from the lie.
- One's feelings of guilt.
- One's feelings about getting away with the lie (i.e., Will you be apt to feel guilty even if you get away with it, or would you feel relieved or glad?).
- The existence of alternatives to the lie.
- The likelihood that the person lied to will seek to learn the truth or will collaborate in a continuation of the lie.
- The likelihood and the dangers of having to create other lies to cover up this one, the risk of getting caught, and the degree of penalties possible with the discovery of these future lies.
- The way the person lied to will react if he or she discovers the lie. Will the lie be likely to be forgiven? Will there be a crisis of trust? Or perhaps an end to the relationship?

And so on. You may think of other considerations that apply for yourself. The point is to be aware of the possible gains and losses and other repercussions under the particular circumstances affecting the lie. Also, it is useful to better understand your own attitudes and values about lying to decide what is appropriate for you to do in the future.

For others, moral or spiritual considerations can be especially important, and they may find their personal values compelling. This was a major factor for Alison, the counselor. As she explained:

Generally, 1 feel like a lie is going to come back to haunt me, so that even if I get away with it now, there will still be some effect.

For some, feelings of guilt discourage the lie, even the white lie. As Roger, the philosophy teacher, reported:

The times I've lied, I've felt badly about it. I've felt like I was short-changing myself and the other person. I have lied to save someone's feelings, but I have felt bad about that as well.

For example, this once happened at a conference where there was a man I was trying to impress, and he asked me what I thought of someone who I know has a good reputation with many people because he is known as a very peaceful sort of leader who works for peace. But in fact, I have not liked this person's style, because he is so evangelical. But I didn't tell this man what I really thought, because I didn't want him to think I didn't like this person when so many other people did. So I just made up a comfortable, placating answer.

But I think the man suspected that I didn't say what I was really thinking. I think he could tell I was being evasive and withholding something, and I think this created a sense of separation between us. I think it was worse to withhold something than tell him what I really wanted to say.

The most important questions for you to answer are: What are your own considerations, values, and priorities about lying? What seems to work for you?

Ultimately, you have to decide what is right for yourself.

When to Reveal or Confess the Lie

Once you have lied, should you reveal it or confess? Or is it better to keep it hidden? There is no right answer for everyone. These considerations may help you to decide:

- *How long has it been since you told the original lie?* With a passage of time, it may become easier to admit it, because the other person may be more accepting.
- *How significant is the original lie to your current relationship with the person?* It may be that the revelation of the lie will disrupt the whole relationship. If so, do you feel the relationship should continue, based on this lie? Or should the relationship be reconstructed on true foundations? Are you willing to take the risk of maybe losing the relationship? Is revealing the lie important enough to take this risk?
- *How major or important was the original lie?* If trivial enough, maybe it could be ignored. But if it is so trivial, perhaps there would be little risk in revealing it.

- *How do you feel about the lie?* Do you have a strong desire to open up about it? Or are you more apt to feel: "Just let things lie. Why rock the boat?"
- *How likely is the lie to come out if you don't reveal it?* This might be a reason to reveal it first. Then you can better control the revelation, and the repercussions may be easier on you.
- *How is the person you have lied to likely to respond?* Is he or she likely to appreciate your candor, to be forgiving, which may be more the case for the pragmatic fibber, Pinocchio, or frequent liar? Or is he or she more likely to be upset, perhaps even end the relationship, more likely to be the case for the model of absolute integrity or the straight shooter?
- *How much better is it likely to be if you reveal the lie yourself rather than have the person find out?* What is the risk of discovery if you do not tell? And how important is it to you to reveal the lie if the person reacts badly to it?
- *What would be the best way to make the revelation?* Would you prefer to explain in a letter what happened? Would you rather just come right out with the lie? If so, what would be the best way to do this? In person? On the phone? At their home? At yours? In an office setting?

Sometimes the pressures to reveal can become complex, such as when there are conflicting considerations such as a moral imperative against lying combined with a realization of the potential losses that confessing can bring. This dilemma occurred to a friend of Don's, the engineer. As Don told me:

My friend had herpes, and he had started this relationship with a woman. In the beginning he didn't want to announce it. After all, they had just started to date, didn't have an intimate relationship, and this wasn't the kind of thing one announces to the world.

But as the relationship started to get serious, he felt he had a need to tell her, because now this was something she should know. Yet, at the same time, he dreaded telling her, because he knew this might be the end of the relationship.

He agonized over this for many days. But finally he decided he needed to tell. So he told her, and that blew the whole relationship. Morally and ethically, he felt he had to do it, and then it was up to her to decide if the relationship would continue.

THE ROLE OF FORGIVENESS

If you find that someone has lied to you or someone confesses a lie, how willing are you to forgive? There seem to be general patterns in how people respond to lies and are willing to forgive.

- *If the lie isn't too serious,* especially if it just happens once, whether confessed or revealed, there is a tendency to forgive and let bygones be bygones.
- *If the lies are only occasional ones,* particularly in the beginning of a relationship, usually the person lied to will forgive, though the models of absolute integrity and straight shooters are apt to be less forgiving. The

reason for the initial tolerance is that people recognize that others might sometimes lie as a kind of convenience or because people weren't totally consistent or perfect in their statements and behavior. But then, if people started to show a pattern of lying, that's when the victims would start to be unforgiving, because the repeated lies would undermine their ability to trust the person and count on the relationship.

- *If a person starts to lie consistently or shows a pattern of lies*, then it may become increasingly hard to forgive, especially for those with a greater concern for doing the moral or right thing. For every person, of course, the tolerance point is different—just when do a few lies turn into a pattern? But once they do, that's when people start to become unwilling to forgive.
- *Forgiveness is encouraged if the liar shows a sense of remorse or a willingness to change.* Again, people differ widely in how much they are wiling to accept another person's remorse or expressed desire to change, but this kind of attitude can help to cushion the effects of the lie and promote healing.

At some point forgiveness is necessary, though hard to do, because otherwise the hate and hostility generated by the lie could be self-destructive. For example, Frances, the computer systems supervisor, had this kind of experience when she continued to feel hostility to two men she had been involved with who used lies and unfulfilled promises to get money out of her, which they never repaid. As she described it:

Eventually, I forgave those two people for what they did to me, and they came back in my life and established a kind of friendship. But before then, when I still felt that hate, it ate at me, and I learned that this hate didn't really hurt them—it hurts me. It hurts with the emotional pain, and I know it contributes to things like cancer and stress. So I felt better when I gave it up.

Finally, there is the question of self-forgiveness. Can you forgive yourself after you've either lied or have felt duped by having someone lie to you? This can be equally important to the process of healing.

TOWARD A SOLUTION IN DEALING WITH LYING

Given the pervasiveness of lying and its paradoxical nature, what should we do about it? I think we need to be aware of this dual nature and come to be more clear about when lying may be constructive and when it may be dangerous. We also need to be aware of these different propensities to lie in ourselves and in others, so we can better understand where we are each coming from and respond accordingly.

For example, individuals who are models of absolute integrity and straight shooters may be more comfortable dealing with others who have a similar moralistic attitude toward lying, as well as working in an organizational culture that supports this approach. That's because they may find they are more judgmental and critical of others who are more pragmatic when it comes to lying, and this could become a source of conflict both in a relationship and the workplace. Conversely, those with a more pragmatic approach to lying, especially the Pinocchios and frequent liars may be more comfortable in a relationship or work situation together, because they know they can count on each other if it is practical to be open and forthright about something and understand not to trust one another, should circumstances change. By the same token, individuals with this more pragmatic attitude may find that those with a more moral perspective are too rigid in their attitude; so unless they are willing to change themselves and become more truthful themselves with that person, even if only for pragmatic reasons, they may be in for a lot of conflict.

Those differences noted, in general, I think we need to make a commitment to the truth and integrity, where it is at all possible to do this, including in these everyday social situations where the so-called social lie is so common. For example, tactful but true explanations might be used to turn down invitations. At the same time we need to recognize that lies to help social relations may be more beneficial than the truth, such as when the assurances of "you'll get better" will help a person heal, though the outcome may seem uncertain and more probably grim. And to facilitate social relationships, we may need to look the other way when we know or suspect others have lied to us.

On the other hand, we also need to be aware when lies become serious and disruptive, when they threaten bonds of trust, and seek to avoid such lies ourselves as well as be ready to handle such lies by others. In short, we need this awareness so we can make choices and manage the lying we encounter in our lives.

To some extent, this process may be conscious and analytical, based on assessing, evaluating, and choosing. But part of it is intuitive, based in effect on listening to yourself and following that "little voice" within.

To help you decide what to do, consider the following.

Look at the Whys behind the Lie

It may be that the lies are covering up some important truth or hidden negative feelings that would be better revealed. A good example of this might be the person who comes to work constantly late and then makes excuses. He could be doing this because he really doesn't like the job. So if you're the one who's lying about the situation, maybe you have to look at whether this is the right job for you. If you're the supervisor, you should discuss this with the person who is lying and try to find his reasons. Maybe there is something in the office that could be changed so he feels better about the job.

If there are lies in a relationship, it might be good to see what these are saying about the relationship, particularly if it has been a good one. Certainly, breaking up the relationship over the lie is one possibility, but maybe looking at the underlying reasons for the lie might be a way of renewing or rebuilding it. If the lie is brought up and addressed and the problems resolved, the lie could lead to healing.

Be Ready to Call People on Their Lies

Let people know the lies are not okay. Otherwise, this suggests you either aren't aware of them or are willing to accept them, which only encourages more lies, and can leave you feeling resentful.

Create a Supportive Environment for Truth Telling

Creating a supportive environment for those who have lied can make it safe for them to reveal or explain their lies. If the lies are designed to cover up failure in the workplace, it may be important to give people permission to acknowledge failure and acknowledge they are not perfect. By giving people this space to see that their failures, mistakes, or weaknesses can be forgiven or will be treated like learning experiences, it takes away some of the fear and insecurity that causes the lies.

Tell the Truth to Yourself

It is important to tell the truth to yourself, even if it is initially painful, because that self-awareness is the beginning step to self-healing.

Marketing and management consultant Robert Middleton put it very well when he observed that:

Telling the truth to yourself is transformational. It is crucial to say the way things really are and really work, instead of creating some pretense as to how we think things ought to be, hope it should be, or wish it would be.

If we really tell the truth about ourselves, what's in it for us is aliveness and satisfaction and joy and love and understanding and connection. It helps us build bridges to others, and it contributes to our ultimate success. And we discover who we really are and what we are. So telling the truth is very powerful.

Use the Truth for Building and Healing Relationships

Telling the truth can be healing. Relationship counselor Susan Scott has advocated these benefits in assisting her clients toward more honest relationships based on personal integrity. As she told me:

I think people should adopt the cardinal rule of telling the truth. That's how you heal everything that's happened in the past in relationships. And by telling the truth to yourself as well as to others, that's how you get or create for yourself what it is that you really want and need in the future generally, and in relationships. So telling the truth can add to your own self-esteem and the quality of life.

On the other hand, if there are lies in a relationship, I think it's important to clean it up or the lies will always be there between the people. Yes, there may be a risk of breaking up the relationship if the lie comes out. But if the lie remains, the relationship isn't going to last anyway. Because the truth always comes out.

Recognize the Long-Term Advantages of Being Committed to the Truth

Finally, recognize that in the long run a commitment to truth does pay off. There may be short-term gains for many lies, but there is always the risk that lies will come out, and in the meantime, they can create guilt and anxiety. People in business, for example, have found that a long-term orientation toward integrity and service is what makes a business strong, and this kind of larger commitment not only helps the individual business but also the economy as a whole.

I think most of us can agree that the last few decades' focus on greed and all manner of manipulation, including lies, helped to contribute to the economic crisis we now face.

Similarly, lies and cover-ups have proved dangerous in the development of science and technology (some examples include the failure of the *Challenger* space shuttle, the fabricated evidence in the Korean cloning experiments, and the concealment of testing failures that have raised questions about the effectiveness of some new drugs).

In short, what I am suggesting is that we need to recognize and embrace the value of truth and integrity, while realizing that in some circumstances there may be benefits to using lies to a limited degree or letting the lies of others pass.

When we encounter lying or consider lying ourselves, we should control how we deal with lying, combining a sense of awareness with an understanding of the pros and cons and issues involved. Using intuition and listening to that inner voice will then help us decide what to do. With this combination of awareness, reason, and intuition, we can take charge and better choose how to deal with lying in everyday life.

Appendix: Ethical Choices Mapping Instrument

Select one of the following approaches, which you are more likely to use:

Personal Ethics

1. A. When I have to make a tough decision, I usually figure out what to do by weighing the pros and cons, thinking about the alternatives, and decide based on what makes the most sense. (R)

   B. When I have a major decision to make, I usually know what to do when the time is right or I have a gut feeling about the best approach to take. (N)

2. A. I generally go by a strong set of principles I follow about what's right and wrong; some of these are ideals I learned as a child or from my parents and role models. (M)

   B. I generally decide what to do based on what seems to make the most sense in that particular situation; I consider such things as the means and the ends and the benefits to me and others. (P)

3. A. I usually prefer to follow the rules or go along with what others are doing in a particular situation. (F)

   B. I tend to follow the rules if it makes sense to do so; but I think it makes sense to break rules or make new ones if the old ones aren't working, and I often do that. (I)

4. A. I tend to put the interests of other people first or do what is in the best interest of the most people. (O)

   B. I tend to think about how something will benefit me first; I prefer to do what's best for me most of the time. (S)

5. A. When I chose the work I'm doing now, I spent some time thinking about I wanted to do, such as my skills, interests, financial considerations, my family's interests, and other factors. (R)
B. When I chose the work I'm doing now, I felt like this was just something I was called to do—or it just happened, because I just drifted into it. (N)
6. If I was working in a job and I had agreed to stay there for two or three years in return for getting hired and trained to do the job, I would:
A. Keep my agreement even if I had a better job offer during this time. (M/O)
B. Take the better job offer if it was better for me to do so. (P/S)
7. If I was in a situation where I had to choose between helping my family handle some financial or personal problems or take an opportunity I've always wanted for a career, move, or relationship, I would:
A. Help my family overcome its problems first and then go after the career, move, or relationship I wanted. (O)
B. Choose to go after the career, move, or relationship I want first, then help my family. (S)
8. A. When I was growing up, I was generally well-behaved at home or one of the gang with my friends. (F)
B. When I was growing up, I was often the one who came up with new ideas or was something of a troublemaker or the one to rock the boat. (I)

Family Ethics

9. When one is a child, I think in general:
A. One should follow the guidelines and principles of one's parents or teachers. (F/M)
B. One should regard this as a period of self-discovery and learning, and follow the guidelines and principles that seem sensible, but otherwise feel free to make one's own choices. (I/P/S)
10. If I was a teenager who got into trouble for committing a petty crime, like joyriding or shoplifting, I would:
A. Confess, tell my parents I was sorry, take my punishment, and promise not to do it again. (F/O)
B. Do what I can to avoid getting punished by the authorities or my parents, and be more careful in the future. (I/S/P)
11. When one is a parent, I think in general:
A. One should put the needs of one's kids first in making choices, like where to move or whether to stay together with a mate for the sake of the child. (O)
B. One should set a good example for the kids and expect them to behave properly. (M)

12. As a parent with a teenager who misbehaves or gets into trouble, I would:
A. Talk about the importance of behaving properly or decide on an appropriate punishment if the problem continues or is serious enough. (M/F)
B. Try to understand why the teenager is having problems from his or her point of view and show my support to help him or her overcome the problem. (P/I/O)

13. As a parent, I think in general:
A. There are certain codes of behavior I think every child should know and follow, such as don't lie, cheat, or steal. (M/F)
B. Each child is an individual, and it is important to help the child develop to his fullest potential. (I/P)

Ethics with Friends, Dates, and Distant Relatives

14. A. In choosing my friends, it's important that a friend shares certain core values or beliefs with me; otherwise, it would be difficult for me to consider that person a friend. (M)
B. In choosing my friends, what's most important is that we share certain common interests, enjoy each other's company, and get along well. (P/S)

15. If I think something a friend has done is wrong, I will generally:
A. Tell the other person what I think, since I tend to be very honest and frank, and it might help the person correct his own behavior, even if it means the end of the relationship. (M/O)
B. Decide whether to tell or not depending on what the person has done, how I think the person will react, how valuable continuing the relationship is to me, and other factors. (P/S)

16. If a friend going through hard times comes to me for help, I would be likely to:
A. Give what I can, feeling I want to help, even if I'm not sure the person can pay me back, because I feel a strong sense of altruism or compassion. (O)
B. Give what I can to help, but work out an agreement that the person will pay me back, or advise the person on ways he can help himself, because I want to be practical and encourage personal responsibility. (P)

17. If I was in a dating relationship that was getting serious, and I had some personal information in my background that would put me in a bad light and might damage the relationship, I would:
A. Tell the person, because he or she should know, and I want a relationship built on honesty and openness, whatever the consequences. (M/O)
B. Not tell the person, because I think this is private information that happened in the past, and I think the relationship should be based on what's happening now and don't want to damage it. (S)

18. If I was in a serious dating relationship, and family members and friends advised me not to continue seeing this person because he or she didn't measure up because he or she didn't have a good enough background (i.e., from the wrong ethnic group, lower social class, etc.) I would:
A. Pay attention to their warnings and probably break up with the person because the attitudes of my family and social group are important to me, and I wouldn't want to lose my relationship with them. (F/R)
B. Listen to my heart and continue the relationship, hoping my friends and family members would finally come around, even if I was risking some of these past relationships. (I/N)

Ethics in Work, Business, and Professional Relationships

19. If I found that the company I was working for or an associate I was dealing with was involved in activities I considered wrong or unethical, I would:
A. Report that company or person, urge them to change their policies, and/or quit, regardless of the career risks because I can't condone such actions. (M/I)
B. Continue to work with that company or individual as long as I have to avoid risking my career, while trying to leave as soon as I can. (P/F/S)

20. Generally, when I am part of an organization or work with one, I tend to:
A. Go along with the current practices or corporate culture, because I think that's the best way to get along. (F/P/S)
B. Think of myself more as a leader, idea person, change maker, or rule breaker, because I feel that's the way to make improvements to help everyone. (I/O)

21. If I was in a profession that had a formal code of ethics, and I found that others in my local peer group were participating in various practices that were a breach of these ethics, such as sharing confidential information or engaging in informal personal relationships with clients, I would:
A. Adhere to the formal code of ethics, because I think that's right and in the best interests of clients. (M/O)
B. Do what seems to work best for myself in the current situation to get along with my peers, advance my career, and only share information or engage in personal relationships if I can do so in a beneficial way, since I think the formal code of ethics is overly restrictive. (I/P/S)

22. Generally, I would prefer to work in a company or in a field where:
A. I can earn a good income based doing a good job. (S/F)
B. I can contribute to helping others, even if I earn less. (M/O)

Ethics in Local Community and Public Issues

23. If a clerk in a store made a mistake, such as giving me too much money back as change or charging me too little for a purchase, I would:
A. Keep the extra money or not say anything about being charged too little, since it was the clerk's mistake, and I would consider this like a gift I can use. (S/P)

B. Tell the clerk about the mistake, since I would be concerned the clerk might be charged, and I would feel I was taking advantage of the situation. (O/M)

24. If I didn't like someone who was a member of a group I belonged to, I would:
A. Keep my feelings to myself, and hope that others might feel the same way and do something to get this person out of the group. (F)
B. Take the lead in talking to others who might feel the same way and showing how he or she is hurting the group. (I)

25. If I saw my neighbors involved in some kind of illegal activity, though it wasn't a threat to me personally or a danger to the neighborhood, I would be likely to:
A. Look the other way and not complain about it, because I don't want to have trouble with the neighbors and consider it their private business. (P)
B. Report them to the authorities, since they were doing something wrong, but I wouldn't use my name to avoid problems with them knowing I complained. (M)

26. If I was asked to lend my name to an unpopular cause that I believe in, such as by a group putting out literature or advertising about its cause, I would:
A. Let the group use my name, because I believe in the cause and want to help. (O)
B. Not let the group use my name, because I would be concerned if my public support for the cause might damage me, though I might help privately. (S)

Ethics in Society as a Whole

27. A. I believe there are some fundamental moral principles that are true for all societies at all times. (M)
B. I believe that moral principles vary from society to society and over history in response to changing times and cultures. (P)

28. A. I believe that one should do what helps the most people, because it is most important to be of service to others, be unselfish, and contribute to others. (O)
B. While I believe one shouldn't hurt others, one also has to consider oneself first because most other people consider themselves first and can take advantage of you if you aren't careful. (S)

29. A. I believe one should help low-income or disadvantaged people as one can, because this is the ethical or moral thing to do. (M/O)
B. I believe that low-income or disadvantaged people should be helped to find jobs or get training if possible; but each of us is personally responsible for himself or herself. (P/S)

30. When it comes to some of the recent technological developments creating ethical challenges for us (like new developments in medicine, fertility, life extension, reproduction, etc.), I think we should generally:
A. Follow time-tested moral principles. (F)

B. Change our traditional moral principles to adapt to the times. (I)
And I think we can determine what these moral principles should be
because:
A. We have a deep sense of knowing about what is right and wrong. (N)
B. We choose the moral principles we do because they are what make
the most sense for us as a society; they help to make society work. (R)

Scoring the Ethical Choices Mapping Instrument

Circle the letters below that you circled on each item of the questionnaire.

	Style of Choosing		Orientation		Philosophy		Attitude to Rules	
	Intuitive (N)	Rational (R)	Other (O)	Self (S)	Moralist (M)	Pragmatist (P)	Follower (F)	Innovator (I)
1.	B	A						
2.					A	B		
3.							A	B
4.			A	B				
5.	B	A						
6.			A	B	A	B		
7.			A	B				
8.							A	B
9.				B	A	B	A	B
10.			A	B		B	A	B
11.			A		B			
12.				B	A	B	A	B
13.					A	B	A	B
14.				B	A	B		
15.			A	B	A	B		
16.			A			B		
17.			A	B	A			
18.	B	A					A	B
19.				B	A	B	B	A

#	Intuitive	Rational	Other	Self	Moralist	Pragmatist	Follower	Innovator
20.			B	A		A	A	B
21.			A	B	A	B		B
22.			B	A	B		A	
23.			B	A	B	A		
24.							A	B
25.					B	A		
26.			A	B				
27.					A	B		
28.			A	B				
29.			A	B	A	B		
30.	A	B					A	B

Total in each column:

____ ____ ____ ____ ____ ____ ____ ____

Intuitive Rational Other Self Moralist Pragmatist Follower Innovator

% of Total

___(4) ___(4) ___(16) ___(16) ___(16) ___(16) ___(12) ___(12)

Notes

CHAPTER 1

1. Sissela Bok, *Lying: Moral Choice in Public and Private Life*, New York: Vintage House, 1978, p. 17.

2. Thomas E. Carson, "On the Definition of Lying: A Reply to Jones and Revisions," *Journal of Business Ethics*, Vol. 7, No. 7, 1988, p. 509.

3. Harry Frankfurt, "Reflections on Bullshit," *Harpers Magazine*, February 1987, pp. 14–15.

4. Erica E. Good, "Nature's Knaves and Tricksters: Some Animals Show a Penchant for Dissembling and Deceit," *U.S. News and World Report*, October 23, 1989, pp. 61–63.

5. Ibid., p. 62.

6. Ibid.

7. R. W. Bryne and A. Whitten, "Tactical Deception of Familiar Individuals in Baboons," *Animal Behavior*, Vol. 33, No. 2, May 1985, pp. 669–73.

8. As recounted by Joseph Campbell in the PBS film of his lecture series: "Transformations of Myth through Time," 9 volumes, Public Media Video, 1989.

9. R. H. Wiley, "The Evolution of Communication: Information and Manipulation," T. R. Halliday and P. J. B. Slater (eds.), *Communication Behavior*, Vol. 2, New York: Freeman, 1983.

10. Charles F. Bond, Jr., Karen Nelson Kahler, and Lucia M. Paolicelli, "The Miscommunication of Deception: An Adaptive Perspective," *Journal of Experimental Social Psychology*, Vol. 21, No. 4., 1985, pp. 331–45.

11. Ibid., pp. 332–33.

12. Michael P. Carroll, "The Trickster as Self-Buffoon and Culture Hero," *Ethos*, Vol. 12, pp. 105–31.

13. Francis E. Kazemek, Muriel Radebaugh, and Pat Rigg, "Old Man Coyote Makes the World: Using Native American Tales," *English Journal*, Vol. 76, February 1987, pp. 100–105.

14. William Manson, "Trickster's Triumph: Sublimation and Culture," *The Journal of Psychohistory*, Vol. 15, No. 3, Winter 1988, pp. 325–32.

15. Kazemek, Radebaugh, and Rigg, p. 102.

16. Manson, p. 325.

17. Claudia V. Camp, "Wise and Strange: An Interpretation of the Female Imagery in Proverbs in Light of Trickster Mythology," *Semia*, No. 42, 1988, pp. 14–36.

18. Naomi Steinberg, "Israelite Tricksters, Their Analogues and Cross-Cultural Study," *Semia*, No 42, 1988, pp. 1–13.

19. Joseph E. Brown, "The Wisdom of the Contrary," interview by D.M. Dooling, *Parabola: The Magazine of Myth and Tradition*, Vol. 4, No. 1, 1979, pp. 54–65.

20. Ingvild Saelid Gilhus, "The Gnostic Demiurge—An Agnostic Trickster," *Religion: Journal of Religion and Religions*, Vol. 14, October 1984, pp. 301–11.

21. Ibid., p. 307.

22. Spaceandmotion.com, "On Truth and Reality: Plato's Republic," http://www.spaceandmotion.com/society/plato-republic.htm (accessed November 5, 2009.

23. St. Augustine, "Lying," *Treatises on Various Subjects*, in R.J. Deferari (ed.), *Fathers of the Church*, New York: Catholic University of America Press, 1952, Vol. 14, Chapter 14.

24. St. Augustine, "The Enchiridion," quoted in Bok, p. 34.

25. Thomas Aquinas, *Summa Theologica*, 2.2, qus. 110, art. 2.

26. Immanuel Kant, *Critique of Pure Reason and Other Writings in Moral Philosophy*, ed. and trans. Lewis White Beck, Chicago: University of Chicago Press, 1949, pp. 346–349; quoted in Mark Dratch, "Nothing But the Truth?" *Judaism: A Quarterly Journal*, Vol. 37, Spring 1988, pp. 218–28.

27. Hugo Grotius, *On the Law of War and Peace*, trans. F.M. Kelsy and others, Indianapolis, IN: Bobbs Merrill Co. 1925, bk. 3, ch. 1, quoted in Dratch, p. 219.

28. Henry Sidgwick, *The Methods of Ethics*, London: Macmillan and Company, 1907, p. 316; quoted in Dratch, p. 219.

29. Dratch, 218–28.

30. Dafna Allon, "Reflections on the Art of Lying," *Commentary*, Vol. 81, No. 6, June 1986, 47–54.

31. Daniel Goleman, "The Truth about Liars," *San Francisco Chronicle*, 1988.

32. Quoted in Ibid.

33. Charles V. Ford, Bryan H. King, and Marc H. Hollender, "Lies and Liars: Psychiatric Aspects of Prevarication," *American Journal of Psychiatry*, Vol. 145, No. 5, May 1988, pp. 554–62.

34. Mark Hosenball, "The Culture of Lying," *The New Republic*, July 13 and 20, 1987, pp. 16–18.

35. Ann Landers, "The Third Biggest Lie," *San Francisco Examiner* (from the Los Angeles Times Syndicate and Creators Syndicate).

36. "The Truth about Lying (Views of Beverly Palmer)," *USA Today*, December 1987, pp. 3–4.

CHAPTER 2

1. Elizabeth Kamarck Minnich, "Why Not Lie?" *Soundings: An Interdisciplinary Journal*, Vol. 68, No. 4, Winter 1985, pp. 493–508.

CHAPTER 3

1. Gini Graham Scott, *Making Ethical Choices, Resolving Ethical Dilemmas*, St. Paul, MN: Paragon, 1998.
2. Ibid.
3. Ibid., p. 56.
4. Ibid., p. 62.

CHAPTER 5

1. Ervin Goffman, *The Presentation of Self in Everyday Life*, New York: Doubleday, 1959.

CHAPTER 8

1. Owen Edwards, "Thrice-Told Tales," *The New York Times Magazine*, March 20, 1988, p. 16.
2. Ibid., p. 17.
3. Ibid.

CHAPTER 10

1. The book describing this research is *Erotic Power*, now published by Contemporary Books. (Originally published as *Dominant Women, Submissive Men*, Westport, CT: Praeger Publishers)
2. Her books were previously cited in Judith Briles, *Women to Women: From Sabotage to Support*, Far Hills, NJ: New Horizon Press, 1995; and *The Confidence Factor*, Aurora, CO: Mile High Press, 2008.

CHAPTER 11

1. Estimates and questionnaire results on the percent of married individuals having affairs vary widely—anywhere from 10 percent to 70 percent. I have used 30 to 50 percent as the more conservative middle-range figures that are more widely agreed upon by those in the field.

CHAPTER 12

1. Paul Ekman, *Why Kids Lie*, New York: Macmillan Publishing Company, 1989.
2. Paul Ekman, "Would a Child Lie?" *Psychology Today*, July–August 1989, p. 62.
3. Ibid.
4. Ibid., p. 65.

CHAPTER 13

1. Daniel Goleman, *Vital Lies, Simple Truths: The Psychology of Self-Deception*, New York: Simon and Schuster, 1985.

2. Ibid., p. 22.
3. Ibid., p. 32.
4. Ibid., p. 37.
5. Ibid., p. 39.
6. Ibid., pp. 52–53.
7. Ibid., p. 90.
8. Ibid., p. 98.
9. Ibid., p. 100.

CHAPTER 14

1. Charles F. Bond, Jr., Karen Nelson Kahler, and Lucia M. Paolicelli, "The Miscommunication of Deception: An Adaptive Perspective," *Journal of Experimental Social Psychology*, Vol. 21, 1985, pp. 331–45.

2. Ibid., p. 341.

3. R.E. Kraut, "Humans as Lie Detectors: Some Second Thoughts," *Journal of Communication*, Vol. 39, 1980, pp. 209–16.

4. Bond, Kahler, and Paolicelli, p. 241.

5. R.E. Kraut and D. Poe, "On the Line: The Deception Judgments of Customs Inspectors and Laymen," *Journal of Personality and Social Psychology*, Vol. 39, 1980, pp. 784–98.

6. Bond, Kahler, and Paolicelli, p. 341.

7. Charles F. Bond, Jr., and William E. Fahey, "False Suspicion and the Misperception of Deceit," *British Journal of Social Psychology*, Vol. 26, 1987, pp. 41–46.

8. Bruce Bower, "Sales Pitches: The Lies Have It," *Science News*, Vol. 134, 1988, p. 140; Bond and Fahey.

9. Bella M. DePaulo, Julie I. Stone, and G. Daniel Lassiter. "Telling Ingratiating Lies: Effects of Target Sex and Target Attractiveness on Verbal and Nonverbal Deceptive Success," *Journal of Personality and Social Psychology*, Vol. 48, No. 5, May 1985, pp. 1191–203.

10. Ibid.

11. Ibid., pp. 1200–1201.

12. Paul Ekman, *Telling Lies: Clues to Deceit in the Marketplace, Politics, and Marriage*, New York: W.W. Norton & Company, 1985, p. 39.

13. Ibid., p. 43.
14. Ibid., p. 44.
15. Ibid.
16. Ibid., p. 79.
17. Ibid., pp. 47–48.
18. Ibid., p. 51.
19. Ibid.
20. Ibid., p. 60.
21. Ibid., p. 65.
22. Ibid., p. 70.
23. Ibid., p. 78.
24. Ibid., pp. 81–82.
25. Ibid., p. 84.
26. Ibid., p. 85.

27. Ibid.

28. Ibid., p. 88.

29. Ibid., p. 90.

30. Ibid., p. 91.

31. Ibid., p. 92–93.

32. Ibid.

33. Ibid., pp. 102–3.

34. Ibid., p. 105–7.

35. Ibid., p. 109–13.

36. Ibid., p. 114.

37. Ibid., p. 115.

38. Ibid., p. 123.

39. Ibid., p. 124.

40. Ibid., p. 126.

41. Ibid., p. 129.

42. Ibid., p. 131.

43. Ibid., p. 142.

44. Ibid., p. 143.

45. Ibid.

46. Ibid., p. 142–43.

47. John Leo, "The Fine Art of Catching Liars," *Time*, April 22, 1985, p. 59; also, Ekman, p. 146.

48. Leo, p. 59; also, Ekman, p. 146.

49. Valerie Adler, "Lying Smiles," *Psychology Today*, Vol. 22, July–August, 1988, p. 16. From Ekman's article: Paul Ekman, Wallace V. Friesen, and Maureen O'Sullivan, "Smiles When Lying," *Journal of Personality and Social Psychology*, Vol. 54, No. 3, March 1988, pp. 414–20.

50. Ekman, p. 149.

Index

About the Author

GINI GRAHAM SCOTT, PhD, JD, is a nationally known writer, consultant, speaker, and seminar/workshop leader, specializing in business and work relationships and in professional and personal development. She has published over 50 books on diverse subjects. Her latest books include: *Want It, See It, Get It!*; *Enjoy! 101 Little Ways to Add More Fun to Your Work Every Day;* and *A Survival Guide for Working with Humans . . . Managing Employees from Hell and Working with Bad Bosses*. She is founder and director of Changemakers and of E-Book Publishing, and has been a featured expert guest on hundreds of TV and radio programs, including *Oprah* and *Good Morning America*. She is the host of a weekly syndicated talk radio show, *Changemakers*, featuring interviews and commentary on various topics. She is also a script writer and indy film producer through her company Changemakers Productions. Her Web site is at www.ginigraham scott.com. She has a PhD in sociology from the University of California in Berkeley, a JD from the University of San Francisco Law School, and MAs in anthropology; mass communications and organizational/consumer/audience behavior, and popular culture and lifestyles from California State University, East Bay.